INTRODUCTION

The retail prices index (RPI) is the primary measure of price inflation as it affects consumers in the United Kingdom. Monthly figures have been compiled on a similar basis since 1947 and an earlier series - the cost of living index - goes back as far as 1914. Besides the overall ("all items") index there are component indices covering particular categories of goods and/or services. Currently about a hundred such indices are compiled but the amount of detail available for years before 1974 is rather less and for years before 1956 much less.

This volume contains the longest possible time series for each of the indices currently compiled. As the grouping and nomenclature of component indices have changed over the years (most notably in January 1987) uniformity of presentation here has meant showing some of the indices in a somewhat different form from that in which they were originally released. Most of the figures have either been published or are readily derivable from published material but in a few cases data which have previously been disclosed only on special request have now been used to provide "back runs" of currently-published indices. It is hoped that the results will be of use both for analytical purposes and for reference.

In addition to the time series themselves the volume contains various tables of supplementary information, relating to the coverage and construction of the indices, which have often been requested by users and are here brought together in a convenient format.

Further information about the retail prices index can be obtained from the

Central Statistical Office
(Branch E2),
Millbank Tower,
London SW1P 4QU.

CONTENTS

CENTRAL STATISTICAL

Retail Prices
1914—1990

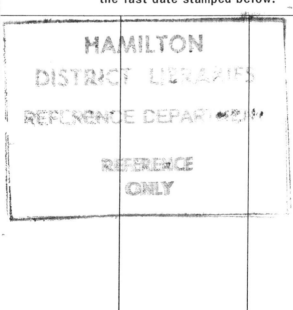

London: HMSO

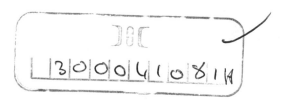

ISBN 0 11 620499 0

THE RETAIL PRICES INDEX :
A brief guide by A J Machin

The retail prices index -the RPI- is an important barometer of the economy of the UK and shows the impact of inflation on family budgets. The inflation figures are eagerly watched by the media, wage-bargainers, business people and politicians. The index affects us all. It can affect your tax allowances, your savings, state benefits and pensions since these and many other payments are often up-dated using the index.

Not all prices move in the same way. The prices of tomatoes or hi-fi equipment might fall while the prices of apples or petrol rise. The index represents the **average change** in prices of millions of consumer purchases which take place in the market. This is achieved by using a large sample of shops and other places up and down the country and carefully recording the prices of a typical selection of products from month to month.

Shopping basket

A convenient way of thinking about the RPI is to imagine a very large " shopping basket" full of goods and services on which people typically spend their money : from bread to ready-made meals, from electricity bills to clothes, from the cost of a cinema seat to the price of a pint at the local pub. The contents of the basket are fixed but as the prices of individual products vary so does the total cost of the basket. The RPI, as a measure of that total cost, only measures **price changes**. If people spend more because they buy more goods this does not affect the index.

We all spend different amounts on various goods and services which show different price movements. No-one is "average". But many prices are ultimately subject to similar market pressures and we all buy a good variety of things, some of which change in price more than others. For all of us, therefore, there is an element of "swings and round-abouts" in the way we are affected by inflation. It is convenient to have one simple measure which, though it may not strictly apply to any one individual or family, nevertheless provides most of us with a useful yardstick of the impact of inflation on our own pocket or purse.

Considerable care is taken to ensure that the shopping basket is kept up-to date and is representative of people's shopping patterns; the places and shops we go to, the goods and services which we buy and the amounts we spend on them.

The cost of living ?

The RPI is not strictly a "cost of living" index, a concept which means different things to different people. To many it may suggest the changing costs of basic essentials, but in practice it would be very difficult to agree on a definition of "essentials". The index simply gives an indication of what we would need to spend in order to purchase the same things we **chose** to buy in an earlier period, irrespective of whether particular products are "needed" or "good for you". For example, some people buy cigarettes, so these are included in the index. However the calculations reflect the average shopping basket and so take account of the fact that a majority of people do not buy tobacco at all.

What is included in the basket ?

The RPI includes virtually all types of household spending as shown in the chart. There are some exceptions such as savings and investments, charges for credit, betting and cash gifts which are out of the scope of the index.

Indirect taxes such as VAT, which are part of the price of the goods and services, are included but income tax and national insurance payments are excluded. (The latter are taken into account in a separate index -the tax and price index - which shows how much tax-payers' **gross** incomes need to change in order to maintain their spending power after taking account of the tax that has been deducted as well as changes in prices.)

The various principles and concepts underlying the construction of the RPI have been determined by recommendations of the Retail Prices Index Advisory Committee which reports to the Chancellor of the Exchequer and includes members from outside Government.

Structure of the Retail Prices Index in 1991

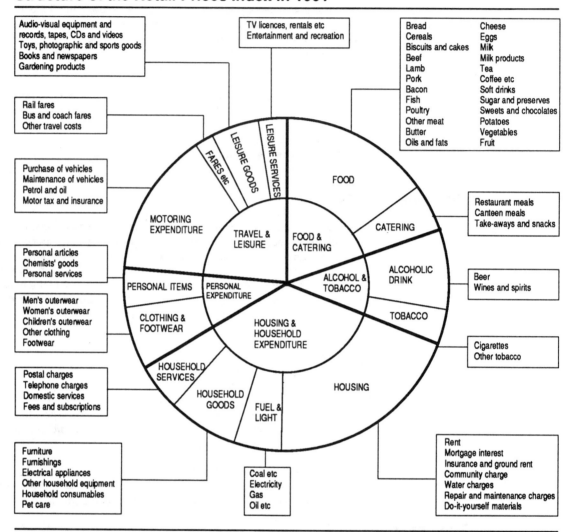

Price indicators

It would be unnecessary and impracticable to monitor the prices of everything on sale in every single shop. The prices of similar items can reasonably be assumed to move in line with one another in response to market forces. It is therefore sufficient to compile the index using prices of a large and varied sample of products at selected places. There are some 600 separate indicators used in compiling the RPI. The movements of these are taken to represent the price changes for all goods and services covered by the index, including those for which prices are not specifically monitored. For example there are six price indicators for bread which are combined together to estimate the overall change in all bread prices.

Price collection

About the middle of every month price collectors (mainly staff from the Employment Service who act on behalf of the Central Statistical Office), obtain well over 100,000 prices altogether for some 500 of the 600 specified types of goods and services. They go to a variety of shops in 180 areas throughout the country. They visit most of the shops in person to see goods at first hand but some of the work is done by telephone. The price collectors go to the same places and note the prices of the same things each month so that over time they compare like with like. The reliability of the index is very much dependent on the goodwill of retailers in allowing this information to be collected.

For many goods and services it is more efficient to collect prices centrally. Information on charges such as those for gas, water, newspapers, council rents and rail fares - about 100 indicators in all - are all obtained from central sources. Also some large chain-stores, which charge the same prices at their various branches, help by sending information direct from their headquarters to the Central Statistical Office.

Weighting

We spend more on some things than others and we would expect, for example, that an increase in mortgage interest payments would have a considerably greater impact on the RPI than an increase of similar proportion in the price of tea. The components of the index are therefore carefully "weighted" to ensure that the index reflects the importance of the various contents of the average shopping basket and the amounts we spend in different regions of the country and in different types of shops.

The weights for the index are obtained from a number of sources but mainly from the Family Expenditure Survey. A sample of about 7,000 households throughout the country each year keep records of what they spend over a fortnight and also give details of their major purchases over a longer period.

In calculating the weights, the expenditure of two groups of people is excluded on the grounds that their pattern of spending is significantly different from the great majority. These are people in households with the top 4 % of the incomes, and low income pensioners who are mainly dependent on state benefits. (Separate 'pensioner' indices are published for these.) These restrictions are designed to make the RPI more representative of the "typical household".

Keeping the index up-to-date

It is clearly important that the index is representative and kept up-to-date. The basket of goods and services is fixed for a year at a time, but is reviewed every year and up-dated as necessary to reflect changing markets, fashions and new products. For example black and white televisions were dropped from the index when sales declined; micro-wave ovens, video-recorders and compact discs were introduced. The weights for the index are also changed each year to keep abreast of the general changes in people's spending patterns. Over the years people have tended to spend a reducing proportion of their money on basics such as food, while electrical goods , travel and leisure etc have accounted for an increasing share of their budgets.

Central Statistical Office, 1991

HMSO £18.00 net
ISBN 0 11 620448 6

APPENDIX

Calculating the index

Once all the price data have been fed onto a computer, checked and processed, all the resulting price indicators are combined together. Changes in prices are measured by comparing them to their levels in the previous January and then weighted together using the latest weights for the current year to produce an overall average price change. The final stage in the calculation is to link this average price change with the figures for earlier years. It is only by "chain-linking" the calculations in this way that the index can **both** take account of changes in the make-up of the shopping basket from year to year **and** provide comparisons between different years. The procedure ensures that if something is dropped from the basket or introduced, this does not distort the index.

Reference dates

The RPI measures price changes, not price levels; so it is expressed in terms of the comparison of prices relative to January 1987, when the index is given a value of 100. For example the index for January 1991 was 130.2, indicating that £130.20 would buy the same amount in January 1991 as £100 would have bought in January 1987, a rise in prices of 30.2 per cent. The headline figure - the annual rate of inflation - is simply the percentage change in the index obtained by comparing the latest index with the value recorded twelve months ago.

The reference date of January 1987 is arbitrary and merely provides a convenient landmark for comparison. The choice of date has no material effect on the measurement of price changes between one month and another. The reference date has been changed several times, for example in 1962 and 1974. Long term comparisons are obtained by linking the various official indices, if necessary back as far as 1914. The longer term comparisons should of course be treated with some caution as the things people buy have changed so much since the days of mangles and candles.

Index dates

The index always refers to a Tuesday near the middle of each month. Since it can often take longer than one day to collect all the local shop prices, for the sake of efficiency some prices are collected on the Monday or the Wednesday. However, some prices such as those for petrol, which can fluctuate markedly from day to day, and all the centrally collected prices, relate to the Tuesday.

Publication

The figures are first published in a press release as soon as they are ready, usually on a Friday a month after the Tuesday index date. The publication dates for each year are announced in advance. Further details and analysis of the results subsequently appear in the *"Employment Gazette"* and in several CSO publications, for example the *"Monthly Digest of Statistics"* and *"Economic Trends"*.

Central Statistical Office , 1991

1   "ALL ITEMS" RETAIL PRICES INDEX (RPI)

	Jan	Feb	Mar	Apr	May	Jun	Jul	Aug	Sep	Oct	Nov	Dec
Indices: June 1947 = 100												
1947						100.0	100.7	100.1	100.6	101.3	103.4	103.7
1948	104.2	106.1	106.4	107.9	107.8	109.7	108.0	108.0	108.2	108.4	108.7	108.8
1949	109.0	109.2	108.9	108.6	110.6	111.1	111.2	111.3	111.7	112.3	112.3	112.6
1950	112.9	113.2	113.5	113.9	114.2	113.6	113.6	113.2	113.9	115.1	115.6	116.2
1951	117.3	118.4	119.2	121.1	124.1	124.5	126.4	127.0	127.9	128.8	129.3	130.2
1952	132.5											
Indices: January 1952 = 100												
1952	100.0	100.1	100.6	102.2	102.2	103.9	103.8	103.2	103.0	103.9	103.8	104.5
1953	104.4	104.7	105.4	106.4	106.0	106.6	106.6	105.9	105.7	105.7	106.0	105.6
1954	105.8	105.6	106.6	107.0	106.7	107.3	109.1	108.4	108.2	108.7	109.2	109.8
1955	110.2	110.2	110.2	110.8	110.6	112.9	113.3	112.5	113.2	114.4	116.2	116.2
1956	115.8											
Indices: January 1956 = 100												
1956	100.0	100.0	101.3	102.7	102.5	102.4	102.0	102.3	102.1	102.7	103.1	103.4
1957	104.4	104.3	104.1	104.5	104.6	105.7	106.6	106.4	106.1	107.1	107.7	108.2
1958	108.1	107.6	108.4	109.6	109.2	110.2	108.5	108.3	108.4	109.4	109.8	110.2
1959	110.4	110.3	110.3	109.5	109.1	109.3	109.0	109.3	108.7	109.2	110.0	110.2
1960	109.9	109.9	109.7	110.3	110.3	110.9	111.1	110.4	110.5	111.4	111.9	112.2
1961	112.3	112.3	112.7	113.3	113.6	114.6	114.6	115.7	115.5	115.7	116.9	117.1
1962	117.5											
Indices: January 1962 = 100												
1962	100.0	100.1	100.5	101.9	102.2	102.9	102.5	101.6	101.5	101.4	101.8	102.3
1963	102.7	103.6	103.7	104.0	103.9	103.9	103.3	103.0	103.3	103.7	104.0	104.2
1964	104.7	104.8	105.2	106.1	107.0	107.4	107.4	107.8	107.8	107.9	108.8	109.2
1965	109.5	109.5	109.9	112.0	112.4	112.7	112.7	112.9	113.0	113.1	113.6	114.1
1966	114.3	114.4	114.6	116.0	116.8	117.1	116.6	117.3	117.1	117.4	118.1	118.3
1967	118.5	118.6	118.6	119.5	119.4	119.9	119.2	118.9	118.8	119.7	120.4	121.2
1968	121.6	122.2	122.6	124.8	124.9	125.4	125.5	125.7	125.8	126.4	126.7	128.4
1969	129.1	129.8	130.3	131.7	131.5	132.1	132.1	131.8	132.2	133.2	133.5	134.4
1970	135.5	136.2	137.0	139.1	139.5	139.9	140.9	140.8	141.5	143.0	144.0	145.0
1971	147.0	147.8	149.0	152.2	153.2	154.3	155.2	155.3	155.5	156.4	157.3	158.1
1972	159.0	159.8	160.3	161.8	162.6	163.7	164.2	165.5	166.4	168.7	169.3	170.2
1973	171.3	172.4	173.4	176.7	178.0	178.9	179.7	180.2	181.8	185.4	186.8	188.2
1974	191.8											
Indices: January 1974=100												
1974	100.0	101.7	102.6	106.1	107.6	108.7	109.7	109.8	111.0	113.2	115.2	116.9
1975	119.9	121.9	124.3	129.1	134.5	137.1	138.5	139.3	140.5	142.5	144.2	146.0
1976	147.9	149.8	150.6	153.5	155.2	156.0	156.3	158.5	160.6	163.5	165.8	168.0
1977	172.4	174.1	175.8	180.3	181.7	183.6	183.8	184.7	185.7	186.5	187.4	188.4
1978	189.5	190.6	191.8	194.6	195.7	197.2	198.1	199.4	200.2	201.1	202.5	204.2
1979	207.2	208.9	210.6	214.2	215.9	219.6	229.1	230.9	233.2	235.6	237.7	239.4
1980	245.3	248.8	252.2	260.8	263.2	265.7	267.9	268.5	270.2	271.9	274.1	275.6
1981	277.3	279.8	284.0	292.2	294.1	295.8	297.1	299.3	301.0	303.7	306.9	308.8
1982	310.6	310.7	313.4	319.7	322.0	322.9	323.0	323.1	322.9	324.5	326.1	325.5
1983	325.9	327.3	327.9	332.5	333.9	334.7	336.5	338.0	339.5	340.7	341.9	342.8
1984	342.6	344.0	345.1	349.7	351.0	351.9	351.5	354.8	355.5	357.7	358.8	358.5
1985	359.8	362.7	366.1	373.9	375.6	376.4	375.7	376.7	376.5	377.1	378.4	378.9
1986	379.7	381.1	381.6	385.3	386.0	385.8	384.7	385.9	387.8	388.4	391.7	393.0
1987	394.5											
Indices: January 1987 = 100												
1987	100.0	100.4	100.6	101.8	101.9	101.9	101.8	102.1	102.4	102.9	103.4	103.3
1988	103.3	103.7	104.1	105.8	106.2	106.6	106.7	107.9	108.4	109.5	110.0	110.3
1989	111.0	111.8	112.3	114.3	115.0	115.4	115.5	115.8	116.6	117.5	118.5	118.8
1990	119.5	120.2	121.4	125.1	126.2	126.7	126.8	128.1	129.3	130.3	130.0	129.9
1991	130.2											

2 "ALL ITEMS" RETAIL PRICES INDEX (RPI)

	Jan	Feb	Mar	Apr	May	Jun	Jul	Aug	Sep	Oct	Nov	Dec
Percentage changes over 12 months												
1948						9.7	7.2	7.9	7.6	7.0	5.1	4.9
1949	4.6	2.9	2.3	0.6	2.6	1.3	3.0	3.1	3.2	3.6	3.3	3.5
1950	3.6	3.7	4.2	4.9	3.3	2.3	2.2	1.7	2.0	2.5	2.9	3.2
1951	3.9	4.6	5.0	6.3	8.7	9.6	11.3	12.2	12.3	11.9	11.9	12.0
1952	13.0	12.0	11.8	11.8	9.1	10.6	8.8	7.6	6.7	6.9	6.3	6.4
1953	4.4	4.6	4.8	4.1	3.8	2.5	2.7	2.6	2.6	1.7	2.2	1.0
1954	1.4	0.9	1.1	0.6	0.6	0.7	2.4	2.4	2.4	2.8	3.0	4.0
1955	4.1	4.4	3.4	3.5	3.6	5.2	3.8	3.8	4.6	5.3	6.4	5.8
1956	5.1	5.1	6.4	7.3	7.3	5.0	4.3	5.2	4.4	3.9	2.7	3.0
1957	4.4	4.3	2.8	1.8	2.0	3.2	4.5	4.0	3.9	4.3	4.5	4.6
1958	3.5	3.2	4.1	4.9	4.4	4.3	1.8	1.8	2.2	2.1	1.9	1.8
1959	2.1	2.5	1.8	-0.1	-0.1	-0.8	0.5	0.9	0.3	-0.2	0.2	0.0
1960	10.5	-0.4	-0.5	0.7	1.1	1.5	1.9	1.0	1.7	2.0	1.7	1.8
1961	2.2	2.2	2.7	2.7	3.0	3.3	3.2	4.8	4.5	3.9	4.5	4.4
1962	4.6	4.7	4.8	5.6	5.7	5.5	5.1	3.2	3.3	2.9	2.3	2.6
1963	2.7	3.5	3.2	2.1	1.7	1.0	0.8	1.4	1.8	2.3	2.2	1.9
1964	1.9	1.2	1.4	2.0	3.0	3.4	4.0	4.7	4.4	4.1	4.6	4.8
1965	4.6	4.5	4.5	5.6	5.0	4.9	4.9	4.7	4.8	4.8	4.4	4.5
1966	4.4	4.5	4.3	3.6	3.9	3.9	3.5	3.9	3.6	3.8	4.0	3.7
1967	3.7	3.7	3.5	3.0	2.2	2.4	2.2	1.4	1.5	2.0	1.9	2.5
1968	2.6	3.0	3.4	4.4	4.6	4.6	5.3	5.7	5.9	5.6	5.2	5.9
1969	6.2	6.2	6.3	5.5	5.3	5.3	5.3	4.9	5.1	5.4	5.4	4.7
1970	5.0	4.9	5.1	5.6	6.1	5.9	6.7	6.8	7.0	7.4	7.9	7.9
1971	8.5	8.5	8.8	9.4	9.8	10.3	10.1	10.3	9.9	9.4	9.2	9.0
1972	8.2	8.1	7.6	6.3	6.1	6.1	5.8	6.6	7.0	7.9	7.6	7.7
1973	7.7	7.9	8.2	9.2	9.5	9.3	9.4	8.9	9.3	9.9	10.3	10.6
1974	12.0	13.2	13.5	15.2	16.0	16.5	17.1	16.9	17.1	17.1	18.3	19.1
1975	19.9	19.9	21.2	21.7	25.0	26.1	26.3	26.9	26.6	25.9	25.2	24.9
1976	23.4	22.9	21.2	18.9	15.4	13.8	12.9	13.8	14.3	14.7	15.0	15.1
1977	16.6	16.2	16.7	17.5	17.1	17.7	17.6	16.5	15.6	14.1	13.0	12.1
1978	9.9	9.5	9.1	7.9	7.7	7.4	7.8	8.0	7.8	7.8	8.1	8.4
1979	9.3	9.6	9.8	10.1	10.3	11.4	15.6	15.8	16.5	17.2	17.4	17.2
1980	18.4	19.1	19.8	21.8	21.9	21.0	16.9	16.3	15.9	15.4	15.3	15.1
1981	13.0	12.5	12.6	12.0	11.7	11.3	10.9	11.5	11.4	11.7	12.0	12.0
1982	12.0	11.0	10.4	9.4	9.5	9.2	8.7	8.0	7.3	6.8	6.3	5.4
1983	4.9	5.3	4.6	4.0	3.7	3.7	4.2	4.6	5.1	5.0	4.8	5.3
1984	5.1	5.1	5.2	5.2	5.1	5.1	4.5	5.0	4.7	5.0	4.9	4.6
1985	5.0	5.4	6.1	6.9	7.0	7.0	6.9	6.2	5.9	5.4	5.5	5.7
1986	5.5	5.1	4.2	3.0	2.8	2.5	2.4	2.4	3.0	3.0	3.5	3.7
1987	3.9	3.9	4.0	4.2	4.1	4.2	4.4	4.4	4.2	4.5	4.1	3.7
1988	3.3	3.3	3.5	3.9	4.2	4.6	4.8	5.7	5.9	6.4	6.4	6.8
1989	7.5	7.8	7.9	8.0	8.3	8.3	8.2	7.3	7.6	7.3	7.7	7.7
1990	7.7	7.5	8.1	9.4	9.7	9.8	9.8	10.6	10.9	10.9	9.7	9.3
1991	9.0											

3   "ALL ITEMS" RETAIL PRICES INDEX (RPI)

	Jan	Feb	Mar	Apr	May	Jun	Jul	Aug	Sep	Oct	Nov	Dec
Percentage changes over 1 month												
1947							.7	-.6	.5	.7	2.1	.3
1948	.5	1.8	.3	1.4	-.1	1.8	-1.5	.0	.2	.2	.3	.1
1949	.2	.2	-.3	-.3	1.8	.5	.1	.1	.4	.5	.0	.3
1950	.3	.3	.3	.4	.3	-.5	.0	-.4	.6	1.1	.4	.5
1951	.9	.9	.7	1.6	2.5	.3	1.5	.5	.7	.7	.4	.7
1952	1.8	.1	.5	1.6	.0	1.7	-.1	-.6	-.2	.9	-.1	.7
1953	-.1	.3	.7	.9	-.4	.6	.0	-.7	-.2	.0	.3	-.4
1954	.2	-.2	.9	.4	-.3	.6	1.7	-.6	-.2	.5	.5	.5
1955	.4	.0	.0	.5	-.2	2.1	.4	-.7	.6	1.1	1.6	.0
1956	-.3	.0	1.3	1.4	-.2	-.1	-.4	.3	-.2	.6	.4	.3
1957	1.0	-.1	-.2	.4	.1	1.1	.9	-.2	-.3	.9	.6	.5
1958	-.1	-.5	.7	1.1	-.4	.9	-1.5	-.2	.1	.9	.4	.4
1959	.2	-.1	.0	-.7	-.4	.2	-.3	.3	-.5	.5	.7	.2
1960	-.3	.0	-.2	.5	.0	.5	.2	-.6	.1	.8	.4	.3
1961	.1	.0	.4	.5	.3	.9	.0	1.0	-.2	.2	1.0	.2
1962	.3	.1	.4	1.4	.3	.7	-.4	-.9	-.1	-.1	.4	.5
1963	.4	.9	.1	.3	-.1	.0	-.6	-.3	.3	.4	.3	.2
1964	.5	.1	.4	.9	.8	.4	.0	.4	.0	.1	.8	.4
1965	.3	.0	.4	1.9	.4	.3	.0	.2	.1	.1	.4	.4
1966	.2	.1	.2	1.2	.7	.3	-.4	.6	-.2	.3	.6	.2
1967	.2	.1	.0	.8	-.1	.4	-.6	-.3	-.1	.8	.6	.7
1968	.3	.5	.3	1.8	.1	.4	.1	.2	.1	.5	.2	1.3
1969	.5	.5	.4	1.1	-.2	.5	.0	-.2	.3	.8	.2	.7
1970	.8	.5	.6	1.5	.3	.3	.7	-.1	.5	1.1	.7	.7
1971	1.4	.5	.8	2.1	.7	.7	.6	.1	.1	.6	.6	.5
1972	.6	.5	.3	.9	.5	.7	.3	.8	.5	1.4	.4	.5
1973	.6	.6	.6	1.9	.7	.5	.4	.3	.9	2.0	.8	.7
1974	1.9	1.7	.9	3.4	1.4	1.0	.9	.1	1.1	2.0	1.8	1.5
1975	2.6	1.7	2.0	3.9	4.2	1.9	1.0	.6	.9	1.4	1.2	1.2
1976	1.3	1.3	.5	1.9	1.1	.5	.2	1.4	1.3	1.8	1.4	1.3
1977	2.6	1.0	1.0	2.6	.8	1.0	.1	.5	.5	.4	.5	.5
1978	.6	.6	.6	1.5	.6	.8	.5	.7	.4	.4	.7	.8
1979	1.5	.8	.8	1.7	.8	1.7	4.3	.8	1.0	1.0	.9	.7
1980	2.5	1.4	1.4	3.4	.9	.9	.8	.2	.6	.6	.8	.5
1981	.6	.9	1.5	2.9	.7	.6	.4	.7	.6	.9	1.1	.6
1982	.6	.0	.9	2.0	.7	.3	.0	.0	-.1	.5	.5	-.2
1983	.1	.4	.2	1.4	.4	.2	.5	.4	.4	.4	.4	.3
1984	-.1	.4	.3	1.3	.4	.3	-.1	.9	.2	.6	.3	-.1
1985	.4	.8	.9	2.1	.5	.2	-.2	.3	-.1	.2	.3	.1
1986	.2	.4	.1	1.0	.2	-.1	-.3	.3	.5	.2	.8	.3
1987	.4	.4	.2	1.2	.1	.0	-.1	.3	.3	.5	.5	-.1
1988	.0	.4	.4	1.6	.4	.4	.1	1.1	.5	1.0	.5	.3
1989	.6	.7	.4	1.8	.6	.3	.1	.3	.7	.8	.9	.3
1990	.6	.6	1.0	3.0	.9	.4	.1	1.0	.9	.8	-.2	-.1
1991	.2											

4 ALL ITEMS EXCEPT FOOD

	Jan	Feb	Mar	Apr	May	Jun	Jul	Aug	Sep	Oct	Nov	Dec
Indices: June 1947 = 100												
1947						100.0	100.5	100.5	101.1	101.7	103.5	103.9
1948	104.5	104.9	105.1	107.1	107.5	107.7	107.9	108.3	108.6	108.9	109.0	109.2
1949	109.4	109.5	109.4	108.6	108.6	108.7	108.8	108.8	108.9	108.7	108.8	108.9
1950	109.0	109.2	109.3	109.6	108.8	108.6	108.9	109.1	109.5	110.0	110.7	111.3
1951	112.2	113.5	114.5	116.0	118.1	118.5	119.2	120.2	121.1	121.4	121.7	122.3
1952	123.3											
Indices: January 1952 = 100												
1952	100.0	100.1	100.5	101.0	100.8	100.7	100.6	100.8	100.9	100.9	101.1	101.3
1953	101.3	101.4	101.8	102.3	101.6	101.7	101.9	102.0	102.2	102.4	102.8	103.0
1954	102.9	103.1	103.2	103.3	103.1	103.2	103.2	103.3	103.5	103.7	104.1	104.2
1955	104.3	104.5	104.6	104.7	104.5	104.9	105.1	105.9	106.4	106.8	108.4	108.9
1956	109.4											
Indices: January 1956 = 100												
1956	100.0	100.2	100.4	101.0	101.6	102.1	102.6	102.6	102.8	103.2	103.4	104.1
1957	104.6	104.7	105.1	105.4	105.1	105.2	105.7	106.1	106.8	108.3	109.2	109.4
1958	109.5	109.7	109.8	110.1	109.6	109.8	109.9	110.0	109.9	110.1	110.6	110.8
1959	110.8	110.9	111.0	110.0	109.6	109.8	109.9	110.0	110.2	110.2	111.0	111.0
1960	111.1	111.2	111.3	112.3	111.9	112.1	112.3	112.5	112.9	113.5	114.2	114.4
1961	114.7	114.9	115.6	116.1	115.8	116.3	116.7	118.8	119.2	119.9	120.8	120.9
1962	121.2											
Indices: January 1962 = 100												
1962	100.0	100.2	100.3	100.9	101.1	101.3	101.5	101.5	101.7	101.9	102.1	102.3
1963	102.2	102.3	102.5	102.9	102.8	103.0	103.2	103.3	103.4	103.5	104.0	104.1
1964	104.3	104.5	104.8	105.3	106.5	106.6	106.7	107.4	107.6	107.7	108.4	108.9
1965	109.2	109.3	109.6	112.2	112.6	112.8	112.9	113.2	113.6	113.8	114.3	114.4
1966	114.8	115.0	115.3	116.3	116.3	116.5	116.8	117.8	118.0	118.2	118.7	118.8
1967	119.0	119.1	119.1	119.4	119.1	119.2	119.5	119.6	119.8	120.8	121.4	121.7
1968	121.9	122.4	122.8	125.3	125.5	125.9	126.1	126.6	127.0	127.6	127.8	129.5
1969	130.2	130.5	130.7	131.6	131.6	131.8	132.1	132.3	132.6	133.7	134.1	134.9
1970	135.8	136.3	136.9	138.9	139.1	139.4	140.5	141.4	141.9	143.7	144.6	145.4
1971	147.0	147.9	148.9	151.8	152.3	152.9	154.1	154.5	154.8	156.0	156.5	156.6
1972	157.4	158.1	158.5	160.9	161.4	161.9	162.6	163.4	164.5	167.4	167.8	168.1
1973	168.4	168.8	169.1	172.5	173.2	174.1	175.0	175.7	176.6	179.1	180.4	181.3
1974	184.0											
Indices: January 1974=100												
1974	100.0	102.0	102.8	107.0	108.7	109.6	111.1	111.1	112.1	114.2	115.8	117.7
1975	120.4	122.1	123.8	128.7	135.0	137.5	139.2	140.3	141.5	143.8	145.0	146.6
1976	147.9	149.1	149.8	152.7	154.7	155.9	157.2	158.6	159.5	161.8	163.8	165.6
1977	169.3	171.1	172.6	177.6	179.3	180.8	181.5	182.7	183.8	184.9	185.9	186.6
1978	187.5	188.8	189.9	192.7	193.6	194.5	195.9	197.6	198.6	199.8	201.1	202.4
1979	204.3	206.2	207.9	212.1	213.7	216.7	228.6	230.6	233.4	235.9	238.0	239.3
1980	245.5	249.4	252.5	262.7	265.3	267.9	270.1	271.2	273.3	275.4	278.0	279.2
1981	280.3	282.8	287.7	297.2	298.9	300.2	302.0	305.3	306.9	309.5	312.9	314.4
1982	314.6	314.4	317.2	324.5	326.6	328.2	329.4	330.7	330.3	332.2	333.7	332.5
1983	332.6	334.2	335.0	340.3	341.7	341.9	344.3	345.9	346.9	347.9	349.0	349.4
1984	348.9	350.3	351.0	355.9	357.0	357.8	358.0	362.5	364.0	366.4	367.6	367.0
1985	367.8	371.0	374.6	383.5	385.5	386.3	386.7	388.0	387.6	388.4	389.5	389.6
1986	390.2	391.4	391.5	395.6	395.8	395.3	394.9	396.1	398.5	399.6	403.7	404.7
1987	405.6											
Indices: January 1987 = 100												
1987	100.0	100.4	100.6	101.8	101.8	101.9	102.1	102.4	102.8	103.3	103.8	103.5
1988	103.4	103.8	104.2	106.0	106.4	106.9	107.2	108.5	109.1	110.4	110.9	111.0
1989	111.7	112.5	113.0	115.2	115.9	116.3	116.6	116.9	117.6	118.5	119.5	119.7
1990	120.2	120.9	122.1	126.3	127.4	128.0	128.4	129.6	131.1	132.2	131.7	131.4
1991	131.6											

5 ALL ITEMS EXCEPT SEASONAL FOOD

	Jan	Feb	Mar	Apr	May	Jun	Jul	Aug	Sep	Oct	Nov	Dec
Indices: January 1956 = 100												
1956	100.0	99.9	100.4	100.8	101.2	101.7	102.0	102.1	102.4	103.2	103.3	104.0
1957	104.8	105.0	105.1	105.2	105.0	105.2	105.5	105.5	106.0	106.9	107.3	107.3
1958	107.4	107.3	107.7	108.1	107.8	108.3	108.3	108.4	108.7	108.9	109.5	109.8
1959	109.9	110.0	109.9	109.0	108.8	108.9	109.1	109.5	109.6	109.6	110.3	110.3
1960	110.2	110.2	110.0	110.5	110.4	110.4	110.8	111.1	111.4	111.8	112.3	112.6
1961	112.8	112.8	113.2	113.7	113.5	113.9	114.1	115.5	115.7	116.0	116.7	117.0
1962	117.3											
Indices: January 1962 = 100												
1962	100.0	100.2	100.4	100.7	101.2	101.6	101.8	101.8	102.2	102.3	102.5	102.8
1963	102.7	102.9	102.9	103.0	103.1	102.9	103.3	103.5	103.7	104.3	104.6	104.8
1964	105.1	105.3	105.7	106.3	107.3	107.5	107.8	108.4	108.6	108.7	109.3	109.8
1965	110.2	110.2	110.4	112.3	112.6	112.8	112.9	113.4	113.6	113.7	114.1	114.3
1966	114.6	114.8	115.1	116.1	116.2	116.5	116.8	117.6	117.7	117.9	118.2	118.3
1967	118.6	118.8	118.8	119.3	119.1	119.1	119.2	119.2	119.3	120.2	120.6	121.3
1968	121.7	122.3	122.6	124.8	124.9	125.4	125.7	126.1	126.4	127.0	127.2	128.6
1969	129.3	129.8	129.9	130.7	130.8	131.4	131.8	131.9	132.4	133.5	133.8	134.5
1970	135.5	136.0	136.6	138.3	138.7	139.2	140.5	141.3	142.2	143.7	144.6	145.5
1971	147.1	148.0	148.9	151.9	152.8	153.6	155.1	155.5	155.9	157.0	157.6	158.0
1972	159.1	159.8	160.2	161.8	162.3	163.3	164.0	165.1	166.2	168.7	169.1	169.7
1973	170.8	171.4	171.9	174.6	175.5	176.7	177.8	179.0	180.4	183.5	184.9	186.1
1974	189.4											
Indices: January 1974=100												
1974	100.0	101.9	102.8	106.3	107.7	108.6	110.0	110.3	111.5	113.7	115.6	117.4
1975	120.5	122.5	124.8	129.4	134.8	137.1	138.5	139.7	140.9	142.8	144.5	146.1
1976	147.6	149.0	149.5	152.2	154.2	155.4	156.8	158.5	160.0	162.8	164.8	166.8
1977	170.9	172.5	174.3	178.7	180.5	182.4	183.5	184.9	186.2	187.3	188.2	189.0
1978	190.2	191.4	192.4	195.0	196.1	197.2	198.7	200.4	201.4	202.4	203.8	205.1
1979	207.3	209.1	210.6	214.0	215.9	219.4	230.1	232.1	234.6	237.0	238.9	240.5
1980	246.2	249.8	253.2	262.0	264.7	267.1	269.3	270.5	272.3	274.1	276.3	277.6
1981	279.3	281.8	285.9	294.1	295.8	297.3	298.9	301.8	303.3	305.7	308.9	310.4
1982	311.5	311.6	314.1	320.2	322.0	323.4	324.6	325.9	325.9	327.6	329.2	328.4
1983	328.5	329.8	330.4	334.8	336.2	336.7	338.7	340.2	341.0	342.1	343.1	343.7
1984	343.5	344.8	345.8	350.1	351.3	352.5	352.7	356.5	357.9	360.0	361.3	361.0
1985	361.8	364.7	367.8	375.5	377.3	378.1	378.5	379.7	379.5	380.0	381.1	381.3
1986	381.9	383.3	383.4	387.0	387.3	387.0	386.8	387.9	390.0	390.9	394.3	395.3
1987	396.4											
Indices: January 1987 = 100												
1987	100.0	100.3	100.6	101.6	101.7	101.8	101.9	102.2	102.6	103.1	103.6	103.3
1988	103.3	103.6	104.0	105.7	106.1	106.6	106.9	108.1	108.7	109.8	110.3	110.5
1989	111.2	111.9	112.4	114.4	115.1	115.6	115.9	116.2	117.0	117.9	118.9	119.0
1990	119.6	120.3	121.4	125.1	126.3	126.9	127.3	128.5	129.8	130.7	130.4	130.2
1991	130.4											

6 ALL ITEMS EXCEPT HOUSING

	Jan	Feb	Mar	Apr	May	Jun	Jul	Aug	Sep	Oct	Nov	Dec
Indices: June 1947 = 100												
1947						100.0	100.8	100.1	100.7	101.4	103.7	104.0
1948	104.6	106.7	107.0	108.7	108.6	110.7	108.8	108.8	109.1	109.3	109.6	109.7
1949	109.9	110.1	109.8	109.4	111.6	112.2	112.3	112.4	112.8	113.5	113.5	113.8
1950	114.1	114.4	114.8	115.1	115.4	114.8	114.8	114.3	115.1	116.4	117.0	117.6
1951	118.8	120.0	120.9	122.8	126.1	126.5	128.6	129.2	130.2	131.2	131.7	132.7
1952	135.2											
Indices: January 1952 = 100												
1952	100.0	100.1	100.6	102.2	102.2	104.0	103.9	103.2	103.0	103.9	103.8	104.6
1953	104.5	104.7	105.5	106.3	105.8	106.5	106.4	105.7	105.5	105.4	105.7	105.3
1954	105.5	105.3	106.3	106.6	106.3	106.9	108.9	108.1	107.9	108.4	108.9	109.5
1955	109.9	109.9	109.9	110.5	110.3	112.7	113.2	112.3	113.0	114.2	116.2	116.2
1956	115.6											
Indices: January 1956 = 100												
1956	100.0	100.0	101.4	102.7	102.5	102.4	101.9	102.2	101.9	102.5	102.9	103.3
1957	104.3	104.2	104.0	104.1	104.1	105.3	106.3	106.0	105.7	106.4	106.9	107.4
1958	107.2	106.6	107.4	108.6	108.1	109.1	107.2	106.9	107.0	108.0	108.4	108.8
1959	108.9	108.8	108.8	107.8	107.4	107.5	107.1	107.5	106.8	107.3	108.2	108.4
1960	108.1	108.1	107.8	108.3	108.2	108.9	109.1	108.3	108.4	109.4	109.9	110.2
1961	110.2	110.2	110.6	111.0	111.3	112.4	112.4	113.5	113.3	113.4	114.7	114.9
1962	115.3											
Indices: January 1962 = 100												
1962	100.0	100.1	100.5	101.7	102.1	102.8	102.3	101.3	101.1	101.0	101.4	102.0
1963	102.4	103.4	103.4	103.6	103.4	103.3	102.6	102.3	102.6	103.0	103.3	103.5
1964	104.0	104.1	104.5	105.2	106.2	106.6	106.6	107.0	107.0	107.0	108.0	108.4
1965	108.8	108.7	109.2	111.0	111.4	111.7	111.7	111.9	112.0	112.0	112.6	113.0
1966	113.2	113.3	113.5	114.5	115.4	115.7	115.1	115.8	115.6	115.9	116.7	116.9
1967	117.0	117.1	117.1	117.9	117.7	118.3	117.4	117.1	116.9	117.7	118.4	119.2
1968	119.6	120.2	120.7	123.0	123.1	123.6	123.6	123.8	123.9	124.5	124.8	126.7
1969	127.4	128.2	128.7	130.0	129.8	130.4	130.4	130.0	130.4	131.3	131.6	132.6
1970	133.8	134.5	135.3	136.9	137.3	137.7	138.8	138.7	139.4	140.7	141.7	142.8
1971	145.0	145.9	147.2	149.8	150.9	152.1	153.1	153.1	153.3	154.0	154.9	155.7
1972	156.7	157.6	158.1	158.7	159.5	160.6	161.1	162.5	163.5	164.8	165.4	166.3
1973	167.5	168.7	169.8	172.8	174.0	174.8	175.7	176.2	178.0	181.4	182.5	184.0
1974	187.9											
Indices: January 1974=100												
1974	100.0	101.7	102.7	105.9	107.6	108.8	109.9	110.5	111.7	114.1	116.1	118.0
1975	121.3	123.4	125.8	129.6	135.6	138.3	139.8	140.6	141.8	143.8	145.7	147.7
1976	149.7	151.8	152.6	154.9	157.0	157.8	158.1	160.5	162.7	165.8	168.3	170.0
1977	175.0	176.8	178.6	182.3	184.1	186.3	186.7	187.5	188.7	189.8	190.8	191.8
1978	193.0	194.7	196.0	198.0	199.2	200.7	201.4	202.4	203.3	203.9	205.4	206.7
1979	209.5	211.3	213.0	215.3	217.1	220.6	231.1	232.9	235.4	237.8	239.9	241.8
1980	246.2	249.6	253.1	259.1	261.6	264.0	266.2	266.6	268.4	269.8	272.0	273.5
1981	275.9	278.7	283.5	288.0	289.8	291.5	292.9	295.2	297.0	298.6	300.8	302.1
1982	304.3	305.2	308.2	312.6	315.3	316.1	316.0	315.9	317.0	318.7	320.5	321.5
1983	322.1	323.5	324.1	327.4	329.0	329.8	330.6	331.9	333.4	334.3	335.6	336.4
1984	336.1	337.6	338.9	342.7	344.6	345.6	345.0	345.3	345.6	347.6	348.5	349.3
1985	350.7	352.4	355.8	360.6	362.1	362.7	361.6	362.5	363.8	364.5	365.5	365.8
1986	366.4	367.8	368.1	370.0	370.9	372.3	370.8	371.9	373.7	374.3	375.3	376.3
1987	377.8											
Indices: January 1987 = 100												
1987	100.0	100.4	100.6	101.2	101.6	101.6	101.4	101.7	102.1	102.6	103.0	103.2
1988	103.2	103.6	104.0	105.0	105.5	105.9	106.0	106.4	106.9	107.4	107.8	108.0
1989	108.5	109.0	109.4	110.6	111.3	111.6	111.6	111.8	112.5	113.3	113.8	114.0
1990	114.6	115.3	115.9	117.6	118.8	119.1	119.1	120.3	121.6	122.6	122.7	122.6
1991	122.7											

7 ALL ITEMS EXCEPT MORTGAGE INTEREST PAYMENTS

	Jan	Feb	Mar	Apr	May	Jun	Jul	Aug	Sep	Oct	Nov	Dec
Indices: January 1974 = 100												
1975	120.5	122.6	125.0	130.0	135.6	138.2	139.6	140.4	141.6	143.7	145.4	147.2
1976	149.1	151.1	151.8	154.8	156.7	157.5	157.8	160.0	162.1	165.1	167.4	169.0
1977	173.5	175.2	177.0	181.6	183.3	185.3	185.7	186.6	187.6	188.7	189.7	190.7
1978	191.8	193.3	194.6	197.4	198.5	200.0	200.7	201.6	202.4	203.2	204.6	205.9
1979	208.4	210.1	211.7	215.4	217.0	220.4	230.2	232.0	234.2	236.6	238.7	240.4
1980	244.5	247.6	251.0	259.9	262.2	264.7	266.8	267.3	268.9	270.5	272.6	274.1
1981	276.2	278.9	283.2	292.1	294.3	295.9	297.1	299.3	300.9	303.6	305.6	306.8
1982	308.5	308.4	311.1	318.7	321.2	322.0	322.0	322.0	322.9	324.6	326.2	327.2
1983	327.7	329.1	329.6	334.3	335.7	336.4	337.1	338.3	339.8	340.9	342.0	342.9
1984	342.5	343.9	344.9	350.7	352.1	352.9	352.4	352.8	353.1	355.1	356.0	356.8
1985	358.2	359.6	362.8	369.4	370.9	371.6	370.7	371.6	372.8	373.5	374.7	375.1
1986	375.7	377.0	377.4	381.8	382.6	384.0	382.7	383.8	385.6	386.0	387.0	388.0
1987	389.4											
Indices: January 1987 = 100												
1987	100.0	100.4	100.6	101.6	102.0	102.1	101.9	102.2	102.5	103.0	103.4	103.6
1988	103.7	104.0	104.4	105.9	106.5	106.9	107.0	107.3	107.8	108.3	108.7	108.9
1989	109.4	109.9	110.4	112.2	112.9	113.2	113.2	113.4	114.1	114.9	115.3	115.5
1990	116.1	116.7	117.3	121.1	122.1	122.5	122.6	123.7	124.9	125.8	125.9	125.9
1991	126.0											

8 ALL ITEMS EXCEPT MORTGAGE INTEREST PAYMENTS AND RATES / COMMUNITY CHARGE

	Jan	Feb	Mar	Apr	May	Jun	Jul	Aug	Sep	Oct	Nov	Dec
Indices: January 1987 = 100												
1975	31.5	32.1	32.8	33.7	35.2	35.9	36.3	36.5	36.8	37.4	37.8	38.3
1976	38.9	39.4	39.6	40.3	40.8	41.0	41.1	41.7	42.3	43.1	43.7	44.1
1977	45.3	45.8	46.3	47.3	47.8	48.3	48.4	48.7	48.9	49.2	49.5	49.8
1978	50.1	50.5	50.8	51.4	51.7	52.1	52.3	52.6	52.8	53.0	53.4	53.7
1979	54.4	54.8	55.3	56.0	56.4	57.3	60.0	60.4	61.0	61.7	62.2	62.7
1980	63.8	64.6	65.6	67.4	68.1	68.7	69.3	69.4	69.9	70.3	70.9	71.2
1981	71.8	72.5	73.7	75.6	76.1	76.6	76.9	77.5	77.9	78.4	78.9	79.3
1982	79.8	80.1	80.8	82.3	82.9	83.1	83.1	83.1	83.4	83.9	84.3	84.6
1983	84.7	85.1	85.2	86.2	86.6	86.8	87.0	87.3	87.7	88.0	88.3	88.6
1984	88.5	88.8	89.1	90.4	90.8	91.1	90.9	91.0	91.1	91.6	91.9	92.1
1985	92.5	92.8	93.7	95.2	95.6	95.7	95.5	95.7	96.0	96.2	96,5	96.6
1986	96.8	97.2	97.3	98.0	98.2	98.5	98.2	98.5	98.9	99.1	99.4	99.6
1987	100.0	100.4	100.6	101.3	101.7	101.8	101.6	101.9	102.3	102.8	103.2	103.4
1988	103.5	103.9	104.2	105.4	106.0	106.4	106.5	106.9	107.4	107.9	108.4	108.5
1989	109.1	109.6	110.0	111.6	112.2	112.6	112.6	112.8	113.5	114.3	114.8	115.0
1990	115.5	116.2	116.8	118.9	120.0	120.4	120.5	121.7	122.9	123.9	124.0	123.9
1991	124.1											

9 PRESENT STRUCTURE OF THE RPI

Groups	Sub-groups	Sections
FOOD & CATERING	FOOD	Bread Cereals Biscuits & cakes Beef Lamb *of which* Home-killed lamb Pork Bacon Poultry Other meat Fish *of which* Fresh fish Butter Oils & fats Cheese Eggs Milk, fresh Milk products Tea Coffee & other hot drinks Soft drinks Sugar & preserves Sweets & chocolates Potatoes *of which* Unprocessed potatoes Vegetables *of which* Fresh vegetables Fruit *of which* Fresh fruit Other foods
	CATERING	Restaurant meals Canteen meals Take-aways & snacks

ALCOHOL & TOBACCO	ALCOHOLIC DRINK	Beer
		of which On sales
		           Off sales
		Wines & spirits
		of which On sales
		           Off sales

	TOBACCO	Cigarettes Tobacco
HOUSING & HOUSEHOLD EXPENDITURE	HOUSING	Rent Mortgage interest payments Rates Water & other charges Repair & maintenance charges Do-it-yourself materials House insurance & ground rent
	FUEL & LIGHT	Coal & solid fuels Electricity Gas Oil & other fuel
	HOUSEHOLD GOODS	Furniture Furnishings Electrical appliances Other household equipment Household consumables Pet care
	HOUSEHOLD SERVICES	Postage Telephones, telemessages etc Domestic services Fees & subscriptions
PERSONAL EXPENDITURE	CLOTHING & FOOTWEAR	Men's outerwear Women's outerwear Children's outerwear Other clothing Footwear

Groups	Sub-groups	Sections
PERSONAL EXPENDITURE (cont.)	PERSONAL GOODS & SERVICES	Personal articles Chemists' goods Personal services
TRAVEL & LEISURE	MOTORING EXPENDITURE	Purchase of motor vehicles Maintenance of motor vehicles Petrol & oil Vehicle tax & insurance
	FARES & OTHER TRAVEL COSTS	Rail fares Bus & coach fares Other travel costs
	LEISURE GOODS	Audio-visual equipment Records & tapes Toys, photographic/sports gds Books & newspapers Gardening products
	LEISURE SERVICES	Television licences & rentals Entertainment & recreation

	1947-1951	1952-1955	1956-1961	1962-1967	1968-1973	1974	1975	1976-1979	1980-1986	1987-1990
Bread						X	X	X	X	X
Cereals	O	O	X	X	X	X	X	X	X	X
Biscuits & cakes						X	X	X	X	X
Beef						X	X	X	X	X
Lamb						X	X	X	X	X
of which Home-killed lamb						X	X	X	X	X
Pork	O	O	X	X	X	X	X	X	X	X
Bacon						X	X	X	X	X
Poultry						X	X	X	X	X
Other meat						X	X	X	X	X
Fish	O	O	X	X	X	X	X	X	X	X
of which Fresh fish	O	O	O	O	O	X[1]	X[1]	X[1]	X[1]	X
Butter						X	X	X	X	X
	O	O	X	X	X					
Oils & fats						X	X	X	X	X
Cheese						X	X	X	X	X
Eggs						X	X	X	X	X
	O	O	X	X	X					
Milk, fresh						X	X	X	X	X
Milk products						X	X	X	X	X
Tea						X	X	X	X	X
Coffee & other hot drinks	O	O	X	X	X	X	X	X	X	X
Soft drinks						X	X	X	X	X
Sugar & preserves						X	X	X	X	X
	O	O	X	X	X					
Sweets & chocolates						X	X	X	X	X
Potatoes						X	X	X	X	X
of which Unprocessed potatoes						X	X	X	X	X
	O	O	X	X	X					
Other vegetables						X	X	X	X	X
of which Fresh vegetables						X	X	X	X	X
Fruit	O	O	X	X	X	X	X	X	X	X
of which Fresh fruit	O	O	O	O	O	X	X	X	X	X
Other foods	O	O	X[2]	X[2]	X[2]	X	X	X	X	X
FOOD	X[2]	X[2]	X[2]	X[2]	X[2]	X	X	X	X	X
Seasonal food	O	O	X	X	X	X	X	X	X	X
Non-seasonal food	O	O	X	X	X	X	X	X	X	X
Canteen meals	O	O	O	O	O	X	X	X	X	X
Restaurant meals									X	X
	O	O	O	O	O	X	X	X		
Take-away meals & snacks									X	X
CATERING	O	O	O	O	X	X	X	X	X	X
Beer	O	O	O	O	O	X	X	X	X	X
- "On" sales	O	O	O	O	O	O	O	O	O	X
- "Off" sales	O	O	O	O	O	O	O	O	O	X
Wines & spirits	O	O	O	O	O	X	X	X	X	X
- "On" sales	O	O	O	O	O	O	O	O	O	X
- "Off" sales	O	O	O	O	O	O	O	O	O	X
ALCOHOLIC DRINK	O	X	X	X	X	X	X	X	X	X
Cigarettes	O	O	O	O	O	X	X	X	X	X
Other tobacco	O	O	O	O	O	X	X	X	X	X
TOBACCO	O	X	X	X	X	X	X	X	X	X
Rent	O	O	O	X[3]	X[3]	X[3]	X	X	X	X
Mortgage interest payments	O	O	O	O	O	O	X	X	X	X
Rates								X	X	X[4]
	O	O	O	X	X	X	X			
Water charges								X	X	X
Repair & maintenance charges						X	X	X	X	X
	O	O	O	X	X					
Do-it-yourself materials						X	X	X	X	X
HOUSING	X	X	X	X	X	X	X	X	X	X
Coal & solid fuels	O	O	X	X	X	X	X	X	X	X
Electricity				X	X	X	X	X	X	X
Gas	O	O	X	X	X	X	X	X	X	X
Oil & other fuel				O	O	X	X	X	X	X
FUEL & LIGHT	X	X	X	X	X	X	X	X	X	X
Furniture						X	X	X	X	X
	O	O	X	X	X					
Furnishings						X	X	X	X	X
Electrical appliances	O	O	O	O	O	X	X	X	X	X
Other household equipment	O	O	X	X	X	X	X	X	X	X
Household consumables	O	O	O	X[5]	X[5]	X	X	X	X	X
Pet care	O	O	O	O	O	X[6]	X[6]	X[6]	X[6]	X
HOUSEHOLD GOODS	O	O	O	O	O	X	X	X	X	X

	1947-1951	1952-1955	1956-1961	1962-1967	1968-1973	1974	1975	1976-1979	1980-1986	1987-1990
Postage	O	O	X	X	X	X	X	X	X	X
Telephone charges etc						X	X	X	X	X
Domestic services						X	X	X	X	X
	O	O	O	O	O					
Fees & subscriptions						X	X	X	X	X
HOUSEHOLD SERVICES	O	O	O	O	O	X	X	X	X	X
Men's outerwear	O	O	X	X	X	X	X	X	X	X
Women's outerwear	O	O	X	X	X	X	X	X	X	X
Children's outerwear	O	O	O	O	O	X	X	X	X	X
Other clothing	O	O	O	O	O	X	X	X	X	X
Footwear	O	O	X	X	X	X	X	X	X	X
CLOTHING & FOOTWEAR	X	X	X	X	X	X	X	X	X	X
Personal articles	O	O	O	O	O	O	O	O	O	X
Chemists' goods	O	O	O	X	X	X	X	X	X	X
Personal services	O	O	O	O	O	X	X	X	X	X
PERSONAL GOODS & SERVICES	O	O	O	O	O	O	O	O	O	X
Purchase of motor vehicles	O	O	O	O	O	X	X	X	X	X
Maintenance of motor vehicles	O	O	O	O	O	X	X	X	X	X
Petrol & oil	O	O	O	O	O	X	X	X	X	X
Vehicle tax & insurance	O	O	O	O	O	X	X	X	X	X
MOTORING EXPENDITURE	O	O	X [7]	X [7]	X [7]	X]	X	X	X	X
Rail fares	O	O	X	X	X	X	X	X	X	X
Bus & coach fares						X	X	X	X	X
Other travel costs	O	O	O	O	O	X	X	X	X	X
FARES & OTHER TRAVEL COSTS	O	O	O	O	O	X	X	X	X	X
Audio-visual equipment	O	O	O	O	O	X	X	X	X	X
Records & tapes	O	O	O	O	O	O	O	O	O	X
Toys, photo & sports goods	O	O	O	O	O	O	O	O	O	X
Books & newspapers	O	O	X	X	X	X	X	X	X	X
Gardening products	O	O	O	O	O	X	X	X	X	X
LEISURE GOODS	O	O	O	O	O	O	O	O	O	X
TV licences & rentals	O	O	O	O	O	X	X	X	X	X
Entertainment & recreation	O	O	O	O	O	X	X	X	X	X
LEISURE SERVICES	O	O	X	X	X	X	X	X	X	X
FOOD & CATERING	O	O	O	O	O	X	X	X	X	X
ALCOHOL & TOBACCO	X	X	X	X	X	X	X	X	X	X
HOUSING & H'HOLD EXPENDITURE	O	O	O	O	O	X	X	X	X	X
PERSONAL EXPENDITURE	O	O	O	O	O	O	O	O	O	X
TRAVEL & LEISURE	O	O	O	O	O	O	O	O	O	X
ALL ITEMS EXCEPT:-										
FOOD	X	X	X	X	X	X	X	X	X	X
SEASONAL FOOD	O	O	X	X	X	X	X	X	X	X
HOUSING	X	X	X	X	X	X	X	X	X	X
MORTGAGE INTEREST PAYMENTS	O	O	O	O	O	O	X	X	X	X
MORTGAGE INTEREST PAYMENTS & RATES / COMMUNITY CHARGE	O	O	O	O	O	O	X	X	X	X
CONSUMER DURABLES	O	O	O	O	O	O	O	O	O	X
NATIONALISED INDUSTRIES	O	O	O	X	X	X	X	X	X	X [8]

[1]   Includes smoked fish
[2]   Includes petfood
[3]   Includes imputed rent
[4]   Includes community charge in 1989 and 1990
[5]   Excludes stationery
[6]   Petfood only
[7]   Includes cycling costs
[8]   Discontinued November 1989

X   Available
O   Not available

11 FOOD & CATERING

	Jan	Feb	Mar	Apr	May	Jun	Jul	Aug	Sep	Oct	Nov	Dec
Indices: January 1974 = 100												
1974	100.0	100.9	102.0	103.4	104.7	106.1	105.9	106.7	108.1	110.8	113.5	114.6
1975	118.3	121.1	125.3	130.2	132.3	135.4	136.2	136.4	137.6	138.8	141.8	144.3
1976	148.1	151.7	153.3	156.4	156.9	156.9	154.4	158.9	164.2	168.8	172.0	175.2
1977	182.1	183.4	185.6	188.7	189.4	193.0	191.9	192.2	193.6	193.5	194.2	195.9
1978	196.5	197.7	198.8	201.8	203.4	206.5	206.4	206.9	207.0	206.8	209.0	211.2
1979	217.7	218.9	220.4	222.3	224.7	230.5	233.9	234.7	236.6	239.2	241.3	244.1
1980	249.0	251.4	255.5	259.0	261.4	263.5	265.8	265.1	265.7	266.1	267.0	269.4
1981	273.3	275.4	284.1	280.6	283.2	286.3	286.4	284.5	286.9	290.0	292.6	295.5
1982	302.5	303.7	306.1	308.9	312.0	310.7	307.2	303.9	304.7	305.5	307.6	308.9
1983	310.6	311.2	311.5	313.8	315.1	318.3	318.3	319.3	322.8	324.4	326.1	328.5
1984	330.2	331.7	334.0	337.4	340.2	341.6	339.8	338.5	336.9	338.3	339.1	340.2
1985	342.9	344.6	347.3	350.9	351.8	352.8	348.8	349.4	349.9	349.9	351.6	353.7
1986	355.7	358.2	359.7	362.4	364.8	366.8	363.4	364.8	365.0	364.7	364.9	367.5
1987	371.5											
Indices: January 1987 = 100												
1987	100.0	100.6	100.7	101.5	102.1	101.7	100.9	101.3	101.2	101.8	102.4	103.1
1988	103.7	104.3	104.7	105.3	105.7	105.9	105.2	105.7	106.2	106.4	107.1	107.8
1989	108.7	109.0	109.6	110.8	111.5	111.9	111.6	112.1	112.8	113.8	114.8	115.8
1990	117.2	118.1	118.7	119.9	121.2	121.3	120.6	121.7	122.2	122.5	123.4	124.1
1991	124.9											

	Jan	Feb	Mar	Apr	May	Jun	Jul	Aug	Sep	Oct	Nov	Dec
Indices: June 1947 = 100												
1947						100.0	100.0	100.0	100.0	100.0	104.0	104.1
1948	104.1	104.1	104.1	110.8	110.8	110.8	110.8	110.8	110.8	110.8	110.8	110.8
1949	110.8	110.8	110.8	107.6	107.5	107.5	107.5	107.5	107.5	107.5	107.5	107.5
1950	107.5	107.5	107.5	107.5	104.0	103.9	103.9	103.9	103.9	103.9	104.0	104.1
1951	104.1	104.1	104.3	104.3	106.6	106.8	106.8	106.8	108.0	108.0	108.0	108.0
1952	108.5											
Indices: January 1952 = 100												
1952	100.0	100.0	100.0	100.0	100.4	100.4	100.6	100.6	100.6	100.5	100.5	100.5
1953	100.5	100.6	100.6	100.6	100.6	100.6	100.8	100.8	100.8	100.8	100.8	100.8
1954	100.9	100.9	100.9	100.8	100.8	100.8	100.9	100.9	100.9	100.9	100.9	101.4
1955	101.3	101.3	101.3	101.4	101.4	101.4	101.7	101.7	101.8	101.8	103.0	103.0
1956	103.0											
Indices: January 1956 = 100												
1956	100.0	100.0	100.0	100.0	103.1	103.3	103.7	103.7	103.7	104.0	104.0	104.0
1957	104.0	104.0	104.5	104.6	104.6	104.6	104.7	105.0	106.3	106.8	106.8	106.8
1958	106.9	106.9	106.9	106.8	106.8	106.8	106.9	106.9	106.9	106.9	106.9	106.9
1959	106.9	106.9	106.9	103.1	103.1	103.1	103.2	103.2	103.5	103.4	103.4	103.4
1960	103.4	103.4	103.4	106.1	106.0	106.0	106.1	106.1	106.1	106.1	106.1	106.1
1961	106.2	106.2	106.2	106.2	106.2	107.2	108.5	115.3	115.7	116.3	116.3	116.3
1962	116.4											
Indices: January 1962 = 100												
1962	100.0	100.0	100.0	100.0	100.0	100.0	100.1	100.2	100.3	100.3	100.3	100.3
1963	100.4	100.4	100.4	100.4	101.0	101.3	101.3	101.3	101.4	101.4	101.4	101.4
1964	101.4	101.6	101.6	101.6	108.5	108.5	108.5	109.8	109.8	109.7	109.8	109.8
1965	110.1	110.5	110.3	119.8	120.0	120.0	120.0	120.0	120.0	120.0	120.0	120.0
1966	120.0	120.0	120.0	120.0	120.0	120.0	120.0	122.8	123.1	123.0	123.0	122.9
1967	122.9	123.0	122.9	123.0	123.0	123.0	123.0	123.0	123.0	122.9	122.9	122.8
1968	122.8	122.8	122.8	126.4	126.4	126.4	126.4	127.9	127.9	126.7	126.8	134.4
1969	135.3	135.4	135.4	135.6	135.8	135.9	136.2	136.3	136.3	136.5	136.4	138.9
1970	139.0	139.0	139.0	139.1	139.1	139.1	139.4	139.4	139.4	139.9	141.6	142.3
1971	144.6	144.6	144.6	145.0	145.0	145.0	145.6	145.6	145.6	145.6	145.6	145.6
1972	145.9	146.0	146.3	147.8	148.1	148.2	148.6	149.1	151.4	152.0	151.9	151.9
1973	152.2	152.2	152.2	152.6	152.3	152.3	152.5	152.5	152.5	152.9	152.9	153.0
1974	154.0											
Indices: January 1974 = 100												
1974	100.0	101.1	102.1	111.4	114.7	114.8	115.5	114.4	115.4	117.8	118.1	119.2
1975	120.4	121.3	122.6	123.7	142.9	146.4	147.9	149.1	149.9	150.2	150.4	152.3
1976	154.0	155.3	156.0	157.5	163.2	165.4	167.2	167.8	168.3	168.4	170.4	171.6
1977	180.8	182.9	184.7	190.2	192.0	195.3	195.7	196.9	198.1	198.9	198.9	198.9
1978	200.8	202.2	204.8	206.5	206.5	206.5	207.1	208.0	208.7	210.0	210.0	210.0
1979	210.4	211.2	213.8	215.8	217.5	217.9	235.9	237.1	241.4	244.0	245.1	245.8
1980	251.7	254.0	257.8	271.4	272.5	273.4	275.8	277.1	282.1	283.6	283.6	283.6
1981	285.3	292.5	306.5	325.4	325.4	325.4	328.6	332.7	337.5	342.2	342.7	342.7
1982	345.2	347.6	354.6	360.9	366.5	367.2	369.2	370.5	372.7	376.7	376.2	374.6
1983	378.0	381.0	382.3	389.4	392.3	393.6	394.3	395.6	396.0	397.3	398.1	398.9
1984	401.2	404.5	406.1	418.8	423.2	423.8	423.8	424.6	427.5	431.7	430.9	431.1
1985	433.5	436.2	437.5	448.1	451.1	451.6	453.0	455.1	458.0	461.1	462.5	460.2
1986	463.0	465.7	467.0	475.5	480.2	481.4	482.5	483.8	485.5	487.4	487.6	486.9
1987	491.3											
Indices: January 1987 = 100												
1987	100.0	100.2	100.4	100.5	100.7	100.9	101.0	101.2	101.7	102.5	102.6	102.5
1988	103.0	103.4	103.6	105.2	105.6	105.7	105.9	106.4	106.9	107.5	107.8	107.7
1989	108.5	108.9	109.2	109.6	109.9	110.2	110.6	111.3	112.0	113.0	113.1	113.1
1990	113.7	114.3	114.8	118.6	120.9	121.3	122.4	123.0	123.5	124.4	124.6	125.1
1991	126.0											

13 HOUSING & HOUSEHOLD EXPENDITURE

	Jan	Feb	Mar	Apr	May	Jun	Jul	Aug	Sep	Oct	Nov	Dec
Indices: January 1974 = 100												
1974	100.0	101.5	102.2	105.8	107.1	108.3	110.4	109.9	110.7	112.3	114.5	115.6
1975	117.6	119.2	121.1	129.7	133.6	136.6	138.4	139.4	140.3	144.5	145.7	147.2
1976	148.0	149.1	149.7	154.0	154.8	156.0	157.1	158.2	158.9	162.4	163.7	166.9
1977	168.5	169.6	170.8	177.3	178.4	179.6	179.8	180.4	180.7	182.0	183.0	184.0
1978	185.4	185.3	186.3	191.0	191.5	193.2	194.6	196.9	197.6	198.9	200.3	202.4
1979	204.8	206.6	208.2	214.7	216.1	219.4	226.6	229.2	232.0	235.0	238.1	239.7
1980	249.0	253.3	256.4	270.1	273.8	278.1	281.2	282.8	285.5	288.9	294.6	296.1
1981	296.1	297.7	..	314.6	317.9	320.3	321.7	323.8	325.2	330.1	337.7	340.5
1982	341.0	340.1	342.1	352.2	353.4	356.0	357.3	359.3	355.7	357.2	359.7	355.4
1983	355.5	356.0	356.9	364.0	363.8	364.2	368.2	369.8	371.0	372.8	374.6	375.6
1984	375.9	377.8	378.8	383.8	383.2	384.0	384.7	395.4	398.0	400.2	402.7	400.2
1985	400.9	407.2	410.2	424.2	426.2	428.1	429.0	430.4	426.8	427.4	429.9	431.4
1986	431.7	433.4	434.7	442.2	442.1	437.0	436.8	437.9	439.6	440.7	450.3	452.0
1987	452.0											
Indices: January 1987 = 100												
1987	100.0	100.3	100.5	102.8	102.2	102.1	102.2	102.5	102.7	103.1	103.7	102.9
1988	102.9	103.2	103.5	106.4	106.6	107.1	107.7	110.5	111.1	113.2	114.1	114.3
1989	115.4	116.8	117.4	120.7	121.4	122.0	122.7	123.2	123.9	124.9	127.2	127.7
1990	128.4	129.0	131.3	138.5	139.8	140.7	141.4	142.5	143.6	144.8	143.8	143.8
1991	144.2											

14 PERSONAL EXPENDITURE

	Jan	Feb	Mar	Apr	May	Jun	Jul	Aug	Sep	Oct	Nov	Dec
Indices: January 1987 = 100												
1987	100.0	100.3	100.8	101.1	101.1	101.2	100.1	100.7	101.8	102.4	103.2	103.6
1988	102.2	102.9	103.7	104.1	105.3	105.8	104.6	104.7	105.8	107.4	108.1	108.3
1989	107.4	108.4	108.9	111.0	111.6	111.7	110.7	110.9	112.5	113.7	114.3	114.6
1990	113.4	114.7	115.6	117.0	117.6	117.5	116.0	117.2	119.3	120.3	121.1	121.1
1991	118.6											

15 TRAVEL & LEISURE

	Jan	Feb	Mar	Apr	May	Jun	Jul	Aug	Sep	Oct	Nov	Dec
Indices: January 1987 = 100												
1987	100.0	100.6	100.8	101.6	102.2	102.5	103.2	103.4	103.7	104.2	104.5	104.3
1988	104.5	104.5	104.9	106.4	106.7	107.3	107.9	108.3	108.6	109.0	109.1	109.0
1989	109.8	110.2	110.7	112.3	113.3	113.6	113.7	113.4	113.9	114.4	114.5	114.0
1990	114.8	115.4	115.9	118.0	118.6	119.1	119.6	121.4	123.5	124.6	123.7	122.4
1991	122.8											

16 FOOD

	Jan	Feb	Mar	Apr	May	Jun	Jul	Aug	Sep	Oct	Nov	Dec
Indices: June 1947 = 100												
1947						100.0	101.2	99.4	99.6	100.6	103.2	103.4
1948	103.6	108.3	108.8	109.3	108.4	113.5	108.2	107.5	107.4	107.6	108.1	107.9
1949	108.2	108.6	108.0	108.5	114.3	115.5	115.6	116.0	116.8	119.0	118.9	119.5
1950	120.3	120.6	121.3	122.0	124.5	123.1	122.3	120.9	122.1	124.6	124.7	125.4
1951	126.9	127.5	128.0	130.6	135.4	135.9	139.8	139.7	140.6	142.8	143.5	144.9
1952	149.7											
Indices: January 1952 = 100												
1952	100.0	100.1	100.8	103.9	104.4	108.7	108.5	106.8	106.1	108.3	107.9	109.3
1953	109.2	109.6	110.7	112.5	112.7	113.8	113.7	111.7	111.0	110.6	110.9	109.6
1954	110.2	109.5	111.6	112.6	112.1	113.6	118.0	116.2	115.2	116.1	116.9	118.2
1955	119.2	118.8	118.6	119.9	119.8	124.8	125.6	122.4	123.6	125.9	128.0	127.1
1956	125.4											
Indices: January 1956 = 100												
1956	100.0	99.6	102.9	106.0	104.2	102.9	101.1	101.7	100.8	101.8	102.5	102.3
1957	104.0	103.5	102.1	102.7	103.9	106.7	108.4	106.9	104.8	104.7	104.8	106.0
1958	105.4	103.9	105.7	108.7	108.5	110.9	106.0	105.2	105.6	108.1	108.4	109.2
1959	109.8	109.1	108.9	108.6	108.1	108.4	107.4	108.1	106.1	107.4	108.2	108.7
1960	107.8	107.4	106.8	106.6	107.3	108.9	108.8	106.4	106.1	107.4	107.6	108.1
1961	107.7	107.5	107.4	108.0	109.5	111.4	110.7	109.9	108.5	108.0	109.8	110.2
1962	110.7											
Indices: January 1962 = 100												
1962	100.0	99.8	100.9	104.1	104.7	106.4	104.6	101.9	101.1	100.5	101.1	102.3
1963	103.8	106.5	106.5	106.5	106.4	105.8	103.7	102.3	103.0	104.2	104.1	104.6
1964	105.4	105.4	105.8	107.4	107.8	109.1	108.9	108.7	108.1	108.0	109.4	109.9
1965	110.3	109.9	110.4	111.6	111.9	112.5	112.0	112.1	111.7	111.4	112.2	113.3
1966	113.0	112.8	113.1	115.2	118.0	118.4	116.2	116.1	115.1	115.4	116.6	117.0
1967	117.6	117.5	117.5	119.6	120.1	121.8	118.4	117.3	116.7	117.0	118.2	120.1
1968	121.1	121.8	122.1	123.5	123.6	124.1	123.8	123.2	122.6	123.4	123.9	125.4
1969	126.1	128.2	129.4	132.1	131.6	133.3	132.0	130.5	131.3	131.8	132.0	133.4
1970	134.7	136.3	137.6	140.1	141.0	141.6	142.1	139.5	140.6	141.4	142.4	144.1
1971	147.0	147.6	149.4	153.7	156.3	158.5	158.5	158.0	157.6	158.0	160.1	162.8
1972	163.9	165.1	166.0	164.6	166.3	169.2	169.2	172.3	172.4	172.8	174.3	176.9
1973	180.4	183.7	187.1	189.9	193.3	194.3	194.6	194.4	198.5	205.1	207.0	210.5
1974	216.7											
Indices: January 1974 = 100												
1974	100.0	100.9	102.0	103.2	104.5	105.9	105.5	106.1	107.5	110.4	113.3	114.4
1975	118.3	121.3	126.0	130.7	132.7	135.9	136.3	136.3	137.3	138.4	141.6	144.2
1976	148.3	152.1	153.8	156.7	157.1	156.7	153.4	158.4	164.4	169.3	172.7	176.1
1977	183.1	184.5	186.5	189.6	189.9	193.7	192.0	191.9	192.5	192.3	192.9	194.8
1978	196.1	197.3	198.4	201.6	203.2	206.7	206.1	206.2	206.3	205.6	207.9	210.5
1979	217.5	218.7	220.2	221.6	224.0	230.0	231.2	231.8	232.6	234.8	237.0	239.9
1980	244.8	246.7	251.1	254.1	255.7	257.9	259.9	259.0	259.0	259.3	260.0	262.7
1981	266.7	268.9	270.6	274.2	276.7	280.0	279.6	277.3	279.6	282.7	285.5	288.5
1982	296.1	297.2	299.8	302.6	305.6	304.1	299.5	295.5	295.9	296.5	298.8	300.1
1983	301.8	302.1	302.4	304.6	305.6	308.8	308.7	309.4	313.0	314.5	316.1	318.5
1984	319.8	321.4	323.8	327.3	329.4	330.6	328.5	326.9	324.9	326.2	326.6	327.6
1985	330.6	332.5	335.4	338.8	339.3	340.1	335.3	335.3	335.8	335.5	337.4	339.4
1986	341.1	343.6	345.2	347.4	349.8	351.4	347.4	348.6	348.3	347.6	347.5	349.8
1987	354.0											
Indices: January 1987 = 100												
1987	100.0	100.7	100.7	101.6	102.2	101.6	100.4	100.7	100.4	101.1	101.6	102.4
1988	102.9	103.6	103.9	104.4	104.7	104.8	104.0	104.4	104.8	104.9	105.7	106.5
1989	107.4	107.7	108.3	109.6	110.3	110.7	110.1	110.6	111.3	112.4	113.5	114.5
1990	116.0	117.0	117.7	118.8	120.1	120.0	118.8	120.0	120.3	120.4	121.3	122.1
1991	122.9											

17 CATERING *

	Jan	Feb	Mar	Apr	May	Jun	Jul	Aug	Sep	Oct	Nov	Dec
Indices: January 1962 = 100												
1968	121.4	121.9	122.4	126.3	126.8	127.5	127.9	128.6	129.4	129.7	130.1	130.3
1969	130.5	131.0	131.4	133.2	133.6	134.5	136.0	137.1	137.2	138.1	138.5	138.9
1970	139.4	139.7	140.5	143.3	144.3	145.0	146.2	147.7	148.1	149.9	150.7	151.3
1971	153.1	156.5	158.1	163.5	164.5	166.0	167.4	168.1	169.3	170.2	171.2	171.9
1972	172.9	173.4	174.1	176.3	177.4	180.1	181.8	182.7	183.9	185.6	187.2	188.3
1973	190.2	191.8	193.5	211.6	212.8	214.0	214.9	216.9	218.1	220.7	222.2	224.7
1974	229.5											
Indices: January 1974 = 100												
1974	100.0	101.0	102.2	104.8	106.1	107.5	109.1	110.4	111.7	113.8	115.3	116.5
1975	118.7	120.5	122.1	128.0	129.9	132.3	135.4	136.6	139.2	140.8	142.1	143.6
1976	146.2	148.3	149.5	153.1	154.6	156.3	158.0	159.9	161.2	164.4	167.0	169.1
1977	172.3	173.8	176.5	178.8	182.0	184.0	186.4	188.7	194.7	195.9	197.4	198.0
1978	199.5	200.6	201.7	203.9	205.4	206.7	208.9	211.1	211.4	213.2	215.1	215.7
1979	218.7	220.1	221.7	225.4	227.3	231.0	246.1	248.4	255.7	259.4	261.4	263.6
1980	267.8	273.3	276.3	281.9	288.9	290.9	294.8	296.5	299.9	301.5	303.7	304.6
1981	307.5	309.2	311.8	312.9	315.5	317.4	319.8	320.4	322.6	325.0	326.3	328.1
1982	329.7	331.9	334.2	336.4	339.1	340.3	342.6	344.5	347.0	349.8	351.6	352.8
1983	353.7	355.3	356.5	358.9	361.4	363.5	364.1	366.1	368.9	370.8	373.4	375.7
1984	378.5	379.7	381.6	383.9	390.1	393.2	392.7	393.6	395.7	398.3	400.1	401.6
1985	401.8	403.0	404.8	408.4	411.2	413.2	414.6	417.1	418.6	420.7	422.4	423.8
1986	426.7	428.9	429.9	434.3	436.2	439.3	440.4	442.6	445.3	447.8	449.5	452.9
1987	454.8											
Indices: January 1987 = 100												
1987	100.0	100.4	100.8	101.4	101.8	102.3	102.9	103.6	104.3	104.7	105.3	105.8
1988	106.4	107.1	107.5	108.5	108.9	109.5	109.7	110.4	111.1	111.7	112.1	112.4
1989	113.1	113.5	114.1	115.0	115.6	116.2	116.8	117.4	118.0	118.9	119.5	120.1
1990	121.2	121.8	122.4	123.9	125.0	125.9	127.1	127.7	129.1	130.0	130.8	131.4
1991	132.2											

* Called Meals bought and consumed outside the home until January 1987

18 ALCOHOLIC DRINK

	Jan	Feb	Mar	Apr	May	Jun	Jul	Aug	Sep	Oct	Nov	Dec
Indices: January 1952 = 100												
1952	100.0	100.1	100.1	100.1	100.8	100.8	101.2	101.2	101.2	101.1	101.1	101.1
1953	101.0	101.0	101.0	101.0	101.0	101.0	101.4	101.4	101.4	101.4	101.4	101.4
1954	101.5	101.5	101.5	101.4	101.4	101.4	101.6	101.6	101.6	101.6	101.6	102.6
1955	102.5	102.5	102.5	102.7	102.7	102.7	102.8	102.8	103.0	103.1	103.1	103.1
1956	103.1											
Indices: January 1956 = 100												
1956	100.0	100.0	100.0	100.0	100.7	101.1	101.9	101.9	101.9	102.6	102.6	102.6
1957	102.6	102.6	103.6	103.9	103.9	103.9	104.1	104.7	104.7	105.7	105.7	105.7
1958	105.8	105.8	105.8	105.6	105.6	105.6	105.8	105.8	105.8	105.8	105.8	105.8
1959	105.9	105.9	105.9	97.8	97.8	97.8	98.1	98.1	98.1	98.0	98.0	98.0
1960	98.1	98.1	98.1	98.0	98.0	98.0	98.2	98.2	98.2	98.3	98.3	98.3
1961	98.4	98.4	98.4	98.4	98.4	99.0	101.7	106.0	106.9	108.0	108.0	108.0
1962	108.2											
Indices: January 1962 = 100												
1962	100.0	100.0	100.0	100.0	100.0	100.0	100.3	100.4	100.6	100.6	100.6	100.6
1963	100.9	100.9	101.0	101.0	102.3	102.8	103.0	103.0	103.2	103.2	103.2	103.2
1964	103.2	103.5	103.5	103.5	110.0	110.0	110.2	110.2	110.2	110.0	110.1	110.1
1965	110.9	111.8	111.3	118.7	119.0	119.1	119.0	119.0	119.0	119.1	119.0	119.0
1966	119.0	119.0	119.0	119.0	119.0	119.0	119.1	125.1	125.7	125.6	125.5	125.2
1967	125.4	125.4	125.3	125.4	125.4	125.4	125.4	125.4	125.4	125.3	125.2	125.0
1968	125.0	125.1	125.0	127.0	127.1	127.1	127.1	127.2	127.2	127.3	127.2	132.7
1969	134.7	134.8	134.8	135.1	135.5	135.6	136.2	136.2	136.2	136.5	136.4	142.7
1970	143.0	143.0	143.0	143.2	143.2	143.2	143.6	143.6	143.6	144.4	145.8	147.0
1971	151.3	151.4	151.4	152.2	152.2	152.3	153.4	153.4	153.4	153.6	153.6	153.6
1972	154.1	154.3	155.0	157.8	158.3	158.6	159.3	160.3	161.8	162.9	162.7	162.7
1973	163.3	163.3	163.3	164.5	164.0	164.0	164.3	164.4	164.3	164.8	164.9	164.9
1974	166.0											
Indices: January 1974 = 100												
1974	100.0	101.2	102.6	109.5	110.5	110.7	111.7	110.7	111.6	115.4	116.0	116.3
1975	118.2	119.5	120.7	122.3	137.3	139.7	141.8	143.5	143.8	144.3	144.5	146.6
1976	149.0	150.9	151.9	154.3	158.7	159.7	162.4	163.3	164.1	164.5	165.8	166.9
1977	173.7	176.4	179.3	181.2	183.9	184.0	184.6	185.7	187.4	188.3	188.3	188.3
1978	188.9	191.0	194.8	196.6	196.6	196.6	197.5	197.5	197.5	198.4	198.4	198.4
1979	198.9	200.1	203.9	206.7	209.2	209.8	224.4	226.2	228.5	231.1	232.7	233.7
1980	241.4	244.7	247.7	259.4	260.4	261.7	265.1	265.2	272.3	274.6	274.6	274.6
1981	277.7	283.0	299.8	306.5	306.5	306.5	311.0	311.0	313.9	318.5	319.3	319.3
1982	321.8	324.4	332.1	338.8	342.3	341.3	344.1	345.7	348.8	352.0	351.7	348.8
1983	353.7	356.0	357.0	363.9	366.7	368.2	369.4	371.4	371.8	373.4	372.7	373.2
1984	376.1	379.0	380.2	385.6	387.6	387.9	387.7	389.0	392.4	397.1	394.8	395.2
1985	397.9	399.7	400.9	409.2	411.2	411.0	412.5	415.5	419.3	423.5	423.7	420.4
1986	423.8	425.9	426.5	427.6	428.8	429.4	431.0	432.5	434.6	436.6	436.0	434.6
1987	440.7											
Indices: January 1987 = 100												
1987	100.0	100.3	100.6	100.8	101.2	101.4	101.7	102.1	102.8	103.5	103.3	103.1
1988	103.7	104.2	104.6	106.1	106.6	106.8	107.1	107.7	108.4	109.1	109.1	108.9
1989	109.9	110.5	110.9	111.5	111.9	112.2	112.9	114.0	114.7	115.5	115.4	115.5
1990	116.3	117.1	117.8	121.5	123.8	124.3	125.8	126.7	127.4	128.2	128.3	128.6
1991	129.7											

19 TOBACCO

	Jan	Feb	Mar	Apr	May	Jun	Jul	Aug	Sep	Oct	Nov	Dec
Indices: January 1952 = 100												
1952	100.0	100.0	100.0	100.0	100.0	100.0	100.0	100.0	100.0	100.0	100.0	100.0
1953	100.0	100.3	100.3	100.3	100.3	100.3	100.3	100.3	100.3	100.3	100.3	100.3
1954	100.3	100.3	100.3	100.3	100.3	100.3	100.3	100.3	100.3	100.3	100.3	100.3
1955	100.3	100.3	100.3	100.3	100.3	100.3	100.7	100.7	100.7	100.7	102.9	102.9
1956	102.9											
Indices: January 1956 = 100												
1956	100.0	100.0	100.0	100.0	105.3	105.3	105.3	105.3	105.3	105.3	105.3	105.3
1957	105.3	105.3	105.3	105.3	105.3	105.3	105.3	105.3	107.8	107.8	107.8	107.8
1958	107.8	107.8	107.8	107.8	107.8	107.8	107.8	107.8	107.8	107.8	107.8	107.8
1959	107.8	107.8	107.8	107.8	107.8	107.8	107.8	107.8	108.2	108.2	108.2	108.2
1960	108.1	108.1	108.1	113.2	113.1	113.1	113.1	113.1	113.1	113.1	113.1	113.1
1961	113.1	113.1	113.1	113.1	113.1	114.4	114.6	123.6	123.6	123.6	123.6	123.6
1962	123.6											
Indices: January 1962 = 100												
1962	100.0	100.0	100.0	100.0	100.0	100.0	100.0	100.0	100.0	100.0	100.0	100.0
1963	100.0	100.0	100.0	100.0	100.0	100.0	100.0	100.0	100.0	100.0	100.0	100.0
1964	100.0	100.0	100.0	100.0	107.2	107.2	107.2	109.5	109.5	109.5	109.5	109.5
1965	109.5	109.5	109.5	120.8	120.8	120.8	120.8	120.8	120.8	120.8	120.8	120.8
1966	120.8	120.8	120.8	120.8	120.8	120.8	120.8	120.8	120.8	120.8	120.8	120.8
1967	120.7	120.8	120.8	120.8	120.8	120.8	120.8	120.8	120.8	120.8	120.8	120.8
1968	120.8	120.8	120.8	125.4	125.4	125.4	125.4	127.8	127.8	125.7	125.9	134.8
1969	135.1	135.2	135.2	135.3	135.3	135.4	135.5	135.7	135.8	135.8	135.8	135.8
1970	135.8	135.8	135.8	135.8	135.8	135.8	136.0	136.0	136.0	136.2	138.2	138.4
1971	138.6	138.6	138.5	138.5	138.5	138.5	138.5	138.5	138.5	138.4	138.4	138.4
1972	138.4	138.4	138.4	138.4	138.4	138.4	138.4	138.4	141.5	141.6	141.6	141.6
1973	141.6	141.6	141.6	141.0	141.0	141.0	141.0	141.0	141.0	141.2	141.2	141.4
1974	142.2											
Indices: January 1974 = 100												
1974	100.0	100.9	101.4	114.6	121.6	121.6	121.6	120.3	121.6	121.6	121.6	123.8
1975	124.0	124.0	125.5	125.7	152.6	158.4	158.7	158.8	160.5	160.7	160.7	162.2
1976	162.6	162.8	162.8	162.8	170.8	175.3	175.3	175.3	175.3	175.0	178.1	179.7
1977	193.2	194.3	193.7	206.5	206.5	216.1	216.1	217.6	217.6	218.2	218.2	218.2
1978	222.8	222.8	222.8	224.2	224.2	224.2	224.2	227.0	229.2	231.1	231.1	231.1
1979	231.5	231.5	231.5	231.9	231.9	231.9	256.7	256.7	264.8	267.5	267.5	267.5
1980	269.7	269.7	275.2	292.9	294.3	294.3	294.3	298.4	298.4	297.9	297.9	297.9
1981	296.6	307.9	315.2	362.2	362.2	362.2	362.2	375.7	384.9	389.7	389.7	389.7
1982	392.1	393.8	399.1	404.4	414.9	419.2	419.5	419.9	420.0	425.8	424.8	426.5
1983	426.2	430.9	432.9	440.3	443.2	444.0	443.5	443.2	443.5	444.0	448.6	450.0
1984	450.8	455.1	457.6	488.0	498.1	499.7	500.1	499.6	501.1	504.0	507.0	506.6
1985	508.1	513.1	514.5	530.8	536.4	538.7	539.6	539.2	539.8	540.0	544.4	544.8
1986	545.7	549.9	553.2	580.8	594.4	597.3	597.1	597.5	598.3	599.9	602.2	603.1
1987	602.9											
Indices: January 1987 = 100												
1987	100.0	99.9	99.9	99.8	99.8	99.8	99.7	99.5	99.7	100.5	101.1	101.2
1988	101.4	101.6	101.6	103.2	103.7	103.6	103.4	103.6	103.7	104.2	105.1	105.2
1989	105.6	105.7	105.8	105.8	105.8	105.9	105.8	105.8	106.4	107.7	108.1	108.2
1990	108.3	108.4	108.4	112.4	114.8	115.0	115.0	115.1	115.2	116.5	116.9	117.6
1991	118.2											

	Jan	Feb	Mar	Apr	May	Jun	Jul	Aug	Sep	Oct	Nov	Dec
Indices: June 1947 = 100												
1947						100.0	100.0	100.0	100.0	100.1	100.1	100.1
1948	100.1	100.1	100.1	99.1	99.1	99.2	99.2	99.2	99.2	99.5	99.5	99.5
1949	99.6	99.6	99.6	100.1	100.1	100.1	100.1	100.1	100.1	100.3	100.3	100.3
1950	100.4	100.4	100.4	101.3	101.3	101.3	101.3	101.3	101.4	101.4	101.4	101.5
1951	101.5	101.5	101.5	103.7	103.8	103.8	103.9	103.9	103.9	104.2	104.2	104.2
1952	104.2											
Indices: January 1952 = 100												
1952	100.0	100.1	100.2	102.1	102.3	102.5	102.6	102.8	102.9	103.3	103.4	103.6
1953	103.7	104.3	104.4	108.2	108.4	108.5	108.7	108.8	108.9	109.5	109.6	109.8
1954	109.9	110.1	110.3	111.6	111.7	111.9	112.0	112.2	112.3	112.5	112.7	113.2
1955	113.5	113.7	113.9	114.4	114.7	114.9	115.0	115.2	115.4	116.4	116.6	116.7
1956	117.9											
Indices: January 1956 = 100												
1956	100.0	100.4	100.5	102.9	102.7	102.9	103.1	103.2	103.7	104.5	104.7	104.8
1957	105.0	105.2	105.4	108.9	109.4	109.7	110.0	110.2	110.5	114.1	115.9	116.9
1958	117.7	118.1	118.4	120.6	121.2	122.2	122.6	123.3	123.3	123.8	124.2	125.1
1959	125.8	126.2	126.2	127.1	127.3	128.1	128.5	128.5	128.7	128.8	129.1	129.2
1960	129.3	129.3	129.5	131.6	131.9	132.1	132.2	132.4	132.5	132.8	133.3	133.6
1961	134.0	134.4	134.7	137.0	137.4	137.8	138.2	138.4	138.7	139.8	140.2	140.3
1962	140.6											
Indices: January 1962 = 100												
1962	100.0	100.3	100.5	103.3	103.5	103.9	104.1	104.3	104.7	104.9	105.1	105.2
1963	105.5	105.7	106.1	107.7	108.0	108.8	109.1	109.5	109.7	109.8	110.1	110.2
1964	110.9	111.1	111.3	113.8	114.1	114.3	114.6	114.9	115.0	115.7	115.8	115.9
1965	116.1	116.2	116.5	120.7	121.0	121.2	121.6	121.7	121.9	122.5	122.8	123.6
1966	123.7	123.9	124.5	129.0	129.2	129.5	129.9	130.1	130.1	130.5	130.7	130.9
1967	131.3	131.8	131.8	133.4	134.0	134.1	134.6	134.9	135.2	136.8	137.6	138.2
1968	138.6	139.4	139.5	140.6	140.9	141.3	141.6	142.0	142.2	142.9	143.3	143.6
1969	143.7	143.9	144.0	146.4	146.6	146.8	147.1	147.5	147.6	149.5	150.0	150.4
1970	150.6	151.4	152.2	157.9	158.3	158.6	158.8	159.3	159.8	162.7	163.7	163.8
1971	164.2	164.4	165.0	173.1	173.4	173.7	173.8	174.3	174.5	177.5	178.2	178.6
1972	178.8	179.3	179.7	188.8	189.5	190.2	190.6	191.3	191.5	202.2	202.5	203.5
1973	203.8	204.2	204.3	210.2	212.0	213.7	213.7	214.0	214.4	219.4	223.6	224.1
1974	225.1											
Indices: January 1974 = 100												
1974	100.0	101.4	101.7	107.2	107.6	108.1	108.2	105.1	105.8	107.1	108.6	109.0
1975	110.3	111.1	111.8	125.8	126.6	128.7	129.3	130.5	131.1	133.1	133.8	134.2
1976	134.8	135.8	136.3	143.5	142.6	143.1	143.8	144.5	145.4	147.5	147.9	153.6
1977	154.1	154.6	155.7	166.3	164.3	164.3	163.3	164.3	164.8	163.3	163.3	163.8
1978	164.3	162.1	162.3	170.6	170.0	172.1	174.1	177.8	178.6	180.5	181.4	185.4
1979	190.3	191.4	192.7	205.0	206.9	211.2	214.0	215.4	216.7	219.5	221.1	222.1
1980	237.4	241.7	243.8	269.8	272.1	275.1	277.0	278.8	280.3	283.7	286.4	287.4
1981	285.0	284.7	285.9	317.7	320.4	321.7	322.6	324.0	325.5	334.5	345.6	351.0
1982	350.0	344.5	345.6	364.9	364.2	365.8	366.8	368.1	359.0	360.4	360.9	348.8
1983	348.1	349.0	349.7	363.5	363.4	364.0	373.0	375.5	376.7	379.6	380.5	381.6
1984	382.6	383.8	383.6	393.1	390.6	390.5	392.0	413.9	417.8	420.8	423.1	416.2
1985	416.4	427.7	431.2	458.4	461.3	463.8	465.8	467.1	457.0	457.0	459.7	462.0
1986	463.7	465.7	467.5	483.5	482.7	471.6	472.8	475.2	477.3	478.4	497.4	501.1
1987	502.4											
Indices: January 1987 = 100												
1987	100.0	100.3	100.7	105.0	103.6	103.4	103.8	104.1	104.4	104.9	105.6	103.9
1988	103.9	104.3	104.7	109.9	109.4	109.8	110.2	115.8	116.5	120.7	122.1	122.5
1989	124.6	127.0	127.7	134.0	134.7	135.5	136.6	137.4	138.2	139.6	143.9	144.8
1990	145.8	146.7	151.0	165.4	166.7	167.6	169.0	170.1	171.0	172.0	169.7	169.6
1991	170.6											

21 FUEL AND LIGHT

	Jan	Feb	Mar	Apr	May	Jun	Jul	Aug	Sep	Oct	Nov	Dec
Indices: June 1947 = 100												
1947						100.0	100.1	100.0	103.6	106.1	106.9	107.1
1948	109.2	110.1	110.1	109.7	110.2	110.4	110.8	111.1	111.2	112.0	112.0	113.7
1949	113.8	113.8	111.8	111.5	111.5	112.5	112.9	112.9	113.2	113.8	114.1	114.7
1950	115.1	115.2	115.4	115.2	116.4	114.0	114.9	115.7	116.8	117.8	119.9	121.9
1951	122.3	125.6	126.3	128.3	126.9	125.6	127.5	127.8	128.8	129.8	132.4	134.2
1952	140.1											
Indices: January 1952 = 100												
1952	100.0	100.3	100.5	101.5	99.6	100.7	100.9	101.1	101.7	101.8	103.3	104.5
1953	104.5	104.4	107.2	107.7	104.7	105.4	105.6	105.8	106.5	106.5	109.6	110.5
1954	110.7	111.1	112.0	112.1	109.6	110.0	110.2	110.2	110.7	111.0	113.7	114.5
1955	114.9	114.8	114.8	114.8	111.4	112.7	113.0	119.2	120.9	121.6	125.7	127.5
1956	127.6											
Indices: January 1956 = 100												
1956	100.0	100.0	100.0	100.1	98.0	100.8	100.9	101.1	101.9	102.4	104.5	105.9
1957	106.2	106.3	106.3	106.3	101.8	102.9	106.3	108.1	109.2	109.9	115.3	115.6
1958	115.6	115.5	115.6	115.7	109.9	110.5	110.7	110.7	110.8	110.9	116.5	116.6
1959	116.6	116.9	117.0	117.0	111.1	111.1	111.1	111.4	111.7	112.2	118.7	119.0
1960	119.0	119.0	119.1	119.0	112.3	112.4	112.4	112.9	113.5	117.6	124.7	125.4
1961	125.8	126.1	126.1	126.2	120.9	121.7	121.8	122.2	122.4	122.8	130.2	130.4
1962	130.6											
Indices: January 1962 = 100												
1962	100.0	100.4	100.5	100.8	99.8	100.1	100.2	100.7	100.9	101.1	105.5	106.1
1963	106.5	106.6	106.8	106.8	103.2	103.9	104.2	104.5	104.8	104.9	109.5	109.7
1964	110.1	110.2	110.0	110.1	106.1	106.5	106.5	108.9	109.4	109.7	110.2	114.4
1965	114.8	115.1	115.7	110.5	111.2	112.1	112.2	112.7	115.2	115.4	119.6	119.6
1966	119.7	120.1	120.1	120.3	119.4	119.5	119.7	120.4	120.7	120.8	124.8	124.9
1967	124.9	124.9	124.9	124.8	120.1	120.2	120.3	120.6	120.9	127.2	130.0	132.4
1968	132.6	132.7	132.7	133.3	130.8	131.9	132.0	132.6	133.2	137.6	138.0	138.2
1969	138.4	138.5	138.5	138.6	134.8	134.8	134.9	135.3	135.4	141.3	141.6	141.7
1970	145.3	145.5	145.6	145.5	142.1	142.1	142.1	143.1	143.9	150.8	150.9	150.9
1971	152.6	154.0	156.5	159.0	157.8	159.1	162.6	162.8	162.8	167.7	167.7	167.7
1972	168.2	169.0	170.5	174.3	172.2	172.8	172.8	173.3	173.3	178.0	178.0	178.0
1973	178.3	178.3	178.3	178.3	175.2	175.2	175.3	175.3	175.3	181.3	183.0	185.8
1974	188.6											
Indices: January 1974 = 100												
1974	100.0	102.6	103.2	103.2	106.2	109.6	113.6	115.7	115.8	116.0	120.4	122.4
1975	124.9	127.8	130.0	136.7	144.0	151.4	154.9	155.0	155.6	159.6	161.9	166.8
1976	168.7	169.4	169.7	174.6	180.0	183.8	185.6	187.0	187.3	191.3	194.9	196.7
1977	198.8	198.0	198.7	202.9	210.4	214.5	216.6	217.3	217.5	220.8	220.3	220.0
1978	219.9	221.1	222.0	223.6	226.4	228.9	230.6	230.6	230.6	230.3	233.7	232.8
1979	233.1	234.4	236.3	237.2	238.0	241.3	251.6	257.2	262.1	265.5	273.5	275.8
1980	277.1	278.2	282.3	289.1	300.5	315.3	322.8	324.1	330.8	337.4	348.8	351.4
1981	355.7	357.4	357.5	363.0	373.3	384.2	389.2	393.0	393.2	396.4	398.5	398.6
1982	401.9	406.5	410.2	416.2	426.1	436.0	441.2	445.4	445.5	449.0	458.1	462.9
1983	467.0	464.8	465.6	465.5	462.6	461.8	461.9	465.2	466.0	466.7	468.8	469.0
1984	469.3	472.1	474.0	475.7	477.6	479.3	479.9	480.3	480.6	483.0	486.0	487.3
1985	487.5	488.7	491.7	497.4	498.5	500.4	501.5	502.6	504.7	504.7	506.8	507.4
1986	507.0	507.0	507.0	506.8	504.2	504.8	505.0	505.8	506.7	506.4	506.1	505.3
1987	506.1											
Indices: January 1987 = 100												
1987	100.0	100.0	99.8	99.9	99.4	99.4	99.1	99.0	98.5	98.0	98.3	98.2
1988	98.3	98.0	97.8	99.1	100.7	102.4	103.6	103.4	103.6	103.7	103.9	104.1
1989	104.2	104.2	104.3	105.4	106.4	107.6	108.4	108.7	109.0	109.4	109.7	110.0
1990	110.6	109.9	110.1	111.7	114.3	116.0	116.7	118.6	119.5	121.9	120.8	120.5
1991	121.6											

22 HOUSEHOLD GOODS

	Jan	Feb	Mar	Apr	May	Jun	Jul	Aug	Sep	Oct	Nov	Dec
Indices: January 1974 = 100												
1974	100.0	101.3	102.5	106.6	107.8	108.7	112.0	112.8	114.0	117.3	119.2	121.0
1975	123.1	125.4	127.0	130.1	134.7	136.4	138.3	139.8	141.3	143.7	145.2	146.2
1976	146.2	147.6	148.4	148.9	149.6	150.2	151.6	153.1	153.9	159.7	161.1	162.3
1977	165.3	168.5	170.5	173.0	175.1	176.1	177.3	180.0	181.8	184.4	186.1	187.1
1978	190.3	192.4	194.3	195.7	196.8	197.6	197.9	200.0	200.8	202.2	203.3	204.6
1979	204.4	207.8	209.7	211.7	212.7	214.6	228.2	231.0	234.1	237.0	238.9	241.0
1980	242.9	247.8	251.3	253.6	255.2	256.1	257.6	259.2	261.3	263.4	265.0	265.7
1981	264.8	268.5	248.7	271.1	271.9	271.9	272.2	273.9	275.6	275.6	276.3	276.3
1982	276.2	278.6	281.2	282.2	282.9	283.6	282.7	284.8	286.0	286.9	289.1	289.9
1983	288.6	290.4	292.1	294.1	294.9	295.4	295.1	294.7	296.5	297.4	298.6	299.5
1984	299.1	302.1	304.2	305.1	305.7	307.5	306.6	308.9	310.8	312.0	312.2	312.8
1985	312.4	315.8	318.6	320.4	321.3	322.8	322.0	323.8	325.6	327.1	328.2	328.6
1986	326.2	328.6	329.6	330.6	332.5	331.7	329.2	328.9	330.6	332.4	334.7	334.9
1987	331.5											
Indices: January 1987 = 100												
1987	100.0	100.4	101.0	101.5	102.0	101.9	101.6	101.9	102.7	103.3	104.2	104.3
1988	103.3	103.9	104.5	105.0	105.5	105.6	105.9	106.5	107.2	107.6	107.9	107.9
1989	107.5	108.3	108.9	109.5	109.9	110.1	110.0	110.5	110.9	111.5	111.8	112.2
1990	112.0	112.8	113.9	114.5	115.1	115.5	114.7	115.7	116.7	117.2	118.0	118.5
1991	116.7											

23 HOUSEHOLD SERVICES

	Jan	Feb	Mar	Apr	May	Jun	Jul	Aug	Sep	Oct	Nov	Dec
Indices: January 1974 = 100												
1974	100.0	100.7	101.6	102.5	105.0	106.0	110.2	112.7	114.0	115.8	117.2	117.7
1975	121.7	122.7	130.9	135.2	144.4	147.4	150.5	150.8	151.6	172.9	173.7	174.7
1976	177.1	177.9	178.7	180.3	180.9	182.1	183.1	183.9	184.1	186.0	186.3	187.0
1977	188.7	189.6	190.1	192.5	193.4	195.6	194.0	186.0	180.0	188.1	195.4	202.7
1978	206.4	207.8	209.7	211.7	211.9	212.4	213.0	213.6	214.9	216.0	217.0	217.7
1979	219.0	220.3	222.1	224.0	225.1	227.0	231.6	233.8	239.0	242.0	246.9	248.3
1980	265.4	273.7	278.0	281.5	282.9	283.7	289.0	289.8	291.7	293.1	315.1	319.3
1981	324.9	328.4 ..	331.0	331.6	331.9	332.6	336.4	338.6	340.6	361.4	364.3	
1982	368.7	370.4	371.1	372.8	368.1	368.1	371.1	372.2	373.1	373.8	374.3	375.4
1983	377.0	375.7	376.1	379.5	379.8	381.1	381.8	382.1	382.6	383.4	391.3	392.5
1984	392.4	392.2	394.2	396.1	396.2	396.8	398.8	399.0	401.0	402.5	412.4	414.4
1985	421.2	421.2	422.5	424.4	427.2	427.6	428.4	429.3	430.0	431.0	437.8	440.5
1986	444.1	445.1	446.1	446.6	447.5	448.2	448.5	449.0	449.7	449.9	455.5	456.8
1987	460.2											
Indices: January 1987 = 100												
1987	100.0	100.1	100.3	100.9	101.4	101.6	102.0	102.4	102.9	103.2	103.8	104.0
1988	105.0	105.3	105.4	105.7	106.0	106.2	107.1	107.4	107.8	108.2	108.7	108.8
1989	110.3	110.8	110.9	111.7	111.8	111.8	112.2	112.2	113.2	114.2	115.1	115.2
1990	116.3	116.7	116.8	117.1	117.9	118.4	119.3	119.5	121.7	123.2	124.0	124.0
1991	125.5											

24 PERSONAL GOODS AND SERVICES

	Jan	Feb	Mar	Apr	May	Jun	Jul	Aug	Sep	Oct	Nov	Dec
Indices: January 1987 = 100												
1987	100.0	100.3	100.7	101.3	101.4	101.9	101.9	102.4	101.9	102.6	103.9	104.1
1988	104.3	104.7	105.1	106.0	106.3	106.6	107.1	107.5	107.8	108.1	108.8	109.1
1989	110.4	110.9	111.1	113.1	113.7	114.0	114.9	115.3	115.6	116.3	116.7	117.3
1990	118.6	119.4	120.2	121.1	121.7	122.0	122.8	123.9	124.9	125.6	126.1	126.2
1991	127.2											

25 CLOTHING AND FOOTWEAR

	Jan	Feb	Mar	Apr	May	Jun	Jul	Aug	Sep	Oct	Nov	Dec
Indices: June 1947 = 100												
1947						100.0	101.5	101.6	101.3	101.6	102.1	102.4
1948	102.7	103.6	104.9	105.7	107.3	108.5	109.6	111.8	113.2	114.1	114.8	115.3
1949	116.1	117.0	117.4	117.8	118.1	118.3	118.6	118.7	119.1	116.8	116.9	117.1
1950	117.1	117.4	117.8	118.4	118.7	119.0	119.4	119.9	120.7	121.9	123.2	124.3
1951	126.0	128.2	130.9	134.2	136.7	138.6	140.7	142.7	144.0	145.1	145.7	147.3
1952	147.1											
Indices: January 1952 = 100												
1952	100.0	99.7	100.0	99.9	99.1	97.9	97.0	96.4	95.9	95.5	95.6	95.3
1953	94.9	95.3	95.6	95.6	95.6	95.6	95.4	95.4	95.6	96.2	96.2	96.3
1954	96.1	96.3	96.3	96.3	96.3	96.3	96.2	96.3	96.3	96.3	96.4	95.8
1955	95.6	96.3	96.3	96.3	96.2	96.2	96.3	96.4	96.4	96.5	97.4	98.3
1956	98.7											
Indices: January 1956 = 100												
1956	100.0	100.2	100.4	100.5	100.4	100.5	100.5	100.6	100.9	101.0	101.1	101.2
1957	101.2	101.6	101.8	101.9	102.0	102.1	102.1	102.3	102.7	102.9	103.0	103.0
1958	103.0	103.3	103.4	103.3	103.1	103.1	102.8	102.7	102.8	102.8	102.7	102.7
1959	102.2	102.2	102.3	102.3	102.3	102.5	102.4	102.5	102.8	102.9	103.1	103.1
1960	103.0	103.5	103.6	103.7	103.8	103.8	103.9	103.9	104.2	104.4	104.5	104.6
1961	104.8	105.0	105.2	105.3	105.4	105.5	105.6	105.8	106.0	106.3	106.4	106.4
1962	106.6											
Indices: January 1962 = 100												
1962	100.0	100.1	100.1	100.9	102.3	102.6	102.6	102.6	102.9	103.0	103.1	103.2
1963	103.2	103.3	103.5	103.5	103.5	103.5	103.5	103.5	103.5	103.7	103.8	103.9
1964	104.0	104.2	104.5	104.5	104.7	104.7	104.8	105.1	105.2	105.5	105.8	105.9
1965	106.0	106.4	106.6	106.7	106.8	106.9	107.0	107.2	107.4	107.6	107.7	107.9
1966	108.1	108.4	108.8	109.1	109.4	109.6	110.2	110.7	111.0	111.1	111.3	111.3
1967	111.4	111.6	111.7	111.7	111.6	111.5	111.6	111.8	112.0	111.9	112.0	112.0
1968	111.9	112.3	112.5	113.0	113.2	113.4	113.4	113.7	114.1	114.4	114.6	114.7
1969	115.1	115.9	116.4	116.7	117.1	117.5	117.6	118.2	118.8	119.2	119.7	120.0
1970	120.5	120.9	121.7	122.5	122.6	123.1	123.4	124.6	125.7	126.0	126.4	127.6
1971	128.4	128.7	130.3	130.7	131.2	131.8	132.2	133.5	133.8	134.5	135.7	135.9
1972	136.7	138.1	138.7	139.9	140.3	140.8	141.1	142.4	144.2	145.9	146.9	147.0
1973	146.8	148.2	148.8	150.7	152.4	154.1	154.6	157.3	159.3	161.3	163.0	164.1
1974	166.6											
Indices: January 1974 = 100												
1974	100.0	102.6	104.2	106.7	108.3	109.0	109.7	110.9	112.9	115.1	116.3	117.2
1975	118.6	121.0	122.5	123.0	123.8	125.1	125.7	127.6	129.3	129.6	130.5	131.4
1976	131.5	134.9	135.9	136.6	137.3	137.7	138.3	140.5	142.4	144.5	145.9	146.8
1977	148.5	151.1	153.4	153.8	154.6	155.7	157.4	160.4	161.8	163.3	164.4	164.7
1978	163.6	167.1	167.9	169.1	169.8	170.3	170.9	172.5	174.0	175.3	175.6	176.3
1979	176.1	178.6	180.1	180.8	181.6	183.7	191.8	192.4	193.2	195.0	196.0	196.5
1980	197.1	199.8	203.1	204.6	205.5	206.7	207.5	207.3	208.4	208.4	208.8	208.1
1981	207.5	207.0	207.6	207.6	207.5	207.1	206.9	208.4	209.4	210.7	210.0	209.3
1982	207.1	209.3	209.6	210.2	210.2	209.6	209.2	210.0	212.4	212.2	212.8	213.2
1983	210.9	213.6	213.8	214.5	214.2	213.7	213.3	215.5	215.8	216.7	218.0	217.1
1984	210.4	212.7	213.0	213.7	214.8	213.5	214.1	215.3	216.7	216.2	216.6	218.5
1985	217.4	216.3	221.0	221.6	221.8	221.1	221.4	223.3	226.2	228.1	228.7	227.9
1986	225.2	225.7	227.9	227.4	227.8	227.5	226.8	229.7	231.5	233.0	234.0	234.2
1987	230.8											
Indices: January 1987 = 100												
1987	100.0	100.3	100.8	101.0	101.0	100.8	99.2	99.8	101.8	102.3	102.9	103.4
1988	101.1	101.9	102.9	103.1	104.8	105.3	103.3	103.3	104.8	106.9	107.6	107.9
1989	105.9	107.2	107.7	109.8	110.5	110.6	108.6	108.7	111.0	112.3	113.0	113.2
1990	110.8	112.4	113.3	115.0	115.6	115.3	112.5	113.8	116.4	117.6	118.6	118.6
1991	114.2											

26 MOTORING EXPENDITURE

	Jan	Feb	Mar	Apr	May	Jun	Jul	Aug	Sep	Oct	Nov	Dec
Indices: January 1974 = 100												
1974	100.0	105.2	105.4	109.4	111.2	111.8	112.8	113.2	113.7	115.4	117.7	125.0
1975	133.5	135.4	136.8	139.2	144.1	145.2	146.4	149.1	150.3	150.8	152.4	154.7
1976	155.9	155.7	156.0	158.7	161.6	162.9	164.1	166.5	167.8	168.7	173.0	174.0
1977	175.6	178.0	179.1	186.7	190.0	191.0	191.6	189.2	190.0	190.6	191.9	192.8
1978	193.7	196.3	197.0	198.3	199.9	201.4	202.6	204.4	205.7	206.8	209.6	211.0
1979	212.9	216.3	218.6	222.8	225.7	232.9	252.0	255.6	256.6	257.6	260.0	259.9
1980	262.5	268.4	271.1	281.5	284.1	286.9	287.9	288.9	287.2	287.2	287.6	288.9
1981	289.9	294.2	307.8	310.5	311.7	314.4	318.1	327.8	327.0	326.9	329.0	327.6
1982	325.1	319.8	323.9	328.8	331.9	334.9	336.6	337.7	336.2	339.2	341.3	343.2
1983	341.6	343.5	344.1	351.9	356.2	357.0	361.7	363.2	364.5	364.5	363.5	362.6
1984	360.9	358.4	358.0	362.1	364.5	366.5	365.8	366.4	365.6	370.2	370.3	368.9
1985	368.5	370.7	377.8	384.5	387.8	387.5	386.7	386.3	385.7	384.1	382.7	381.8
1986	380.8	379.0	374.1	372.4	369.3	373.9	372.3	372.5	379.2	379.3	381.5	382.5
1987	385.3											
Indices: January 1987 = 100												
1987	100.0	101.0	101.3	102.1	102.8	103.2	104.4	104.8	105.1	105.4	105.4	105.0
1988	105.1	105.0	105.6	107.0	107.3	108.2	109.2	109.5	109.7	110.2	110.1	109.8
1989	110.6	111.0	111.8	114.2	115.2	115.5	115.4	114.6	115.1	115.4	115.0	114.0
1990	115.0	115.4	116.0	118.8	119.4	119.9	120.7	123.5	126.3	127.5	125.4	123.0
1991	122.8											

27 FARES AND OTHER TRAVEL COSTS

	Jan	Feb	Mar	Apr	May	Jun	Jul	Aug	Sep	Oct	Nov	Dec
Indices: January 1974 = 100												
1974	100.0	100.3	101.3	105.1	105.9	106.8	109.8	110.5	112.6	113.4	114.0	114.8
1975	115.5	119.6	124.3	133.6	136.1	142.7	144.7	144.9	148.8	152.2	160.3	164.1
1976	163.8	163.9	165.6	173.5	177.9	178.1	182.7	186.2	186.5	188.2	189.1	189.9
1977	196.9	199.6	200.4	202.5	204.0	204.6	206.0	213.5	213.9	214.8	216.4	216.8
1978	226.2	228.3	228.7	231.6	232.3	233.7	237.6	238.3	239.4	239.7	240.8	241.6
1979	250.0	251.5	251.9	252.3	253.6	254.5	261.0	263.1	273.6	275.4	276.6	277.0
1980	299.2	306.7	315.5	322.6	323.7	325.5	326.4	327.3	330.1	338.3	340.5	354.8
1981	354.3	356.1	363.3	365.4	365.7	366.7	366.4	368.8	368.6	349.1	349.3	353.6
1982	356.2	358.4	361.3	423.2	423.4	424.3	424.1	425.4	426.4	427.2	427.8	428.8
1983	436.4	438.5	439.2	440.2	440.6	424.4	424.1	424.9	426.2	425.7	426.9	428.3
1984	433.7	435.0	435.1	436.9	437.0	437.4	437.0	438.6	439.1	439.9	440.8	441.7
1985	453.6	454.4	454.9	457.0	457.8	458.3	458.0	459.3	460.0	460.1	461.5	461.4
1986	477.1	475.0	475.2	488.1	488.8	490.4	492.7	493.5	494.2	493.6	494.2	494.8
1987	504.1											
Indices: January 1987 = 100												
1987	100.0	99.8	99.9	100.2	101.3	101.5	102.2	102.3	102.3	102.6	103.1	103.2
1988	105.1	105.7	105.6	105.8	106.7	106.9	107.9	108.6	108.8	109.2	109.5	109.6
1989	112.9	113.2	113.3	113.4	114.6	115.6	115.9	116.1	116.3	116.6	117.0	117.1
1990	117.5	121.4	121.5	121.8	122.4	123.8	124.2	124.8	125.0	126.0	126.1	126.2
1991	130.8											

28 LEISURE GOODS

	Jan	Feb	Mar	Apr	May	Jun	Jul	Aug	Sep	Oct	Nov	Dec
Indices: January 1987 = 100												
1987	100.0	100.2	100.3	100.9	101.6	102.0	101.6	101.7	101.9	102.6	103.1	103.2
1988	102.8	103.3	103.3	103.9	104.3	104.2	104.4	104.7	104.5	105.0	104.9	105.0
1989	105.1	105.5	105.7	106.0	107.2	107.4	107.6	107.6	107.8	108.7	109.9	110.0
1990	110.1	110.5	111.0	111.5	112.2	112.3	112.1	112.5	112.9	114.2	114.9	115.1
1991	114.9											

29 LEISURE SERVICES *

	Jan	Feb	Mar	Apr	May	Jun	Jul	Aug	Sep	Oct	Nov	Dec
Indices: January 1956 = 100												
1956	100	100	100	100	100	100	104	104	104	104	105	105
1957	105	105	105	105	105	105	105	106	110	110	111	111
1958	111	111	111	111	111	111	111	112	112	112	112	112
1959	112	112	112	112	112	112	112	112	112	113	113	113
1960	115	115	115	116	116	116	116	116	123	124	124	124
1961	124	124	124	125	125	125	125	126	129	130	130	130
1962	132											
Indices: January 1962 = 100												
1962	100	100	100	101	101	101	101	101	102	102	102	102
1963	101	101	102	102	102	102	101	101	101	102	102	102
1964	103	103	103	103	102	102	103	103	104	104	104	104
1965	105	106	106	106	107	107	108	112	113	113	114	114
1966	114	114	114	115	115	115	117	117	117	118	119	119
1967	119	119	119	119	119	119	120	120	120	122	122	122
1968	124	124	124	125	126	126	126	127	127	130	131	132
1969	137	137	137	137	137	138	138	138	139	141	142	143
1970	146	146	150	150	150	150	154	156	157	157	157	159
1971	158	159	159	160	161	161	167	169	169	169	170	170
1972	170	170	171	172	173	173	174	178	178	184	184	184
1973	185	185	185	193	194	194	195	195	197	197	197	197
1974	198											
Indices: January 1974 = 100												
1974	100.0	100.1	100.1	101.0	103.3	103.4	103.6	103.4	103.7	104.4	106.0	106.3
1975	106.7	107.1	107.3	114.4	125.7	127.0	127.9	121.1	123.5	125.6	127.2	128.0
1976	128.3	128.9	129.5	128.4	132.6	132.9	132.9	133.0	133.9	135.4	136.4	136.7
1977	138.5	138.7	138.9	140.0	142.4	142.8	143.0	152.4	154.4	154.6	155.3	155.6
1978	157.2	157.6	157.8	157.9	158.6	158.6	159.0	159.2	161.4	161.8	162.4	167.2
1979	170.5	170.7	170.8	171.7	172.2	172.3	183.6	183.7	185.9	186.9	187.3	196.3
1980	210.0	210.2	210.4	216.7	217.9	218.3	219.2	219.6	220.9	221.4	224.2	224.4
1981	235.7	235.9	236.1	241.9	244.7	244.9	245.7	246.1	246.9	247.7	248.6	261.1
1982	264.3	265.8	265.9	269.7	270.2	270.5	270.9	271.5	272.8	272.2	273.2	273.2
1983	274.9	275.1	275.4	278.3	278.9	278.8	278.9	279.2	279.6	279.6	280.0	280.3
1984	281.7	281.9	281.7	287.1	287.1	287.1	287.2	287.1	288.0	288.3	288.6	288.7
1985	288.7	288.7	288.7	309.3	309.3	309.2	306.7	306.7	307.6	307.7	307.5	307.7
1986	310.3	310.8	310.7	317.8	319.1	319.2	319.0	319.4	320.6	321.1	320.8	321.1
1987	321.1											
Indices: January 1987 = 100												
1987	100.0	100.1	100.1	101.5	101.1	101.3	101.4	101.4	101.9	103.3	103.7	103.6
1988	103.6	103.7	103.8	108.3	108.4	108.4	108.3	108.5	110.6	110.5	111.6	111.7
1989	112.1	122.2	112.3	113.5	114.3	114.5	115.2	115.6	117.2	117.4	118.4	118.4
1990	119.6	119.9	120.0	122.8	123.4	124.1	124.4	124.8	127.7	128.4	129.2	129.6
1991	130.7											

* Called Entertainment until January 1987

30 SEASONAL FOOD *

	Jan	Feb	Mar	Apr	May	Jun	Jul	Aug	Sep	Oct	Nov	Dec
Indices: January 1956 = 100												
1956	100.0	101.2	110.3	121.1	115.5	109.0	101.8	104.2	99.4	97.8	100.8	97.9
1957	100.4	97.9	94.6	97.9	100.8	110.5	117.1	115.4	107.2	109.3	112.0	116.5
1958	114.8	110.8	114.8	123.9	123.3	128.7	110.6	107.1	106.0	113.9	112.9	114.1
1959	115.4	113.1	114.6	114.3	112.2	112.8	108.2	107.7	99.8	105.0	107.2	109.5
1960	106.9	107.3	107.2	108.1	109.7	115.4	114.1	103.7	102.1	107.3	107.8	108.0
1961	107.4	107.5	108.3	109.4	114.4	121.8	119.8	117.4	113.4	113.2	118.4	118.5
1962	119.3											
Indices: January 1962 = 100												
1962	100.0	97.6	103.0	119.3	117.6	122.3	112.3	99.7	91.9	88.6	91.1	95.5
1963	102.2	114.4	117.5	120.0	117.1	118.3	103.8	96.0	96.3	96.0	96.0	97.4
1964	98.4	96.6	97.6	100.9	101.4	105.8	101.1	98.0	95.5	95.4	99.4	100.3
1965	99.9	99.0	102.0	107.8	110.5	112.7	109.0	105.8	103.8	102.7	107.5	111.7
1966	109.7	107.4	107.3	115.5	128.7	127.6	113.8	112.6	107.9	109.9	117.8	119.4
1967	118.5	116.9	116.8	124.3	126.4	135.9	119.9	115.6	111.4	112.5	118.0	121.3
1968	121.0	121.2	122.9	125.7	126.0	127.4	122.5	117.5	113.9	117.4	119.0	125.7
1969	124.6	132.2	138.4	152.4	147.5	148.4	138.3	131.7	129.0	129.2	128.4	134.4
1970	136.8	142.7	147.7	157.2	159.2	156.9	150.0	132.0	129.4	130.3	132.0	136.0
1971	145.2	145.9	152.0	161.3	166.2	172.8	159.0	155.0	147.2	145.5	153.0	161.9
1972	158.5	160.0	167.0	163.7	170.5	174.7	171.5	178.4	174.0	172.2	177.8	184.0
1973	187.1	199.8	213.1	232.6	243.9	238.6	229.8	210.5	218.9	234.9	236.5	243.8
1974	254.4											
Indices: January 1974=100												
1974	100.0	97.6	99.5	102.1	106.9	111.1	103.1	99.1	99.8	104.6	105.7	106.5
1975	106.6	108.9	114.9	124.8	129.4	140.3	140.2	131.7	133.8	137.9	140.1	148.1
1976	158.6	173.5	181.2	189.9	184.8	174.3	149.0	163.6	178.6	184.0	192.8	202.1
1977	214.8	216.8	215.7	223.9	213.7	219.4	194.1	182.8	176.9	168.1	166.9	171.1
1978	173.9	174.5	179.0	186.3	187.5	200.8	185.5	177.9	173.1	168.2	171.4	183.0
1979	207.6	208.2	215.3	221.6	222.1	229.3	208.0	201.0	199.1	200.5	207.1	212.9
1980	223.6	225.1	229.3	233.0	227.6	232.0	234.0	218.9	214.9	215.2	216.8	223.6
1981	225.8	227.7	233.0	245.2	248.2	257.2	250.3	233.2	241.3	250.3	256.8	266.8
1982	287.6	285.7	296.5	308.9	322.8	311.5	281.0	249.5	244.3	244.1	243.1	248.2
1983	256.8	258.2	260.6	270.8	270.8	281.5	279.9	279.7	298.2	304.4	311.0	321.1
1984	321.3	327.0	331.9	343.8	347.7	339.9	325.3	311.5	295.8	296.9	294.0	292.6
1985	306.9	313.3	325.8	333.7	333.2	334.5	303.6	299.1	298.2	299.7	305.3	315.7
1986	322.8	328.2	337.5	343.7	356.8	361.8	332.2	336.5	331.7	324.9	322.8	333.3
1987	347.3											
Indices: January 1987 = 100												
1987	100.0	103.2	103.0	107.4	110.6	105.2	97.0	98.6	95.7	96.8	98.8	102.4
1988	103.7	106.9	107.1	108.5	106.9	105.3	97.9	97.5	97.2	97.1	98.8	101.5
1989	103.2	103.4	104.8	108.0	109.9	109.3	100.6	100.8	100.7	101.5	106.2	111.1
1990	116.3	118.7	119.6	123.4	123.6	118.3	108.1	112.2	111.5	111.8	114.5	119.2
1991	121.2											

* For the purposes of this index seasonal food is defined as:
- Home-killed lamb
- Fresh fish (including smoked fish until January 1987)
- Eggs
- Unprocessed potatoes
- Fresh vegetables
- Fresh fruit.

31 NON-SEASONAL FOOD

	Jan	Feb	Mar	Apr	May	Jun	Jul	Aug	Sep	Oct	Nov	Dec
Indices: January 1956 = 100												
1956	100.0	99.0	100.2	100.6	100.1	100.7	100.8	100.8	101.3	103.3	103.1	103.9
1957	105.3	105.5	104.8	104.4	105.0	105.3	105.2	103.8	103.9	103.0	102.2	102.2
1958	102.0	101.4	102.4	103.2	103.2	104.5	104.3	104.5	105.5	106.0	106.8	107.4
1959	107.8	107.6	106.8	106.6	106.6	106.8	107.1	108.2	108.4	108.3	108.6	108.4
1960	108.1	107.4	106.7	106.1	106.4	106.6	106.9	107.4	107.6	107.4	107.5	108.1
1961	107.8	107.5	107.1	107.5	107.7	107.7	107.4	107.2	106.7	106.1	106.7	107.2
1962	107.6											
Indices: January 1962 = 100												
1962	100.0	100.4	100.4	100.3	101.5	102.4	102.6	102.5	103.4	103.5	103.6	104.0
1963	104.2	104.6	103.8	103.2	103.7	102.7	103.7	103.9	104.7	106.3	106.1	106.4
1964	107.1	107.6	107.9	109.1	109.4	110.0	110.8	111.2	111.2	111.2	111.9	112.3
1965	112.9	112.6	112.6	112.7	112.4	112.8	112.9	113.7	113.7	113.7	113.5	113.8
1966	113.9	114.3	114.6	115.3	115.8	116.5	116.9	117.2	116.9	116.9	116.5	116.7
1967	117.6	117.9	117.9	118.8	119.0	118.9	118.3	117.9	118.1	118.3	118.5	120.1
1968	121.3	122.2	122.2	123.3	123.4	123.7	124.4	124.7	124.8	125.0	125.2	125.6
1969	126.7	127.6	127.7	128.0	128.5	130.3	130.9	130.5	132.1	132.6	133.0	133.4
1970	134.5	135.1	135.7	136.7	137.3	138.6	140.6	141.5	143.5	144.1	145.0	146.2
1971	147.8	148.3	149.2	152.5	154.6	156.0	158.7	159.0	160.1	160.9	162.0	163.3
1972	165.4	166.5	166.2	165.2	165.9	168.5	169.1	171.5	172.5	173.3	174.1	175.9
1973	179.5	181.0	182.4	182.1	184.0	186.2	188.2	191.7	194.9	199.7	201.7	204.5
1974	209.8											
Indices: January 1974=100												
1974	100.0	101.6	102.5	103.4	103.9	104.7	106.1	107.8	109.3	111.8	115.0	116.3
1975	121.1	124.2	128.7	132.2	133.8	135.2	135.7	137.5	138.3	138.9	142.4	143.9
1976	146.6	148.2	148.6	150.4	151.9	153.5	154.8	157.8	161.9	166.8	169.1	171.4
1977	177.1	178.5	181.0	183.2	185.4	189.0	191.8	193.8	195.6	196.9	197.5	198.9
1978	200.4	201.7	202.2	204.7	206.3	207.9	210.0	211.7	212.6	212.7	214.7	215.8
1979	219.5	220.8	221.3	221.9	224.6	230.3	235.8	237.9	239.2	241.4	242.7	245.1
1980	248.9	251.0	255.4	258.3	261.3	263.0	265.1	267.0	267.7	267.9	268.3	270.2
1981	274.7	276.9	278.0	279.8	282.0	284.2	285.1	285.9	287.0	289.0	291.1	292.8
1982	297.5	299.2	300.1	301.1	301.9	302.3	303.0	304.7	306.1	306.7	309.3	309.9
1983	310.3	310.4	310.4	311.0	312.2	314.0	314.0	315.0	315.7	316.7	317.5	318.7
1984	319.8	320.7	322.6	324.5	326.2	329.2	329.5	330.3	330.9	332.1	333.2	334.4
1985	335.6	336.6	337.6	340.0	340.8	341.5	341.9	342.7	343.4	342.7	343.9	344.3
1986	344.9	346.9	347.3	348.7	349.4	350.3	350.7	351.4	351.8	352.2	352.4	353.4
1987	355.9											
Indices: January 1987 = 100												
1987	100.0	100.2	100.3	100.5	100.7	100.9	101.0	101.0	101.2	101.8	102.1	102.4
1988	102.7	103.0	103.4	103.8	104.3	104.7	105.0	105.7	106.1	106.4	107.0	107.4
1989	108.2	108.5	108.9	109.9	110.4	111.0	111.9	112.3	113.2	114.4	114.8	115.1
1990	116.0	116.7	117.3	118.0	119.4	120.3	120.7	121.4	121.8	121.9	122.4	122.6
1991	123.1											

32 IMPORTED LAMB

	Jan	Feb	Mar	Apr	May	Jun	Jul	Aug	Sep	Oct	Nov	Dec
Indices: January 1987 = 100												
1987	100.0	102.4	100.6	100.9	100.9	100.6	100.9	100.3	98.5	99.8	99.5	100.1
1988	99.3	99.9	99.1	100.8	100.1	100.2	101.1	101.5	101.5	101.7	101.0	101.7
1989	103.0	101.9	102.9	103.8	106.5	106.9	107.9	109.5	111.9	111.1	111.7	114.1
1990	113.0	112.7	114.9	112.2	112.4	115.6	114.3	113.7	112.2	112.4	113.9	115.4
1991	113.0											

33 PROCESSED FISH

	Jan	Feb	Mar	Apr	May	Jun	Jul	Aug	Sep	Oct	Nov	Dec
Indices: January 1987 = 100												
1987	100.0	101.1	101.0	102.4	103.4	103.6	103.4	103.4	103.2	103.8	103.8	103.8
1988	103.6	105.3	105.0	104.8	104.5	104.3	102.6	101.9	102.4	102.4	103.2	103.8
1989	105.1	105.7	105.2	105.6	105.9	105.8	106.3	105.7	106.5	106.7	105.5	104.9
1990	106.9	107.8	107.1	108.1	110.6	112.4	113.0	113.0	114.2	114.4	115.2	113.9
1991	115.4											

34 POTATO PRODUCTS

	Jan	Feb	Mar	Apr	May	Jun	Jul	Aug	Sep	Oct	Nov	Dec
Indices: January 1987 = 100												
1987	100.0	100.1	99.8	100.8	100.9	101.3	101.3	101.8	102.0	103.3	101.8	102.1
1988	102.3	101.7	102.1	101.4	102.9	104.3	104.9	105.9	106.0	106.2	106.3	106.7
1989	106.6	106.5	106.6	107.0	107.3	107.5	109.4	111.3	112.6	112.8	114.0	114.1
1990	114.8	115.0	115.8	116.6	118.2	119.6	122.9	124.6	124.1	124.0	124.5	124.2
1991	123.7											

35 PROCESSED VEGETABLES

	Jan	Feb	Mar	Apr	May	Jun	Jul	Aug	Sep	Oct	Nov	Dec
Indices: January 1987 = 100												
1987	100.0	101.6	101.3	102.3	102.3	102.6	100.1	100.8	100.9	101.1	100.0	99.9
1988	101.3	103.0	105.4	108.0	108.8	109.3	109.9	110.1	110.5	110.8	112.2	112.9
1989	114.0	114.9	115.7	116.2	116.7	117.4	118.3	119.2	118.9	120.0	120.3	120.5
1990	120.9	121.4	122.8	123.2	124.3	124.3	123.5	124.5	124.7	125.2	126.8	126.8
1991	127.3											

36 PROCESSED FRUIT

	Jan	Feb	Mar	Apr	May	Jun	Jul	Aug	Sep	Oct	Nov	Dec
Indices: January 1987 = 100												
1987	100.0	101.9	102.3	102.8	106.1	105.3	101.0	103.6	96.4	100.1	98.6	100.4
1988	101.7	103.5	102.9	102.7	101.3	102.5	102.9	102.5	102.0	101.2	99.5	99.5
1989	101.5	102.8	102.1	103.8	104.4	104.8	105.9	106.6	106.4	104.5	104.0	104.3
1990	106.0	109.8	111.4	111.9	113.6	115.1	116.9	117.4	117.3	114.6	114.8	115.2
1991	117.1											

37 BEER "ON" SALES

	Jan	Feb	Mar	Apr	May	Jun	Jul	Aug	Sep	Oct	Nov	Dec
Indices: January 1987 = 100												
1987	100.0	100.2	100.5	100.6	100.7	100.9	101.2	101.6	102.7	103.7	104.3	104.4
1988	104.5	104.9	105.1	106.8	107.3	107.5	108.1	109.0	110.0	110.9	111.5	111.8
1989	112.4	112.6	113.0	113.3	113.7	114.0	114.9	116.6	117.5	118.6	118.8	119.4
1990	119.9	120.3	120.8	124.7	126.7	127.0	128.6	130.5	131.4	132.4	132.9	133.9
1991	134.6											

38 BEER "OFF" SALES

	Jan	Feb	Mar	Apr	May	Jun	Jul	Aug	Sep	Oct	Nov	Dec
Indices: January 1987 = 100												
1987	100.0	100.9	101.8	102.2	102.9	103.1	103.1	103.6	103.5	103.7	102.4	101.1
1988	102.9	104.2	105.0	107.0	107.4	107.8	107.7	107.5	107.8	108.0	106.7	105.9
1989	107.4	109.4	110.5	111.3	111.5	111.5	111.8	112.0	112.2	112.5	111.5	110.9
1990	111.9	114.0	115.3	117.1	120.0	119.9	121.4	120.6	120.9	121.5	120.9	119.9
1991	121.6											

39 WINES & SPIRITS "ON" SALES

	Jan	Feb	Mar	Apr	May	Jun	Jul	Aug	Sep	Oct	Nov	Dec
Indices: January 1987 = 100												
1987	100.0	100.2	100.5	100.8	101.0	101.4	101.7	102.0	102.6	103.3	103.6	103.7
1988	104.0	104.5	104.7	106.3	106.7	107.0	107.1	107.7	108.3	108.7	109.2	109.3
1989	109.8	110.2	110.8	111.4	111.9	112.3	112.9	113.7	114.4	115.1	115.4	115.8
1990	116.1	116.7	117.5	122.2	124.5	125.5	126.0	126.3	127.0	127.6	127.9	128.8
1991	129.7											

40 WINES & SPIRITS "OFF" SALES

	Jan	Feb	Mar	Apr	May	Jun	Jul	Aug	Sep	Oct	Nov	Dec
Indices: January 1987 = 100												
1987	100.0	100.5	100.7	100.9	101.9	102.1	102.7	102.8	102.8	103.1	101.4	100.2
1988	102.0	102.7	103.4	104.2	104.6	104.8	104.9	105.0	105.3	105.5	104.1	103.0
1989	105.3	106.2	106.5	107.4	108.0	108.3	108.6	108.8	109.3	109.7	109.0	107.9
1990	109.8	111.0	111.9	115.2	118.2	118.7	120.8	120.4	120.8	121.2	120.6	119.4
1991	121.4											

41 CONSUMER DURABLES *

	Jan	Feb	Mar	Apr	May	Jun	Jul	Aug	Sep	Oct	Nov	Dec
Indices: January 1987 = 100												
1987	100.0	100.3	100.8	101.0	101.2	101.1	99.9	100.3	101.7	102.2	102.9	103.2
1988	101.2	101.9	102.6	103.0	104.1	104.2	103.1	103.4	104.3	105.3	105.7	105.9
1989	104.5	105.3	105.8	107.0	107.5	107.6	106.5	106.7	107.9	108.8	109.3	109.5
1990	108.0	109.1	109.9	111.0	111.6	111.5	109.7	110.7	112.5	113.2	113.8	114.1
1991	110.7											

*For the purposes of this index consumer durables are defined as:
- Furniture and furnishings
- Electrical appliances and other household equipment
- Men's, women's and children's outerwear and footwear
- Audio-visual equipment, records and tapes
- Toys, photographic and sports goods.

42 GOODS AND SERVICES MAINLY PRODUCED BY NATIONALISED INDUSTRIES *

	Jan	Feb	Mar	Apr	May	Jun	Jul	Aug	Sep	Oct	Nov	Dec
Indices: January 1962 = 100												
1962	100.0	100.2	100.3	100.7	100.1	101.0	101.3	101.9	102.2	102.3	105.2	105.6
1963	105.9	106.0	106.1	106.1	103.9	104.4	105.2	105.6	105.9	106.1	109.1	109.4
1964	109.7	109.7	110.0	110.1	107.6	107.8	108.2	110.5	111.0	111.2	111.6	114.5
1965	114.9	115.5	115.7	112.3	113.6	114.5	114.9	115.5	117.5	117.9	120.8	120.8
1966	121.8	122.2	122.3	122.8	122.2	122.4	122.6	123.2	123.3	123.9	126.6	126.6
1967	126.8	126.8	126.8	126.9	123.8	123.9	124.3	124.8	125.0	129.1	131.1	132.8
1968	133.0	133.4	133.4	133.8	132.2	132.9	133.0	134.2	135.7	139.1	139.4	139.6
1969	139.9	139.9	139.9	140.2	137.8	137.8	137.9	138.2	139.1	143.0	143.3	144.0
1970	146.4	146.7	146.7	146.7	145.2	145.2	147.8	150.5	151.1	155.8	156.6	158.9
1971	160.9	164.2	167.4	170.6	170.6	171.7	174.3	174.6	174.6	178.2	178.2	178.2
1972	179.9	180.5	182.1	185.1	184.0	184.4	184.7	185.0	186.3	190.0	190.0	190.0
1973	190.2	190.2	190.2	191.0	188.9	189.9	190.3	190.5	191.7	195.1	196.2	198.0
1974	198.9											
Indices: January 1974 = 100												
1974	100.0	100.4	101.1	101.8	104.0	106.5	110.5	112.7	113.6	114.0	117.2	118.8
1975	119.9	123.1	128.3	135.0	143.2	150.8	154.0	154.1	155.7	165.1	169.0	171.5
1976	172.8	173.2	173.9	179.1	183.8	186.5	188.9	190.5	190.7	193.4	195.1	196.4
1977	198.7	198.7	199.3	203.1	208.0	211.4	211.6	211.4	209.6	213.3	215.4	217.2
1978	220.1	221.3	221.9	224.1	226.0	227.9	230.0	230.2	230.4	230.2	232.7	232.3
1979	234.5	235.4	236.1	237.9	238.6	239.8	246.0	249.1	255.2	258.0	263.9	265.7
1980	274.7	278.6	283.5	292.3	299.7	308.9	313.5	314.5	319.2	325.1	339.2	345.3
1981	348.9	350.4	351.9	359.0	365.7	372.0	374.9	377.3	377.2	373.8	381.6	383.6
1982	387.0	390.6	393.4	412.5	417.0	423.2	425.9	428.6	428.8	430.4	435.4	438.5
1983	441.4	439.8	440.3	443.4	441.8	437.8	437.8	439.9	440.4	440.5	443.9	444.2
1984	445.8	447.7	448.9	453.3	454.5	455.5	455.8	456.3	456.8	457.6	462.6	463.7
1985	465.9	466.8	469.0	477.9	478.8	480.2	482.0	483.0	484.6	484.9	486.3	486.9
1986	489.7	489.5	489.5	497.8	495.9	496.8	498.3	499.8	500.5	500.4	500.7	499.7
1987	502.1											
Indices: January 1987 = 100												
1987	100.0	100.0	100.0	100.8	100.7	100.7	100.9	101.3	101.4	101.5	101.9	101.9
1988	102.8	103.1	103.0	104.9	106.0	107.3	108.2	108.3	109.0	109.2	109.3	109.3
1989	110.9	110.9	110.9	114.2	114.7	115.9	116.5	116.8	116.9	117.2	117.4	

*For the purposes of this index goods and services mainly produced by nationalised industries are defined as:
- Water charges (from August 1976)
- Coal & solid fuels
- Electricity
- Gas (until December 1986)
- Postage
- Telephone charges (until December 1984)
- Rail fares
- Bus & coach fares (until January 1989).

The index was discontinued in November 1989 when water authorities were privatised.

	Weight *	Jan	Feb	Mar	Apr	May	Jun	Jul	Aug	Sep	Oct	Nov	Dec	Next Jan
Bread, flour, cereals, biscuits & cakes	52	100	100	105	105	105	105	105	105	106	115	115	117	118
Meat & bacon	89	100	100	100	101	100	101	101	101	101	101	100	100	102
Fish	9	100	95	98	98	97	97	96	98	99	102	104	104	116
Butter, oils & fats	19	100	96	93	90	85	88	88	87	92	93	92	93	87
Cheese, eggs & milk	53	100	99	104	98	97	99	106	113	112	108	112	106	104
Tea, coffee & other drinks	22	100	98	97	97	97	97	97	97	97	96	96	99	105
Sugar, preserves, sweets & chocolates	39	100	97	97	99	99	99	99	100	100	100	101	101	104
Potatoes & other vegetables	33	100	106	121	155	142	120	90	86	83	85	87	87	93
Fruit	19	100	102	106	118	117	119	118	118	102	100	102	103	104
Other foods	15	100	100	100	100	101	101	101	101	101	101	101	101	102
FOOD (including petfood)	350	100.0	99.6	102.9	106.0	104.2	102.9	101.1	101.7	100.8	101.8	102.5	102.3	104.0
ALCOHOLIC DRINK	71	100.0	100.0	100.0	100.0	100.7	101.1	101.9	101.9	101.9	102.6	102.6	102.6	102.6
TOBACCO	80	100.0	100.0	100.0	100.0	105.3	105.3	105.3	105.3	105.3	105.3	105.3	105.3	105.3
HOUSING	87	100.0	100.4	100.5	102.9	102.7	102.9	103.1	103.2	103.7	104.5	104.7	104.8	105.0
Coal & solid fuels	28	100	100	100	100	96	101	101	101	102	102	106	107	108
Other fuel & light	27	100	100	100	100	100	100	101	101	102	103	103	105	105
FUEL & LIGHT	55	100.0	100.0	100.0	100.1	98.0	100.8	100.9	101.1	101.9	102.4	104.5	105.9	106.2
Furniture & furnishings	35	100	100	100	101	101	101	102	102	102	102	102	102	103
Electrical appliances & audio-visual equipment	21	100	100	100	101	101	101	100	100	100	100	100	100	100
Other household equipment	10	100	100	101	101	102	102	103	103	103	103	103	103	104
Postage & telephone charges	6	100	100	100	100	100	104	109	109	109	109	109	109	110
Domestic & personal services, fees & subscriptions	29	100	100	103	104	104	105	105	105	106	106	106	107	107
Men's outerwear	20	100	100	101	101	101	101	101	100	101	101	102	102	102
Women's outerwear	22	100	100	100	100	100	101	101	101	101	102	102	102	101
Footwear	19	100	100	101	101	101	101	101	101	102	102	102	102	102
CLOTHING & FOOTWEAR	106	100.0	100.2	100.4	100.5	100.4	100.5	100.5	100.6	100.9	101.0	101.1	101.2	101.2
Chemists' goods & household consumables ex. stationery	26	100	100	100	100	100	101	101	101	101	101	101	104	106
Motoring & cycling	30	100	100	100	100	100	100	100	100	100	101	100	107	108
Fares etc (not cycling)	38	100	100	100	102	103	104	104	104	105	105	105	106	111
Records, toys, photo & sports, pers. articles & stat'nery	17	100	101	101	103	103	103	104	104	104	105	105	105	105
Books & newspapers	16	100	103	103	103	103	104	105	105	105	106	106	106	107
Leisure services	23	100	100	100	100	100	100	104	104	104	104	105	105	105

Index: January 1974 = 100

* Applied to index change since January 1956

	Weight*	Jan	Feb	Mar	Apr	May	Jun	Jul	Aug	Sep	Oct	Nov	Dec	Next Jan
						Index: January 1974 = 100								
Bread, flour, cereals, biscuits & cakes	52	118	119	120	120	120	119	119	119	119	119	119	119	119
Meat & bacon	89	102	103	100	100	102	103	103	101	101	99	98	99	99
Fish	9	116	111	103	112	105	102	102	103	108	110	114	109	119
Butter, oils & fats	19	87	84	84	82	84	88	88	88	89	88	86	83	82
Cheese, eggs & milk	53	104	98	97	93	97	99	109	116	111	110	112	115	106
Tea, coffee & other drinks	22	105	106	106	105	104	102	102	102	102	102	102	102	102
Sugar, preserves, sweets & chocolates	39	104	106	106	106	107	106	106	100	100	100	98	98	98
Potatoes & other vegetables	33	93	95	89	97	98	123	125	110	98	101	102	107	110
Fruit	19	104	103	104	108	111	113	115	115	105	111	114	120	122
Other foods	15	102	102	102	102	102	102	102	102	102	103	103	104	104
FOOD (including petfood)	350	104.0	103.5	102.1	102.7	103.9	106.7	108.4	106.9	104.8	104.7	104.8	106.0	105.4
ALCOHOLIC DRINK	71	102.6	102.6	103.6	103.9	103.9	103.9	104.1	104.7	104.7	105.7	105.7	105.7	105.8
TOBACCO	80	105.3	105.3	105.3	105.3	105.3	105.3	105.3	105.3	107.8	107.8	107.8	107.8	107.8
HOUSING	87	105.0	105.2	105.4	108.9	109.4	109.7	110.0	110.2	110.5	114.1	115.9	116.9	117.7
Coal & solid fuels	28	108	108	108	108	98	100	105	107	108	108	118	118	118
Other fuel & light	27	105	105	105	105	106	106	107	109	111	112	113	113	113
FUEL & LIGHT	55	106.2	106.3	106.3	106.3	101.8	102.9	106.3	108.1	109.2	109.9	115.3	115.6	115.6
Furniture & furnishings	35	103	103	103	102	102	102	101	102	102	102	103	103	103
Electrical appliances & audio-visual equipment	21	100	100	100	99	99	99	99	99	99	99	99	99	99
Other household equipment	10	104	104	105	101	100	100	100	100	100	100	101	101	101
Postage & telephone charges	6	110	110	110	110	110	110	110	110	110	136	136	136	132
Domestic & personal services, fees & subscriptions	29	107	106	108	109	109	110	111	111	111	111	112	112	111
Men's outerwear	20	102	102	103	103	103	103	103	103	104	104	104	104	104
Women's outerwear	22	101	102	102	102	102	103	102	103	104	104	104	104	104
Footwear	19	102	102	102	102	102	102	103	103	103	103	103	103	103
CLOTHING & FOOTWEAR	106	101.2	101.6	101.8	101.9	102.0	102.1	102.1	102.3	102.7	102.9	103.0	103.0	103.0
Chemists' goods & household consumables ex. stationery	26	106	106	106	106	106	106	107	107	107	108	108	108	109
Motoring & cycling	30	108	108	111	106	106	106	107	108	107	107	107	106	106
Fares etc (not cycling)	38	111	111	111	112	110	110	110	111	113	115	117	118	118
Records, toys, photo & sports, pers. articles & stat'nery	17	105	105	105	105	105	106	106	106	106	107	107	107	108
Books & newspapers	16	107	107	107	108	108	108	108	108	108	121	121	123	123
Leisure services	23	105	105	105	105	105	105	105	106	110	110	111	111	111

* Applied to index change since January 1956

45 DETAILED FIGURES FOR GROUPS AND SECTIONS: 1958

Index: January 1974 = 100

	Weight *	Jan	Feb	Mar	Apr	May	Jun	Jul	Aug	Sep	Oct	Nov	Dec	Next Jan
Bread, flour, cereals, biscuits & cakes	52	119	119	118	118	118	119	119	119	118	118	118	118	119
Meat & bacon	89	99	99	100	102	103	106	105	105	107	108	108	109	110
Fish	9	119	110	112	113	111	107	108	111	112	114	112	114	117
Butter, oils & fats	19	82	78	77	73	73	73	74	76	77	78	84	87	87
Cheese, eggs & milk	53	106	101	101	105	100	100	106	107	108	114	116	116	110
Tea, coffee & other drinks	22	102	102	102	102	102	102	102	102	101	100	100	100	100
Sugar, preserves, sweets & chocolates	39	98	98	102	104	104	104	104	104	104	103	104	104	104
Potatoes & other vegetables	33	110	110	118	133	142	157	103	97	99	115	112	114	125
Fruit	19	122	123	130	133	129	133	123	113	103	99	100	102	102
Other foods	15	104	104	104	104	104	104	104	104	104	104	104	104	104
FOOD (including petfood)	350	105.4	103.9	105.7	108.7	108.5	110.9	106.0	105.2	105.6	108.1	108.4	109.2	109.8
ALCOHOLIC DRINK	71	105.8	105.8	105.8	105.6	105.6	105.6	105.8	105.8	105.8	105.8	105.8	105.8	105.9
TOBACCO	80	107.8	107.8	107.8	107.8	107.8	107.8	107.8	107.8	107.8	107.8	107.8	107.8	107.8
HOUSING	87	117.7	118.1	118.4	120.6	121.2	122.2	122.6	123.3	123.3	123.8	124.2	125.1	125.8
Coal & solid fuels	28	118	118	118	118	107	108	109	109	109	109	120	120	120
Other fuel & light	27	113	113	113	113	113	113	113	113	113	113	113	113	113
FUEL & LIGHT	55	115.6	115.5	115.6	115.7	109.9	110.5	110.7	110.7	110.8	110.9	116.5	116.6	116.6
Furniture & furnishings	35	103	103	103	103	103	103	103	103	103	103	103	103	103
Electrical appliances & audio-visual equipment	21	99	99	99	98	95	95	95	95	95	95	95	95	95
Other household equipment	10	101	102	102	102	102	102	102	102	101	101	101	101	102
Postage & telephone charges	6	132	132	132	132	132	132	132	132	132	132	132	132	132
Domestic & personal services, fees & subscriptions	29	111	111	113	113	113	113	114	114	114	114	114	115	114
Men's outerwear	20	104	104	105	105	105	105	104	104	104	104	104	104	104
Women's outerwear	22	104	104	104	104	104	104	104	104	104	104	104	104	102
Footwear	19	103	104	104	104	103	103	103	103	103	103	103	103	103
CLOTHING & FOOTWEAR	106	103.0	103.3	103.4	103.3	103.1	103.1	102.8	102.7	102.8	102.8	102.7	102.7	102.2
Chemists' goods & household consumables ex. stationery	26	109	109	109	109	109	109	110	110	110	110	110	111	111
Motoring & cycling	30	106	106	106	106	106	106	106	106	105	105	105	105	106
Fares etc (not cycling)	38	118	118	118	118	118	119	119	119	119	119	119	119	119
Records, toys, photo & sports, pers. articles & stat'nery	17	108	108	108	109	107	107	107	107	107	107	107	107	105
Books & newspapers	16	123	123	123	124	125	125	125	125	125	126	126	126	126
Leisure services	23	111	111	111	111	111	111	111	112	112	112	112	112	112

* Applied to index change since January 1956

Index: January 1974 = 100

	Weight *	Jan	Feb	Mar	Apr	May	Jun	Jul	Aug	Sep	Oct	Nov	Dec	Next Jan
Bread, flour, cereals, biscuits & cakes	52	119	119	119	119	119	119	119	119	119	119	119	119	119
Meat & bacon	89	110	110	107	107	108	107	107	108	108	107	107	108	108
Fish	9	117	113	113	112	111	111	109	110	110	114	118	122	122
Butter, oils & fats	19	87	86	86	84	84	87	92	97	99	100	106	102	100
Cheese, eggs & milk	53	110	107	106	106	102	102	103	110	106	110	114	115	109
Tea, coffee & other drinks	22	100	100	100	101	100	100	101	101	101	100	100	100	100
Sugar, preserves, sweets chocolates	39	104	104	104	105	105	105	105	105	105	105	105	105	105
Potatoes & other vegetables	33	125	125	129	128	127	129	114	106	94	104	101	101	100
Fruit	19	102	103	106	107	108	109	112	106	99	99	102	106	108
Other foods	15	104	104	104	104	103	103	103	103	103	103	103	101	101
FOOD (including petfood)	350	109.8	109.1	108.9	108.6	108.1	108.4	107.4	108.1	106.1	107.4	108.2	108.7	107.8
ALCOHOLIC DRINK	71	105.9	105.9	105.9	97.8	97.8	97.8	98.1	98.1	98.1	98.0	98.0	98.0	98.1
TOBACCO	80	107.8	107.8	107.8	107.8	107.8	107.8	107.8	107.8	108.2	108.2	108.2	108.2	108.1
HOUSING	87	125.8	126.2	126.2	127.1	127.3	128.1	128.5	128.5	128.7	128.8	129.1	129.2	129.3
Coal & solid fuels	28	120	120	120	120	108	108	108	109	109	109	122	123	123
Other fuel & light	27	113	114	114	114	114	114	114	114	115	115	115	115	115
FUEL & LIGHT	55	116.6	116.9	117.0	117.0	111.1	111.1	111.1	111.4	111.7	112.2	118.7	119.0	119.0
Furniture & furnishings	35	103	103	103	102	102	102	102	102	102	103	103	103	103
Electrical appliances & audio-visual equipment	21	95	95	95	90	90	90	89	89	89	89	88	88	88
Other household equipment	10	102	101	102	101	101	101	101	101	100	100	100	100	100
Postage & telephone charges	6	132	132	132	132	132	132	132	132	132	132	132	132	132
Domestic & personal services, fees & subscriptions	29	114	114	115	115	116	116	116	117	117	117	117	117	117
Men's outerwear	20	104	104	104	104	104	104	104	103	104	104	104	104	104
Women's outerwear	22	102	102	102	102	102	102	102	102	103	102	103	102	102
Footwear	19	103	103	103	103	104	105	105	106	107	107	108	108	108
CLOTHING & FOOTWEAR	106	102.2	102.2	102.3	102.3	102.3	102.5	102.4	102.5	102.8	102.9	103.1	103.1	103.0
Chemists' goods & household consumables ex. stationery	26	111	112	112	111	111	111	111	111	112	112	112	112	112
Motoring & cycling	30	106	107	107	107	107	107	108	108	107	107	107	106	106
Fares etc (not cycling)	38	119	119	119	120	120	120	120	120	121	121	124	124	124
Records, toys, photo & sports, pers. articles & stat'nery	17	105	105	105	104	104	104	104	104	104	104	104	104	103
Books & newspapers	16	126	126	126	126	126	126	127	127	127	128	128	128	128
Leisure services	23	112	112	112	112	112	112	112	112	112	113	113	113	115

* Applied to index change since January 1956

	Weight *	Jan	Feb	Mar	Apr	May	Jun	Jul	Aug	Sep	Oct	Nov	Dec	Next Jan
						Index: January 1974 = 100								
Bread, flour, cereals, biscuits & cakes	52	119	119	119	119	121	121	121	121	121	121	121	122	123
Meat & bacon	89	108	109	108	108	109	108	109	110	111	110	110	112	110
Fish	9	122	118	121	122	118	116	118	118	119	123	124	123	122
Butter, oils & fats	19	100	91	88	83	82	82	85	85	82	84	84	84	84
Cheese, eggs & milk	53	109	106	106	102	102	103	108	110	112	118	118	116	111
Tea, coffee & other drinks	22	100	100	99	99	99	99	99	98	98	98	98	98	98
Sugar, preserves, sweets & chocolates	39	105	105	105	105	105	105	104	105	105	105	105	105	104
Potatoes & other vegetables	33	100	104	101	107	111	127	111	87	84	89	91	93	98
Fruit	19	108	109	109	109	111	113	119	106	96	95	95	97	100
Other foods	15	101	101	101	103	103	103	103	103	103	103	104	105	105
FOOD (including petfood)	350	107.8	107.4	106.8	106.6	107.3	108.9	108.8	106.4	106.1	107.4	107.6	108.1	107.7
ALCOHOLIC DRINK	71	98.1	98.1	98.1	98.0	98.0	98.0	98.2	98.2	98.2	98.3	98.3	98.3	98.4
TOBACCO	80	108.1	108.1	108.1	113.2	113.1	113.1	113.1	113.1	113.1	113.1	113.1	113.1	113.1
HOUSING	87	129.3	129.3	129.5	131.6	131.9	132.1	132.2	132.4	132.5	132.8	133.3	133.6	134.0
Coal & solid fuels	28	123	123	123	123	110	110	110	110	111	118	131	132	132
Other fuel & light	27	115	115	115	115	115	115	115	115	117	117	118	119	119
FUEL & LIGHT	55	119.0	119.0	119.1	119.0	112.3	112.4	112.4	112.9	113.5	117.6	124.7	125.4	125.8
Furniture & furnishings	35	103	103	103	103	103	103	105	105	105	106	106	106	106
Electrical appliances & audio-visual equipment	21	88	88	88	88	88	88	88	88	88	88	88	88	87
Other household equipment	10	100	100	100	100	100	100	100	100	100	101	101	101	101
Postage & telephone charges	6	132	132	132	132	132	132	132	132	129	129	129	129	12
Domestic & personal services, fees & subscriptions	29	117	118	118	118	118	119	119	120	120	121	122	122	120
Men's outerwear	20	104	104	104	104	104	104	105	104	105	105	106	106	106
Women's outerwear	22	102	103	103	103	103	103	103	103	104	104	104	104	104
Footwear	19	108	108	109	109	109	109	109	109	109	109	109	109	109
CLOTHING & FOOTWEAR	106	103.0	103.5	103.6	103.7	103.8	103.8	103.9	103.9	104.2	104.4	104.5	104.6	104.8
Chemists' goods & household consumables ex. stationery	26	112	112	112	112	112	112	112	113	113	113	114	114	114
Motoring & cycling	30	106	106	107	107	107	106	106	104	103	103	104	103	103
Fares etc (not cycling)	38	124	124	124	124	126	128	129	131	132	132	132	132	134
Records, toys, photo & sports, pers. articles & stat'nery	17	103	103	103	103	103	103	103	103	103	104	104	104	106
Books & newspapers	16	128	130	130	131	131	131	131	131	131	134	134	135	139
Leisure services	23	115	115	115	116	116	116	116	116	123	124	124	124	124

* Applied to index change since January 1956

	Weight *	Jan	Feb	Mar	Apr	May	Jun	Jul	Aug	Sep	Oct	Nov	Dec	Next Jan
						Index: January 1974 = 100								
Bread, flour, cereals, biscuits & cakes	52	123	123	123	123	123	124	126	126	126	126	127	127	127
Meat & bacon	89	110	109	108	110	110	109	107	106	105	103	103	104	106
Fish	9	122	125	123	123	124	122	123	124	124	126	130	129	130
Butter, oils & fats	19	84	84	83	82	82	82	82	80	79	79	81	84	85
Cheese, eggs & milk	53	111	109	106	106	106	108	111	114	114	110	115	112	108
Tea, coffee & other drinks	22	98	98	98	97	97	97	98	98	98	98	98	98	98
Sugar, preserves, sweets & chocolates	39	104	105	104	105	105	105	105	105	105	105	105	105	106
Potatoes & other vegetables	33	98	99	104	106	118	137	123	116	106	106	109	110	117
Fruit	19	100	103	106	108	110	114	118	114	112	122	130	134	133
Other foods	15	105	106	106	106	106	106	106	106	106	106	106	106	107
FOOD (including petfood)	350	107.7	107.5	107.4	108.0	109.5	111.4	110.7	109.9	108.5	108.0	109.8	110.2	110.7
ALCOHOLIC DRINK	71	98.4	98.4	98.4	98.4	98.4	99.0	101.7	106.0	106.9	108.0	108.0	108.0	108.2
TOBACCO	80	113.1	113.1	113.1	113.1	113.1	114.4	114.6	123.6	123.6	123.6	123.6	123.6	123.6
HOUSING	87	134.0	134.4	134.7	137.0	137.4	137.8	138.2	138.4	138.7	139.8	140.2	140.3	140.6
Coal & solid fuels	28	132	132	132	132	119	119	119	120	120	120	134	135	135
Other fuel & light	27	119	120	120	120	123	124	124	124	125	125	126	126	126
FUEL & LIGHT	55	125.8	126.1	126.1	126.2	120.9	121.7	121.8	122.2	122.4	122.8	130.2	130.4	130.6
Furniture & furnishings	35	106	106	106	107	107	107	107	108	108	108	108	108	109
Electrical appliances & audio-visual equipment	21	87	87	87	87	87	87	86	87	88	88	88	88	88
Other household equipment	10	101	102	102	102	102	103	104	105	106	106	106	107	107
Postage & telephone charges	6	129	129	129	129	129	129	129	129	129	129	134	134	134
Domestic & personal services, fees & subscriptions	29	120	121	123	124	124	125	126	127	127	128	128	129	128
Men's outerwear	20	106	106	106	106	107	107	107	107	108	108	108	108	108
Women's outerwear	22	104	104	105	105	105	105	105	105	105	106	106	106	106
Footwear	19	109	109	109	109	110	110	110	110	110	111	111	111	111
CLOTHING & FOOTWEAR	106	104.8	105.0	105.2	105.3	105.4	105.5	105.6	105.8	106.0	106.3	106.4	106.4	106.6
Chemists' goods & household consumables ex. stationery	26	114	114	121	121	121	121	121	123	124	125	126	126	126
Motoring & cycling	30	103	104	104	107	107	106	106	107	106	106	106	106	106
Fares etc (not cycling)	38	134	134	134	134	135	135	135	137	138	141	142	143	143
Records, toys, photo & sports, pers. articles & stat'nery	17	106	106	106	107	107	107	107	109	109	110	110	110	110
Books & newspapers	16	139	139	148	148	148	148	148	148	148	149	149	149	150
Leisure services	23	124	124	124	125	125	125	125	126	129	130	130	130	132

* Applied to index change since January 1956

Index: January 1974 = 100

	Weight *	Jan	Feb	Mar	Apr	May	Jun	Jul	Aug	Sep	Oct	Nov	Dec	Next Jan
Bread, flour, cereals, biscuits & cakes	47	100	102	102	102	102	102	103	103	103	103	103	103	103
Meat & bacon	74	100	101	101	101	101	101	101	100	101	101	101	101	102
Fish	11	100	99	96	99	97	96	97	97	97	98	100	98	99
Butter, oils & fats	18	100	99	99	99	99	101	102	102	102	103	104	106	106
Cheese, eggs & milk	46	100	98	95	95	95	96	97	99	103	103	106	109	110
Tea, coffee & other drinks	20	100	100	100	99	102	102	103	103	103	103	103	103	103
Sugar, preserves, sweets & chocolates	31	100	100	101	100	106	111	111	111	111	111	112	113	114
Potatoes & other vegetables	32	100	99	114	143	143	154	132	105	91	88	90	94	106
Fruit	22	100	99	100	101	97	93	94	94	90	85	84	84	84
Other foods	18	100	100	100	100	105	105	105	105	105	105	105	105	104
FOOD (including petfood)	319	100.0	99.8	100.9	104.1	104.7	106.4	104.6	101.9	101.1	100.5	101.1	102.3	103.8
ALCOHOLIC DRINK	64	100.0	100.0	100.0	100.0	100.0	100.0	100.3	100.4	100.6	100.6	100.6	100.6	100.9
TOBACCO	79	100.0	100.0	100.0	100.0	100.0	100.0	100.0	100.0	100.0	100.0	100.0	100.0	100.0
Rent	55	100	100	101	103	103	103	104	104	105	105	105	106	106
Rates & water charges	29	100	100	100	107	107	107	107	107	107	107	107	107	107
Repair & maintenance charges & do-it-yourself materials	18	100	100	100	100	100	100	100	100	100	101	101	101	101
HOUSING	102	100.0	100.3	100.5	103.3	103.5	103.9	104.1	104.3	104.7	104.9	105.1	105.2	105.5
Coal & solid fuels	28	100	100	100	100	98	98	98	98	98	99	108	109	109
Electricity	18	100	100	100	100	101	101	101	102	103	103	103	104	105
Gas	12	100	101	102	103	104	104	104	104	104	104	104	104	104
FUEL & LIGHT	62	100.0	100.4	100.5	100.8	99.8	100.1	100.2	100.7	100.9	101.1	105.5	106.1	106.5
Furniture & furnishings	29	100	101	101	102	102	102	103	103	103	103	103	103	103
Electrical appliances & audio-visual equipment	27	100	100	100	98	98	98	98	98	98	98	98	98	96
Other household equipment	8	100	100	100	100	100	100	100	100	100	100	100	100	100
Household consumables excluding stationery	14	100	100	101	100	100	100	101	101	101	101	101	101	101
Postage & telephone charges	6	100	100	100	100	100	100	100	100	100	100	100	100	100
Domestic & personal services, fees & subscriptions	28	100	100	102	102	103	103	103	103	104	104	104	105	104
Men's outerwear	16	100	100	100	102	103	104	104	103	104	104	104	104	104
Women's outerwear	21	100	100	100	101	102	102	101	102	102	102	102	102	103
Footwear	20	100	100	100	101	103	104	104	105	105	105	105	105	105
CLOTHING & FOOTWEAR	98	100.0	100.1	100.1	100.9	102.3	102.6	102.6	102.6	102.9	103.0	103.1	103.2	103.2
Chemists' goods	16	100	100	100	99	99	99	100	100	100	100	100	100	98
Motoring & cycling	59	100	100	101	100	101	100	100	99	98	99	96	97	97
Fares	33	100	100	100	101	101	103	104	104	105	105	105	105	105
Records, toys, photo & sports, pers. articles & stat'nery	18	100	100	100	101	101	101	101	101	101	101	101	101	102
Books & newspapers	16	100	100	100	101	101	101	101	101	102	102	103	103	103
Leisure services	22	100	100	100	101	101	101	101	101	102	102	102	102	101

* Applied to index change since January 1962

	Weight *	Jan	Feb	Mar	Apr	May	Jun	Jul	Aug	Sep	Oct	Nov	Dec	Next Jan
							Index: January 1974 = 100							
Bread, flour, cereals, biscuits & cakes	46	103	103	103	103	103	104	104	104	104	105	104	106	107
Meat & bacon	73	102	102	100	98	100	100	101	103	104	104	105	105	105
Fish	11	99	100	100	100	101	98	98	99	99	101	101	102	103
Butter, oils & fats	18	106	106	106	106	106	108	109	109	110	110	111	112	112
Cheese, eggs & milk	49	110	113	113	109	103	99	101	102	105	108	109	109	103
Tea, coffee & other drinks	20	103	103	103	103	103	103	103	103	103	103	103	102	103
Sugar, preserves, sweets & chocolates	34	114	116	114	115	117	109	114	111	113	122	119	117	119
Potatoes & other vegetables	32	106	125	130	138	140	140	108	92	94	95	92	94	104
Fruit	17	84	86	87	88	89	95	95	94	85	82	84	86	86
Other foods	19	104	104	104	104	104	104	104	104	104	104	104	106	107
FOOD (including petfood)	319	103.8	106.5	106.5	106.5	106.4	105.8	103.7	102.3	103.0	104.2	104.1	104.6	105.4
ALCOHOLIC DRINK	63	100.9	100.9	101.0	101.0	102.3	102.8	103.0	103.0	103.2	103.2	103.2	103.2	103.2
TOBACCO	77	100.0	100.0	100.0	100.0	100.0	100.0	100.0	100.0	100.0	100.0	100.0	100.0	100.0
Rent	56	106	106	107	107	108	109	109	110	110	110	111	111	112
Rates & water charges	30	107	107	107	112	112	113	113	113	113	114	114	114	114
Repair & maintenance charges & do-it-yourself materials	18	101	101	101	101	102	102	102	102	102	102	102	102	104
HOUSING	104	105.5	105.7	106.1	107.7	108.0	108.8	109.1	109.5	109.7	109.8	110.1	110.2	110.9
Coal & solid fuels	29	109	109	109	109	100	100	100	100	100	100	110	111	111
Electricity	19	105	106	106	106	108	110	111	111	112	112	112	112	112
Gas	12	104	104	104	104	104	104	104	104	105	106	107	107	107
FUEL & LIGHT	63	106.5	106.6	106.8	106.8	103.2	103.9	104.2	104.5	104.8	104.9	109.5	109.7	110.1
Furniture & furnishings	30	103	104	104	104	104	104	104	104	104	104	104	104	106
Electrical appliances & audio-visual equipment	26	96	96	96	96	96	96	96	96	96	96	96	96	96
Other household equipment	8	100	101	101	101	101	101	101	101	101	101	101	101	101
Household consumables excluding stationery	14	101	101	102	102	102	102	102	102	102	102	102	102	102
Postage & telephone charges	6	100	100	100	100	103	103	103	103	103	103	103	103	103
Domestic & personal services, fees & subscriptions	28	104	104	106	106	106	106	107	107	107	107	108	108	107
Men's outerwear	16	104	104	105	105	105	104	105	105	105	105	105	105	105
Women's outerwear	21	103	103	103	103	103	103	103	103	103	103	103	103	103
Footwear	20	105	105	106	106	106	106	105	105	105	106	106	106	106
CLOTHING & FOOTWEAR	98	103.2	103.3	103.5	103.5	103.5	103.5	103.5	103.5	103.5	103.7	103.8	103.9	104.0
Chemists' goods	14	98	98	98	98	98	98	98	98	99	99	99	99	99
Motoring & cycling	61	97	97	97	98	98	98	98	97	97	96	97	97	96
Fares	32	105	105	105	105	105	105	107	108	108	108	109	109	109
Records, toys, photo & sports, pers. articles & stat'nery	19	102	102	102	102	102	102	103	103	103	103	103	103	103
Books & newspapers	16	103	104	104	104	104	105	105	105	107	107	107	107	107
Leisure services	22	101	101	102	102	102	102	101	101	101	102	102	102	103

* Applied to index change since January 1963

	Weight *	Jan	Feb	Mar	Apr	May	Jun	Jul	Aug	Sep	Oct	Nov	Dec	Next Jan
								Index: January 1974 = 100						
Bread, flour, cereals, biscuits & cakes	47	107	107	107	107	108	108	109	109	109	109	111	112	112
Meat & bacon	77	105	107	108	110	111	113	114	115	115	114	114	115	116
Fish	10	103	103	103	103	105	104	105	105	105	106	107	109	111
Butter, oils & fats	18	112	112	112	112	111	111	111	111	111	112	114	115	115
Cheese, eggs & milk	46	103	100	100	104	101	103	104	104	104	102	106	108	106
Tea, coffee & other drinks	19	103	104	104	104	104	104	104	104	104	105	105	104	105
Sugar, preserves, sweets & chocolates	33	119	119	119	119	120	120	120	121	121	121	121	120	121
Potatoes & other vegetables	29	104	103	104	109	111	116	103	99	101	105	108	106	107
Fruit	17	86	88	89	90	91	95	99	95	86	85	85	85	85
Other foods	18	107	108	108	108	108	108	108	108	108	108	108	108	108
FOOD (including petfood)	314	105.4	105.4	105.8	107.4	107.8	109.1	108.9	108.7	108.1	108.0	109.4	109.9	110.3
ALCOHOLIC DRINK	63	103.2	103.5	103.5	103.5	110.0	110.0	110.2	110.2	110.2	110.0	110.1	110.1	110.9
TOBACCO	74	100.0	100.0	100.0	100.0	107.2	107.2	107.2	109.5	109.5	109.5	109.5	109.5	109.5
Rent	58	112	112	112	113	114	114	115	115	116	116	116	116	117
Rates & water charges	31	114	114	114	120	120	120	120	120	120	121	121	121	121
Repair & maintenance charges & do-it-yourself materials	18	104	104	104	105	105	105	105	105	105	107	107	107	107
HOUSING	107	110.9	111.1	111.3	113.8	114.1	114.3	114.6	114.9	115.0	115.7	115.8	115.9	116.1
Coal & solid fuels	28	111	112	111	111	101	101	101	105	106	106	107	117	118
Electricity	22	112	112	112	112	113	114	114	115	116	116	117	117	117
Gas	12	107	107	108	108	109	109	109	109	109	109	109	109	109
FUEL & LIGHT	66	110.1	110.2	110.0	110.1	106.1	106.5	106.5	108.9	109.4	109.7	110.2	114.4	114.8
Furniture & furnishings	29	106	106	106	107	107	107	107	108	108	108	108	108	110
Electrical appliances & audio-visual equipment	25	96	96	96	97	97	97	97	97	97	97	97	97	98
Other household equipment	8	101	102	102	102	102	102	103	103	103	103	103	104	104
Household consumables excluding stationery	13	102	102	102	102	102	103	104	104	105	105	105	107	108
Postage & telephone charges	6	103	103	103	103	103	103	103	103	103	103	103	103	103
Domestic & personal services, fees & subscriptions	28	107	107	109	110	110	110	111	111	111	112	113	113	112
Men's outerwear	15	105	106	106	106	106	106	107	107	107	107	108	108	108
Women's outerwear	20	103	104	104	104	104	104	104	105	105	105	106	106	106
Footwear	19	106	106	106	106	106	106	106	106	106	107	107	107	107
CLOTHING & FOOTWEAR	95	104.0	104.2	104.5	104.5	104.7	104.7	104.8	105.1	105.2	105.5	105.8	105.9	106.0
Chemists' goods	15	99	101	102	102	102	102	102	100	99	100	100	100	102
Motoring & cycling	68	96	96	97	97	97	97	97	96	96	96	98	98	98
Fares	32	109	109	110	111	111	111	112	114	115	115	115	116	116
Records, toys, photo & sports, pers. articles & stat'nery	19	103	103	103	104	104	104	104	104	104	104	104	104	105
Books & newspapers	16	107	107	109	110	110	110	111	111	113	113	121	121	122
Leisure services	22	103	103	103	103	102	102	103	103	104	104	104	104	105

* Applied to index change since January 1964

Index: January 1974 = 100

	Weight *	Jan	Feb	Mar	Apr	May	Jun	Jul	Aug	Sep	Oct	Nov	Dec	Next Jan
Bread, flour, cereals, biscuits & cakes	47	112	113	113	113	113	113	113	113	113	113	113	113	114
Meat & bacon	82	116	115	115	115	115	117	117	118	118	11/	117	118	110
Fish	10	111	108	108	111	110	109	110	110	110	111	114	114	117
Butter, oils & fats	17	115	115	116	116	114	113	112	112	112	112	111	112	111
Cheese, eggs & milk	45	106	105	104	105	101	103	105	113	114	116	119	124	118
Tea, coffee & other drinks	18	105	105	105	105	105	105	105	105	105	105	105	105	105
Sugar, preserves, sweets & chocolates	31	121	121	121	121	120	120	119	118	118	119	118	119	119
Potatoes & other vegetables	28	107	105	110	117	126	126	117	104	103	100	101	102	106
Fruit	15	85	88	91	94	96	98	98	95	91	88	91	91	92
Other foods	18	108	109	109	110	110	111	111	111	111	111	111	111	111
FOOD (including petfood)	311	110.3	109.9	110.4	111.6	111.9	112.5	112.0	112.1	111.7	111.4	112.2	113.3	113.0
ALCOHOLIC DRINK	65	110.9	111.8	111.3	118.7	119.0	119.1	119.0	119.0	119.0	119.1	119.0	119.0	119.0
TOBACCO	76	109.5	109.5	109.5	120.8	120.8	120.8	120.8	120.8	120.8	120.8	120.8	120.8	120.8
Rent	59	117	117	118	119	120	120	121	121	121	122	122	124	124
Rates & water charges	32	121	121	121	132	132	132	132	132	132	133	133	133	133
Repair & maintenance charges & do-it-yourself materials	18	107	107	107	108	108	108	108	108	108	109	109	109	109
HOUSING	109	116.1	116.2	116.5	120.7	121.0	121.2	121.6	121.7	121.9	122.5	122.8	123.6	123.7
Coal & solid fuels	27	118	118	118	104	104	104	104	104	109	110	120	120	120
Electricity	23	117	118	119	120	122	125	125	126	127	127	127	127	127
Gas	11	109	109	109	110	110	110	110	110	110	111	111	111	111
FUEL & LIGHT	65	114.8	115.1	115.7	110.5	111.2	112.1	112.2	112.7	115.2	115.4	119.6	119.6	119.7
Furniture & furnishings	27	110	110	110	111	111	111	111	112	112	112	112	112	112
Electrical appliances & audio-visual equipment	23	98	98	98	98	98	98	98	98	98	98	98	98	98
Other household equipment	9	104	104	105	105	105	106	106	106	106	106	107	107	107
Household consumables excluding stationery	14	108	108	108	109	110	110	110	110	110	111	111	111	111
Postage & telephone charges	6	103	103	103	103	114	114	114	114	114	114	114	114	114
Domestic & personal services, fees & subscriptions	27	112	112	114	115	115	116	117	117	118	118	119	119	119
Men's outerwear	15	108	109	109	109	110	110	110	110	110	111	111	112	111
Women's outerwear	20	106	107	107	107	107	107	107	107	107	107	107	107	107
Footwear	18	107	108	108	108	108	108	109	109	109	109	109	109	110
CLOTHING & FOOTWEAR	92	106.0	106.4	106.6	106.7	106.8	106.9	107.0	107.2	107.4	107.6	107.7	107.9	108.1
Chemists' goods	13	102	94	94	94	94	94	94	94	94	94	94	94	94
Motoring & cycling	74	98	98	99	101	102	102	102	101	101	101	101	101	102
Fares	31	116	117	117	117	117	118	119	120	121	122	122	122	125
Records, toys, photo & sports, pers. articles & stat'nery	19	105	105	105	106	106	106	106	106	106	107	107	107	109
Books & newspapers	17	122	122	125	125	126	126	126	126	127	127	128	128	128
Leisure services	22	105	106	106	106	107	107	108	112	113	113	114	114	114

* Applied to index change since January 1965

Index: January 1974 = 100

	Weight *	Jan	Feb	Mar	Apr	May	Jun	Jul	Aug	Sep	Oct	Nov	Dec	Next Jan
Bread, flour, cereals, biscuits & cakes	45	114	115	116	117	117	117	119	119	119	119	119	119	122
Meat & bacon	76	118	118	119	121	123	125	125	125	124	123	121	122	123
Fish	10	117	115	114	116	115	115	115	115	118	117	117	118	119
Butter, oils & fats	15	111	111	110	110	110	110	110	110	110	110	110	110	110
Cheese, eggs & milk	48	118	111	108	107	109	109	108	111	112	112	117	119	116
Tea, coffee & other drinks	17	105	105	105	105	105	105	105	105	105	107	106	106	106
Sugar, preserves, sweets & chocolates	27	119	119	119	118	118	118	118	119	119	120	120	120	121
Potatoes & other vegetables	26	106	113	116	130	153	151	126	121	112	116	123	122	125
Fruit	16	92	93	96	97	98	100	99	96	95	96	97	96	97
Other foods	18	111	111	112	112	112	112	112	112	112	113	113	113	112
FOOD (including petfood)	298	113.0	112.8	113.1	115.2	118.0	118.4	116.2	116.1	115.1	115.4	116.6	117.0	117.6
ALCOHOLIC DRINK	67	119.0	119.0	119.0	119.0	119.0	119.0	119.1	125.1	125.7	125.6	125.5	125.2	125.4
TOBACCO	77	120.8	120.8	120.8	120.8	120.8	120.8	120.8	120.8	120.8	120.8	120.8	120.8	120.7
Rent	25	124	124	125	128	128	128	129	129	129	129	130	130	131
Rates & water charges	11	133	133	133	143	143	143	143	143	143	144	144	144	144
Repair & maintenance charges & do-it-yourself materials	25	109	109	109	111	112	112	112	112	112	112	113	113	113
HOUSING	113	123.7	123.9	124.5	129.0	129.2	129.5	129.9	130.1	130.1	130.5	130.7	130.9	131.3
Coal & solid fuels	25	120	121	121	121	119	118	119	120	121	121	132	132	132
Electricity	25	127	127	127	127	127	127	127	127	127	127	127	127	127
Gas	11	111	111	111	112	112	113	113	114	114	114	114	114	114
FUEL & LIGHT	64	119.7	120.1	120.1	120.3	119.4	119.5	119.7	120.4	120.7	120.8	124.8	124.9	124.9
Furniture & furnishings	27	112	112	112	113	113	113	114	115	115	116	116	116	116
Electrical appliances & audio-visual equipment	21	98	98	98	98	98	98	99	100	100	100	100	100	100
Other household equipment	9	107	108	108	108	109	109	109	110	111	111	111	111	111
Household consumables excluding stationery	13	111	111	111	111	111	111	112	112	112	112	112	112	113
Postage & telephone charges	7	114	114	114	114	114	114	114	114	114	121	121	121	123
Domestic & personal services, fees & subscriptions	27	119	120	122	123	124	124	125	126	128	130	131	131	130
Men's outerwear	15	111	112	112	113	113	113	114	114	114	114	115	115	115
Women's outerwear	20	107	108	108	108	108	108	109	109	109	109	110	110	110
Footwear	18	110	111	111	112	112	113	113	114	114	115	115	115	115
CLOTHING & FOOTWEAR	91	108.1	108.4	108.8	109.1	109.4	109.6	110.2	110.7	111.0	111.1	111.3	111.3	111.4
Chemists' goods	13	94	95	95	95	95	95	95	98	99	99	99	99	99
Motoring & cycling	85	102	102	102	102	102	102	102	102	102	102	102	103	103
Fares	31	125	125	126	127	127	127	128	128	128	128	128	128	128
Records, toys, photo & sports, pers. articles & stat'nery	19	109	109	109	112	112	112	112	114	114	113	113	113	113
Books & newspapers	16	128	128	130	130	130	130	130	130	130	130	130	130	130
Leisure services	22	114	114	114	115	115	115	117	117	117	118	119	119	119

* Applied to index change since January 1966

Index: January 1974 = 100

	Weight *	Jan	Feb	Mar	Apr	May	Jun	Jul	Aug	Sep	Oct	Nov	Dec	Next Jan
Bread, flour, cereals, biscuits & cakes	44	122	122	122	122	122	122	123	123	123	123	123	123	123
Meat & bacon	73	123	123	123	124	125	125	122	121	122	122	123	128	132
Fish	10	119	119	120	119	119	118	118	117	118	118	118	120	121
Butter, oils & fats	14	110	110	110	110	109	109	107	107	107	107	107	107	107
Cheese, eggs & milk	45	116	111	108	112	111	111	109	111	114	114	118	120	117
Tea, coffee & other drinks	17	106	107	106	106	106	106	106	105	106	106	106	106	106
Sugar, preserves, sweets & chocolates	27	121	123	123	124	124	124	124	123	123	124	124	125	126
Potatoes & other vegetables	30	125	127	129	140	145	160	133	122	116	115	119	119	125
Fruit	16	97	100	102	106	106	110	112	112	104	107	108	109	108
Other foods	17	112	113	113	113	113	113	114	114	113	113	114	114	113
FOOD (including petfood)	293	117.6	117.5	117.5	119.6	120.1	121.8	118.4	117.3	116.7	117.0	118.2	120.1	121.1
ALCOHOLIC DRINK	67	125.4	125.4	125.3	125.4	125.4	125.4	125.4	125.4	125.4	125.3	125.2	125.0	125.0
TOBACCO	72	120.7	120.8	120.8	120.8	120.8	120.8	120.8	120.8	120.8	120.8	120.8	120.8	120.8
Rent	65	131	132	132	134	135	135	136	136	137	140	141	142	143
Rates & water charges	34	144	144	144	145	145	145	145	145	145	145	145	145	145
Repair & maintenance charges & do-it-yourself materials	19	113	113	113	114	114	114	114	114	114	114	114	114	114
HOUSING	118	131.3	131.8	131.8	133.4	134.0	134.1	134.6	134.9	135.2	136.8	137.6	138.2	138.6
Coal & solid fuels	26	132	132	132	132	120	120	120	120	120	132	133	133	134
Electricity	23	127	127	127	127	127	128	128	128	129	133	139	145	145
Gas	11	114	114	114	114	114	114	114	114	114	114	114	114	114
FUEL & LIGHT	62	124.9	124.9	124.9	124.8	120.1	120.2	120.3	120.6	120.9	127.2	130.0	132.4	132.6
Furniture & furnishings	28	116	116	116	116	116	116	116	116	116	117	117	117	118
Electrical appliances & audio-visual equipment	22	100	100	100	100	100	100	100	100	100	100	100	100	101
Other household equipment	9	111	111	112	112	112	112	112	112	112	112	112	113	113
Household consumables excluding stationery	12	113	112	112	112	108	108	108	109	109	109	108	109	110
Postage & telephone charges	8	123	123	123	123	123	123	123	123	123	123	123	123	123
Domestic & personal services, fees & subscriptions	28	130	131	132	132	132	132	133	133	134	133	134	134	133
Men's outerwear	15	115	115	116	116	116	116	116	116	116	116	116	116	116
Women's outerwear	22	110	110	110	110	110	109	109	110	110	110	110	110	109
Footwear	18	115	115	115	115	115	115	115	115	116	116	116	116	116
CLOTHING & FOOTWEAR	92	111.4	111.6	111.7	111.7	111.6	111.5	111.6	111.8	112.0	111.9	112.0	112.0	111.9
Chemists' goods	13	99	97	97	97	98	98	98	97	98	98	99	100	100
Motoring & cycling	89	103	103	103	103	104	104	105	104	104	105	106	106	106
Fares	29	128	128	128	129	129	129	130	131	131	132	132	133	133
Records, toys, photo & sports, pers. articles & stat'nery	21	113	113	113	113	113	113	114	114	114	114	114	114	114
Books & newspapers	15	130	130	130	131	131	131	131	132	133	137	137	138	140
Leisure services	22	119	119	119	119	119	119	120	120	120	122	122	122	124

* Applied to index change since January 1967

	Weight *	Jan	Feb	Mar	Apr	May	Jun	Jul	Aug	Sep	Oct	Nov	Dec	Next Jan
Bread, flour, cereals, biscuits & cakes	38	123	128	128	130	130	130	130	130	130	130	130	131	131
Meat & bacon	69	132	131	131	131	131	132	131	131	131	131	132	133	135
Fish	9	121	120	120	120	121	120	120	122	122	124	125	125	127
Butter, oils & fats	12	107	107	110	110	109	109	108	108	108	107	107	108	108
Cheese, eggs & milk	39	117	116	116	117	114	115	118	119	120	120	122	127	125
Tea, coffee & other drinks	15	106	106	106	108	108	108	108	108	107	108	107	108	109
Sugar, preserves, sweets & chocolates	24	126	126	127	128	129	129	130	131	131	132	133	134	137
Potatoes & other vegetables	26	125	128	131	136	140	136	127	118	116	122	121	124	126
Fruit	16	108	106	105	106	108	115	116	113	108	108	110	112	110
Other foods	15	113	113	114	117	117	118	118	121	119	119	119	119	119
FOOD (including petfood)	263	121.1	121.8	122.1	123.5	123.6	124.1	123.8	123.2	122.6	123.4	123.9	125.4	126.1
CATERING	41	121.4	121.9	122.4	126.3	126.8	127.5	127.9	128.6	129.4	129.7	130.1	130.3	130.5
ALCOHOLIC DRINK	63	125.0	125.1	125.0	127.0	127.1	127.1	127.1	127.2	127.2	127.3	127.2	132.7	134.7
TOBACCO	66	120.8	120.8	120.8	125.4	125.4	125.4	125.4	127.8	127.8	125.7	125.9	134.8	135.1
Rent	71	143	144	144	145	145	146	146	147	147	148	148	149	149
Rates & water charges	32	145	145	145	147	146	146	146	146	146	147	147	147	147
Repair & maintenance charges & do-it-yourself materials	18	114	115	115	118	118	119	119	119	119	120	121	121	121
HOUSING	121	138.6	139.4	139.5	140.6	140.9	141.3	141.6	142.0	142.2	142.9	143.3	143.6	143.7
Coal & solid fuels	24	134	134	134	134	126	126	126	127	129	140	141	142	142
Electricity	25	145	145	145	145	145	145	145	145	145	145	145	145	145
Gas	11	114	114	114	116	120	126	127	127	127	127	127	127	127
FUEL & LIGHT	62	132.6	132.7	132.7	133.3	130.8	131.9	132.0	132.6	133.2	137.6	138.0	138.2	138.4
Furniture & furnishings	29	118	118	119	121	121	121	122	122	122	123	123	123	124
Electrical appliances & audio-visual equipment	22	101	101	101	104	104	104	105	105	105	106	106	106	107
Other household equipment	8	113	114	114	115	115	116	116	116	116	117	117	117	117
Household consumables excluding stationery	12	110	111	112	113	114	114	113	113	113	112	112	113	114
Postage & telephone charges	7	123	123	123	123	123	123	123	123	130	137	137	137	137
Domestic & personal services, fees & subscriptions	26	133	136	136	137	138	138	139	139	140	142	142	143	144
Men's outerwear	15	116	117	117	118	118	118	118	119	119	119	120	120	120
Women's outerwear	21	109	110	110	110	110	110	110	110	111	111	111	111	112
Footwear	18	116	116	116	117	118	118	118	118	118	118	118	118	118
CLOTHING & FOOTWEAR	89	111.9	112.3	112.5	113.0	113.2	113.4	113.4	113.7	114.1	114.4	114.6	114.7	115.1
Chemists' goods	13	100	99	99	105	106	112	114	114	114	115	115	115	117
Motoring & cycling	92	106	106	106	112	113	113	113	113	113	113	113	114	114
Fares	28	133	134	134	134	134	134	134	137	139	139	139	139	139
Records, toys, photo & sports, pers. articles & stat'nery	20	114	115	115	121	122	122	123	123	123	123	123	123	127
Books & newspapers	15	140	147	156	158	158	159	159	159	159	160	160	160	161
Leisure services	23	124	124	124	125	126	126	126	127	127	130	131	132	137

* Applied to index change since January 1968

	Weight *	Jan	Feb	Mar	Apr	May	Jun	Jul	Aug	Sep	Oct	Nov	Dec	Next Jan
Bread, flour, cereals, biscuits & cakes	37	131	133	133	134	135	135	136	136	136	136	137	137	140
Meat & bacon	65	135	135	135	136	137	141	141	141	141	142	142	143	143
Fish	8	127	128	128	129	129	129	130	131	132	135	138	139	142
Butter, oils & fats	12	108	108	108	107	108	108	109	109	110	111	112	111	113
Cheese, eggs & milk	40	125	125	127	127	123	121	121	119	126	127	127	131	129
Tea, coffee & other drinks	14	109	109	109	109	109	109	109	110	109	111	111	111	112
Sugar, preserves, sweets & chocolates	24	137	139	140	141	141	142	142	142	143	143	144	144	147
Potatoes & other vegetables	24	126	139	143	164	163	169	148	138	135	138	136	142	149
Fruit	15	110	111	116	122	120	121	125	120	114	110	109	108	109
Other foods	15	119	119	120	121	121	125	126	127	128	128	129	128	129
FOOD (including petfood)	254	126.1	128.2	129.4	132.1	131.6	133.3	132.0	130.5	131.3	131.8	132.0	133.4	134.7
CATERING	42	130.5	131.0	131.4	133.2	133.6	134.5	136.0	137.1	137.2	138.1	138.5	138.9	139.4
ALCOHOLIC DRINK	64	134.7	134.8	134.8	135.1	135.5	135.6	136.2	136.2	136.2	136.5	136.4	142.7	143.0
TOBACCO	68	135.1	135.2	135.2	135.3	135.3	135.4	135.5	135.7	135.8	135.8	135.8	135.8	135.8
Rent	70	149	149	149	150	151	151	152	152	153	155	156	156	157
Rates & water charges	30	147	147	147	153	153	153	153	153	153	154	154	154	154
Repair & maintenance charges & do-it-yourself materials	18	121	121	121	123	123	123	122	122	122	124	125	125	125
HOUSING	118	143.7	143.9	144.0	146.4	146.6	146.8	147.1	147.5	147.6	149.5	150.0	150.4	150.6
Coal & solid fuels	22	142	142	142	143	132	132	132	133	133	150	151	151	162
Electricity	24	145	145	145	145	145	145	145	145	145	145	145	145	145
Gas	13	127	127	127	127	127	127	127	126	126	126	126	126	126
FUEL & LIGHT	61	138.4	138.5	138.5	138.6	134.8	134.8	134.9	135.3	135.4	141.3	141.6	141.7	145.3
Furniture & furnishings	29	124	124	125	126	126	127	128	128	129	131	131	132	134
Electrical appliances & audio-visual equipment	23	107	107	107	107	107	107	107	107	108	108	108	108	109
Other household equipment	8	117	118	119	119	119	120	121	121	121	122	123	123	124
Household consumables excluding stationery	11	114	114	115	114	115	117	117	118	118	118	118	118	119
Postage & telephone charges	8	137	137	137	137	137	137	137	137	137	137	137	137	137
Domestic & personal services, fees & subscriptions	25	144	144	144	145	145	146	148	148	149	150	150	151	151
Men's outerwear	14	120	121	122	122	122	123	123	123	124	124	125	125	126
Women's outerwear	20	112	113	113	114	114	114	114	115	115	116	117	117	117
Footwear	17	118	120	120	120	120	120	120	121	122	122	123	123	124
CLOTHING & FOOTWEAR	86	115.1	115.9	116.4	116.7	117.1	117.5	117.6	118.2	118.8	119.2	119.7	120.0	120.5
Chemists' goods	16	117	117	117	119	119	119	120	120	120	121	121	121	121
Motoring & cycling	98	114	114	115	116	117	116	116	115	115	115	116	116	116
Fares	26	139	139	140	140	141	141	141	141	144	144	144	147	147
Records, toys, photo & sports, pers. articles & stat'nery	23	127	128	127	129	129	129	130	130	130	131	131	131	132
Books & newspapers	16	161	161	161	162	162	162	162	162	163	166	167	171	174
Leisure services	24	137	137	137	137	137	138	138	138	139	141	142	143	146

Index: January 1974 = 100

* Applied to index change since January 1969

	Weight *	Jan	Feb	Mar	Apr	May	Jun	Jul	Aug	Sep	Oct	Nov	Dec	Next Jan
							Index: January 1974 = 100							
Bread, flour, cereals, biscuits & cakes	37	140	141	141	143	143	144	145	146	147	147	149	152	156
Meat & bacon	65	143	143	144	146	148	150	152	153	154	153	153	154	155
Fish	9	142	145	146	147	148	148	150	150	151	153	154	154	157
Butter, oils & fats	11	113	114	116	116	116	118	120	121	121	123	125	127	128
Cheese, eggs & milk	38	129	129	128	128	127	127	127	127	133	134	137	142	141
Tea, coffee & other drinks	15	112	112	112	113	112	113	117	118	120	121	122	122	123
Sugar, preserves, sweets & chocolates	24	147	149	150	151	152	152	155	155	156	157	157	158	161
Potatoes & other vegetables	27	149	158	167	181	184	179	164	136	136	141	140	140	156
Fruit	13	109	112	113	117	120	121	129	121	113	111	112	113	117
Other foods	16	129	129	130	132	132	136	138	139	140	141	142	142	143
FOOD (including petfood)	255	134.7	136.3	137.6	140.1	141.0	141.6	142.1	139.5	140.6	141.4	142.4	144.1	147.0
CATERING	43	139.4	139.7	140.5	143.3	144.3	145.0	146.2	147.7	148.1	149.9	150.7	151.3	153.1
ALCOHOLIC DRINK	66	143.0	143.0	143.0	143.2	143.2	143.2	143.6	143.6	143.6	144.4	145.8	147.0	151.3
TOBACCO	64	135.8	135.8	135.8	135.8	135.8	135.8	136.0	136.0	136.0	136.2	138.2	138.4	138.6
Rent	71	157	157	158	164	164	164	165	165	165	168	169	170	171
Rates & water charges	30	154	154	154	161	161	161	161	161	161	164	164	164	164
Repair & maintenance charges & do-it-yourself materials	18	125	127	130	134	135	135	135	136	138	141	142	142	142
HOUSING	119	150.6	151.4	152.2	157.9	158.3	158.6	158.8	159.3	159.8	162.7	163.7	163.8	164.2
Coal & solid fuels	23	162	162	162	162	152	152	152	155	156	175	175	175	177
Electricity	23	145	145	145	145	145	145	145	145	146	147	147	147	147
Gas	13	126	126	126	126	126	126	126	126	126	126	127	127	129
FUEL & LIGHT	61	145.3	145.5	145.6	145.5	142.1	142.1	142.1	143.1	143.9	150.8	150.9	150.9	152.6
Furniture & furnishings	29	134	134	134	137	137	137	139	139	139	142	142	142	146
Electrical appliances & audio-visual equipment	22	109	109	109	111	111	111	112	112	112	115	115	115	116
Other household equipment	9	124	125	126	128	128	129	131	131	132	133	134	135	136
Household consumables excluding stationery	11	119	119	119	120	121	120	123	124	124	124	124	125	127
Postage & telephone charges	8	137	137	137	137	137	137	151	151	151	151	151	151	151
Domestic & personal services, fees & subscriptions	25	151	152	152	155	156	157	158	159	159	160	161	162	165
Men's outerwear	14	126	126	127	128	129	130	130	130	132	132	133	137	137
Women's outerwear	20	117	118	119	120	119	120	120	123	124	124	125	125	126
Footwear	17	124	125	126	127	127	127	127	128	128	129	129	130	131
CLOTHING & FOOTWEAR	86	120.5	120.9	121.7	122.5	122.6	123.1	123.4	124.6	125.7	126.0	126.4	127.6	128.4
Chemists' goods	14	121	124	124	127	127	127	127	127	128	134	134	134	135
Motoring & cycling	101	116	117	118	120	121	122	123	124	124	125	126	127	128
Fares	25	147	147	147	147	150	150	155	163	163	163	166	175	179
Records, toys, photo & sports, pers. articles & stat'nery	23	132	132	133	134	134	134	137	138	139	141	141	141	145
Books & newspapers	17	174	175	175	186	186	187	188	189	191	194	195	195	198
Leisure services	22	146	146	150	150	150	150	154	156	157	157	157	159	158

* Applied to index change since January 1970

	Weight *	Jan	Feb	Mar	Apr	May	Jun	Jul	Aug	Sep	Oct	Nov	Dec	Next Jan
Bread, flour, cereals, biscuits & cakes	37	156	156	156	159	159	100	160	160	161	162	165	168	169
Meat & bacon	65	155	156	158	162	165	167	167	167	168	168	168	170	172
Fish	8	157	158	159	163	165	166	169	170	172	176	180	181	190
Butter, oils & fats	11	128	128	132	135	149	154	160	160	164	167	172	175	177
Cheese, eggs & milk	37	141	141	141	149	148	148	157	157	160	157	163	168	162
Tea, coffee & other drinks	14	123	124	124	124	124	125	126	126	125	126	126	125	126
Sugar, preserves, sweets & chocolates	23	161	162	163	166	167	168	169	170	171	170	170	170	177
Potatoes & other vegetables	25	156	155	161	168	178	188	166	161	150	154	157	165	167
Fruit	13	117	120	126	133	134	137	137	135	131	129	132	133	133
Other foods	17	143	144	144	146	147	148	148	148	148	148	148	149	153
FOOD (including petfood)	250	147.0	147.6	149.4	153.7	156.3	158.5	158.5	158.0	157.6	158.0	160.1	162.8	163.9
CATERING	44	153.1	156.5	158.1	163.5	164.5	166.0	167.4	168.1	169.3	170.2	171.2	171.9	172.9
ALCOHOLIC DRINK	65	151.3	151.4	151.4	152.2	152.2	152.3	153.4	153.4	153.4	153.6	153.6	153.6	154.1
TOBACCO	59	138.6	138.6	138.5	138.5	138.5	138.5	138.5	138.5	138.5	138.4	138.4	138.4	138.4
Rent	71	171	171	171	176	177	177	177	178	178	181	182	182	182
Rates & water charges	29	164	164	164	184	184	183	184	184	184	187	187	187	187
Repair & maintenance charges & do-it-yourself materials	19	142	142	144	147	148	148	148	148	149	152	154	154	154
HOUSING	119	164.2	164.4	165.0	173.1	173.4	173.7	173.8	174.3	174.5	177.5	178.2	178.6	178.8
Coal & solid fuels	22	177	177	177	177	167	168	179	179	179	195	195	195	195
Electricity	22	147	148	152	158	163	166	166	166	166	166	166	166	166
Gas	13	129	133	138	138	138	138	138	139	139	139	139	139	140
FUEL & LIGHT	60	152.6	154.0	156.5	159.0	157.8	159.1	162.6	162.8	162.8	167.7	167.7	167.7	168.2
Furniture & furnishings	30	146	146	146	149	149	150	150	150	151	151	152	152	154
Electrical appliances & audio-visual equipment	22	116	116	116	119	119	119	119	119	118	118	119	119	119
Other household equipment	9	136	137	139	140	141	142	142	142	143	143	144	145	145
Household consumables excluding stationery	11	127	127	128	130	130	131	133	132	132	134	133	132	133
Postage & telephone charges	8	151	175	175	175	175	175	175	175	175	175	175	175	175
Domestic & personal services, fees & subscriptions	24	165	166	167	170	171	171	173	173	174	175	176	177	177
Men's outerwear	14	137	138	139	139	140	141	142	145	145	146	147	147	149
Women's outerwear	21	126	126	129	129	129	130	130	132	133	133	134	135	135
Footwear	17	131	132	133	134	134	134	136	136	137	137	137	138	141
CLOTHING & FOOTWEAR	87	128.4	128.7	130.3	130.7	131.2	131.8	132.2	133.5	133.8	134.5	135.7	135.9	136.7
Chemists' goods	14	135	135	135	144	146	147	152	149	148	147	147	148	149
Motoring & cycling	110	128	129	130	131	132	133	134	134	135	135	135	135	136
Fares	26	179	179	185	191	194	195	195	196	196	196	197	197	202
Records, toys, photo & sports, pers. articles & stat'nery	24	145	145	145	150	151	151	151	151	151	151	152	152	156
Books & newspapers	16	198	201	203	206	209	213	223	223	224	229	229	230	232
Leisure services	22	158	159	159	160	161	161	167	169	169	169	170	170	170

Index: January 1974 = 100

* Applied to index change since January 1971

	Weight *	Jan	Feb	Mar	Apr	May	Jun	Jul	Aug	Sep	Oct	Nov	Dec	Next Jan
						Index: January 1974 = 100								
Bread, flour, cereals, biscuits & cakes	36	169	169	169	169	170	170	174	177	178	178	178	178	179
Meat & bacon	64	172	173	174	175	178	188	188	190	192	194	196	203	216
Fish	9	190	188	188	191	191	191	195	199	201	204	209	215	220
Butter, oils & fats	14	177	178	177	176	175	166	161	152	151	150	150	150	147
Cheese, eggs & milk	39	162	164	164	152	153	152	150	161	162	164	165	168	165
Tea, coffee & other drinks	13	126	126	126	126	128	128	128	128	129	130	130	130	131
Sugar, preserves, sweets & chocolates	23	177	180	174	175	175	176	176	176	176	176	177	177	178
Potatoes & other vegetables	24	167	168	179	177	186	192	190	185	180	174	175	182	188
Fruit	13	133	134	136	138	137	141	141	161	155	156	162	157	157
Other foods	16	153	155	155	156	157	158	159	159	160	160	163	163	163
FOOD (including petfood)	251	163.9	165.1	166.0	164.6	166.3	169.2	169.2	172.3	172.4	172.8	174.3	176.9	180.4
CATERING	46	172.9	173.4	174.1	176.3	177.4	180.1	181.8	182.7	183.9	185.6	187.2	188.3	190.2
ALCOHOLIC DRINK	66	154.1	154.3	155.0	157.8	158.3	158.6	159.3	160.3	161.8	162.9	162.7	162.7	163.3
TOBACCO	53	138.4	138.4	138.4	138.4	138.4	138.4	138.4	138.4	141.5	141.6	141.6	141.6	141.6
Rent	71	182	183	183	190	191	192	193	193	193	209	209	211	211
Rates & water charges	31	187	187	187	205	205	206	206	206	206	209	209	209	209
Repair & maintenance charges & do-it-yourself materials	19	154	155	157	159	160	160	161	164	165	170	171	171	171
HOUSING	121	178.8	179.3	179.7	188.8	189.5	190.2	190.6	191.3	191.5	202.2	202.5	203.5	203.8
Coal & solid fuels	20	195	195	195	205	194	194	194	196	196	211	211	211	212
Electricity	24	166	166	168	171	172	174	174	174	174	174	174	174	174
Gas	13	140	143	146	146	146	146	146	146	146	146	146	146	146
FUEL & LIGHT	60	168.2	169.0	170.5	174.3	172.2	172.8	172.8	173.3	173.3	178.0	178.0	178.0	178.3
Furniture & furnishings	28	154	154	154	156	156	156	158	158	159	162	164	164	165
Electrical appliances & audio-visual equipment	21	119	119	119	118	118	118	119	119	119	120	119	119	119
Other household equipment	9	145	147	147	148	148	149	150	150	151	152	152	152	152
Household consumables excluding stationery	11	133	135	133	136	137	137	136	138	138	138	137	137	138
Postage & telephone charges	9	175	175	178	178	178	178	178	178	178	183	183	183	183
Domestic & personal services, fees & subscriptions	22	177	178	178	181	181	183	185	186	187	189	190	191	194
Men's outerwear	15	149	150	151	151	152	152	153	153	155	158	159	159	160
Women's outerwear	22	135	136	137	141	141	141	140	141	144	145	147	146	146
Footwear	17	141	142	143	144	144	145	148	151	151	152	153	153	153
CLOTHING & FOOTWEAR	89	136.7	138.1	138.7	139.9	140.3	140.8	141.1	142.4	144.2	145.9	146.9	147.0	146.8
Chemists' goods	14	149	149	150	147	147	147	147	148	147	149	149	149	149
Motoring & cycling	113	136	137	137	137	139	139	141	141	142	142	143	143	143
Fares	26	202	202	203	205	207	207	208	208	213	213	213	213	213
Records, toys, photo & sports, pers. articles & stat'nery	22	156	157	157	154	154	154	153	154	155	157	156	156	157
Books & newspapers	18	232	235	236	238	238	238	243	244	244	243	243	243	243
Leisure services	21	170	170	171	172	173	173	174	178	178	184	184	184	185

* Applied to index change since January 1972

Index: January 1974 = 100

	Weight *	Jan	Feb	Mar	Apr	May	Jun	Jul	Aug	Sep	Oct	Nov	Dec	Next Jan
Bread, flour, cereals, biscuits & cakes	33	179	179	179	183	184	188	190	191	193	202	204	211	225
Meat & bacon	73	216	220	224	228	235	238	240	246	254	261	264	267	270
Fish	8	220	225	224	240	240	242	244	252	261	277	286	294	319
Butter, oils & fats	10	147	146	147	148	145	145	148	152	155	158	161	164	168
Cheese, eggs & milk	36	165	169	176	178	179	176	176	182	189	194	195	199	202
Tea, coffee & other drinks	12	131	132	132	128	128	129	129	130	130	130	130	130	131
Sugar, preserves, sweets & chocolates	21	178	178	179	165	166	166	168	172	174	178	179	180	188
Potatoes & other vegetables	25	188	199	207	226	240	235	222	186	191	207	206	212	224
Fruit	14	157	162	168	170	175	181	186	179	178	180	185	185	188
Other foods	16	163	163	163	160	160	161	161	164	166	167	168	170	176
FOOD (including petfood)	248	180.4	183.7	187.1	189.9	193.3	194.3	194.6	194.4	198.5	205.1	207.0	210.5	216.7
CATERING	46	190.2	191.8	193.5	211.6	212.8	214.0	214.9	216.9	218.1	220.7	222.2	224.7	229.5
ALCOHOLIC DRINK	73	163.3	163.3	163.3	164.5	164.0	164.0	164.3	164.4	164.3	164.8	164.9	164.9	166.0
TOBACCO	49	141.6	141.6	141.6	141.0	141.0	141.0	141.0	141.0	141.0	141.2	141.2	141.4	142.2
Rent	75	211	212	212	212	214	217	217	217	218	221	228	228	229
Rates & water charges	32	209	209	209	226	226	226	226	226	226	227	227	227	227
Repair & maintenance charges & do-it-yourself materials	19	171	171	171	181	185	186	186	186	186	201	202	204	208
HOUSING	126	203.8	204.2	204.3	210.2	212.0	213.7	213.7	214.0	214.4	219.4	223.6	224.1	225.1
Coal & solid fuels	18	212	212	212	212	199	199	199	199	199	215	215	215	218
Electricity	24	174	174	174	174	174	174	174	174	174	176	180	186	186
Gas	13	146	146	146	146	146	146	146	146	146	146	146	146	148
FUEL & LIGHT	58	178.3	178.3	178.3	178.3	175.2	175.2	175.3	175.3	175.3	181.3	183.0	185.8	188.6
Furniture & furnishings	28	165	165	166	171	171	172	179	181	182	186	187	188	195
Electrical appliances & audio-visual equipment	22	119	119	119	115	115	115	115	115	115	117	117	117	118
Other household equipment	8	152	153	153	159	159	160	161	162	163	165	166	167	169
Household consumables excluding stationery	10	138	139	138	147	148	149	150	150	149	154	156	157	160
Postage & telephone charges	9	183	183	183	191	192	194	195	195	205	208	208	208	208
Domestic & personal services, fees & subscriptions	23	194	195	196	212	213	214	216	217	218	221	222	224	227
Men's outerwear	15	160	161	162	165	168	169	170	173	176	179	181	183	187
Women's outerwear	22	146	147	148	148	150	151	151	155	157	159	162	163	165
Footwear	18	153	155	155	157	160	161	162	164	167	168	168	169	174
CLOTHING & FOOTWEAR	89	146.8	148.2	148.8	150.7	152.4	154.1	154.6	157.3	159.3	161.3	163.0	164.1	166.6
Chemists' goods	13	149	150	149	146	145	145	147	147	146	148	149	149	150
Motoring & cycling	110	143	143	143	145	147	148	149	149	151	153	154	155	159
Fares	25	213	213	213	213	214	217	218	219	220	217	217	218	218
Records, toys, photo & sports, pers. articles & stat'nery	26	157	157	156	157	158	158	161	161	159	162	161	161	168
Books & newspapers	16	243	244	244	244	244	244	243	243	243	249	250	250	259
Leisure services	21	185	185	185	193	194	194	195	195	197	197	197	197	198

* Applied to index change since January 1973

Index: January 1974 = 100

	Weight *	Jan	Feb	Mar	Apr	May	Jun	Jul	Aug	Sep	Oct	Nov	Dec	Next Jan
Bread	15	100.0	108.5	109.0	107.7	107.4	107.2	107.3	107.5	107.6	107.5	107.8	108.1	108.3
Cereals	5	100.0	104.0	109.2	112.1	113.8	117.7	119.8	121.6	122.1	124.7	128.8	131.7	134.8
Biscuits & cakes	15	100.0	101.2	101.9	109.7	110.6	111.3	116.6	119.5	121.3	124.8	126.9	129.3	133.4
Beef	18	100.0	99.1	99.1	99.5	99.5	99.6	98.1	98.7	98.8	98.3	97.4	99.1	102.7
Lamb	11	100.0	98.8	99.0	100.5	101.2	100.5	96.3	94.5	92.8	92.5	91.8	94.2	99.5
of which Home-killed lamb	5.5	100.0	100.6	103.1	108.1	111.3	109.4	103.3	101.1	96.7	94.6	93.6	97.3	103.7
Pork	7	100.0	98.3	96.9	96.5	95.7	95.3	94.0	95.3	98.6	105.6	107.5	109.8	111.3
Bacon	11	100.0	96.4	97.4	95.5	95.6	95.7	96.0	99.0	104.5	108.1	111.8	114.9	115.8
Poultry & other meat	29	100.0	101.2	101.6	102.4	102.3	102.8	102.1	102.6	103.9	106.0	106.8	103.7	105.3
Fish	10	100.0	98.2	97.6	99.1	99.6	99.1	98.4	98.7	99.9	100.0	100.4	100.8	104.5
of which Fresh/smoked fish	5	100.0	95.1	93.4	93.5	94.0	92.9	91.1	91.6	93.6	94.7	96.0	98.5	104.4
Butter	5	100.0	101.5	105.1	101.4	101.6	101.6	103.6	104.6	106.0	108.0	110.6	113.3	118.6
Oils & fats	4	100.0	106.0	109.4	117.8	119.5	121.0	121.0	126.0	127.5	137.0	140.8	143.1	149.4
Cheese	5	100.0	103.8	105.0	107.5	109.2	109.9	110.6	111.6	113.9	117.1	119.9	120.2	121.7
Eggs	12	100.0	84.2	83.4	75.4	79.0	70.9	64.2	67.9	75.6	82.7	83.4	86.9	69.8
Milk, fresh	18	100.0	100.0	100.0	81.8	81.8	81.8	81.8	81.8	81.8	81.8	90.8	90.8	90.8
Milk products	3	100.0	100.7	100.6	102.5	102.8	106.8	113.0	114.5	115.2	115.5	116.0	118.6	131.8
Tea	4	100.0	100.3	102.9	105.6	107.8	112.3	114.7	114.6	110.2	108.6	107.9	107.9	108.7
Coffee & other hot drinks	3	100.0	101.4	103.1	104.4	106.5	109.6	113.3	116.8	118.8	122.7	122.9	122.2	125.7
Soft drinks	4	100.0	100.8	100.7	113.6	115.5	116.0	118.7	119.4	121.5	125.6	126.7	127.1	136.4
Sugar & preserves	6	100.0	101.2	102.1	103.2	103.3	103.9	111.7	118.0	123.9	138.2	168.1	179.8	241.4
Sweets & chocolates	13	100.0	104.5	106.1	117.2	119.4	121.7	125.8	131.4	134.2	136.7	139.8	144.2	152.0
Potatoes	8	100.0	101.2	101.4	105.0	125.5	140.9	126.1	119.2	123.1	130.4	131.5	134.0	138.2
of which Unproc'd potatoes	6	100.0	101.6	101.8	102.3	129.5	150.1	127.8	116.3	121.5	130.6	128.3	129.2	133.4
Other vegetables	17	100.0	105.5	110.3	121.6	121.3	131.7	121.2	107.8	109.7	116.7	119.8	118.2	125.0
of which Fresh vegetables	§	100.0	106.1	111.7	127.7	125.8	142.1	124.2	102.6	104.1	112.2	115.7	112.6	120.5
Fruit	14	100.0	102.8	106.4	109.4	111.2	113.7	118.8	126.1	120.1	121.6	123.7	123.6	126.1
of which Fresh fruit	§	100.0	102.0	106.3	109.2	111.4	113.5	120.4	130.0	118.4	119.5	121.4	120.9	124.3
Other foods (excl. petfood)	11	100.0	101.5	103.1	107.8	108.7	109.2	111.0	114.3	116.3	120.4	125.6	128.6	134.4
FOOD (excluding petfood)	248	100.0	100.9	101.9	103.1	104.4	105.8	105.3	105.9	107.3	110.2	113.1	114.2	118.2
Canteen meals	14	100.0	100.6	101.0	102.8	103.6	104.2	105.0	106.1	106.9	108.0	109.1	110.3	112.7
Other meals & snacks	37	100.0	101.2	102.7	105.6	107.0	108.7	110.6	112.0	113.5	116.0	117.7	118.9	121.0
CATERING	51	100.0	101.0	102.2	104.8	106.1	107.5	109.1	110.4	111.7	113.8	115.3	116.5	118.7
Beer	44	100.0	101.8	103.9	111.1	112.0	112.2	113.0	111.6	112.7	118.0	119.0	119.5	120.0
Wines & spirits	26	100.0	100.3	100.3	106.8	107.9	108.1	109.5	109.1	109.8	110.9	110.9	110.9	115.2
ALCOHOLIC DRINK	70	100.0	101.2	102.6	109.5	110.5	110.7	111.7	110.7	111.6	115.4	116.0	116.3	118.2
Cigarettes	39	100.0	100.9	101.4	114.5	121.4	121.4	121.4	120.1	121.4	121.3	121.3	123.3	123.5
Other tobacco	4	100.0	100.8	101.9	115.2	123.5	123.5	123.5	121.9	123.5	124.4	124.4	128.4	128.8
TOBACCO	43	100.0	100.9	101.4	114.6	121.6	121.6	121.6	120.3	121.6	121.6	121.6	123.8	124.0
Rent and imputed rent	73	100.0	102.0	102.1	102.2	102.3	102.3	102.1	102.4	102.7	102.8	103.0	103.1	103.2
Rates & water charges	30	100.0	100.0	100.0	120.0	120.0	120.0	120.0	120.0	106.0	106.0	108.0	112.0	112.0
Repair/maintenance charges	9	100.0	100.3	100.5	107.0	107.0	108.0	109.0	109.0	110.5	117.0	118.0	119.5	121.0
Do-it-yourself materials	12	100.0	101.7	104.4	105.7	109.2	113.5	114.8	115.9	120.4	123.5	127.3	129.3	141.6
HOUSING #	124	100.0	101.4	101.7	107.2	107.6	108.1	108.2	105.1	105.8	107.1	108.6	109.0	110.3
Coal & solid fuels	13	100.0	100.0	100.0	100.0	102.4	102.4	103.7	104.2	104.7	105.2	123.0	123.5	125.1
Electricity	23	100.0	100.0	100.1	100.1	105.5	113.1	121.4	125.9	125.8	126.0	125.7	129.9	131.9
Gas	13	100.0	102.1	104.0	104.0	104.0	104.0	104.3	104.3	104.3	104.3	104.3	104.3	106.7
Oil & other fuel	3	100.0	136.1	136.9	137.0	137.2	137.4	137.4	137.4	137.4	137.5	137.6	137.8	148.6
FUEL & LIGHT	52	100.0	102.6	103.2	103.2	106.2	109.6	113.6	115.7	115.8	116.0	120.4	122.4	124.9
Furniture	15	100.0	100.5	101.0	105.1	106.1	107.1	109.1	108.9	109.9	113.5	115.5	117.5	117.7
Furnishings	19	100.0	100.1	101.8	107.4	108.4	109.3	113.2	113.9	115.4	117.7	118.7	119.7	121.7
Electrical appliances	14	100.0	100.0	100.0	103.0	103.0	103.0	106.6	107.5	108.5	112.7	114.7	116.7	119.7
Other household equipment	8	100.0	101.9	104.0	105.9	107.7	109.7	111.5	111.9	113.1	115.3	117.4	119.0	121.1
Household consumables	14	100.0	103.3	106.0	110.9	113.7	114.2	117.7	120.5	121.9	126.4	128.7	131.2	135.1
Pet care	5	100.0	103.0	104.7	107.1	107.8	111.1	116.0	115.6	116.4	118.2	120.9	122.6	124.4
HOUSEHOLD GOODS	75	100.0	101.3	102.5	106.6	107.8	108.7	112.0	112.8	114.0	117.3	119.2	121.0	123.1
Postage	3	100.0	100.0	100.0	100.0	100.0	100.0	119.1	119.1	119.1	119.1	119.1	119.1	119.1
Telephone charges etc	7	100.0	100.0	100.0	100.0	100.0	100.0	100.0	107.7	109.8	111.8	114.1	114.1	114.1
Domestic services	7	100.0	102.0	104.6	107.0	109.1	112.4	114.9	118.1	119.7	122.3	124.8	126.4	131.0
Fees & subscriptions	9	100.0	100.4	100.8	102.0	107.3	107.6	111.4	110.2	111.3	112.6	113.1	113.1	121.2
HOUSEHOLD SERVICES	26	100.0	100.7	101.6	102.5	105.0	106.0	110.2	112.7	114.0	115.8	117.2	117.7	121.7
Men's outerwear	16	100.0	101.2	104.0	105.4	106.9	106.9	107.8	108.5	111.4	114.0	115.3	116.4	118.3
Women's outerwear	24	100.0	103.9	104.7	107.5	108.3	108.3	108.6	110.1	112.0	114.1	114.9	115.0	116.2
Children's outerwear	9	100.0	102.6	104.0	106.3	109.7	110.1	111.4	113.7	115.2	116.2	117.2	117.7	119.1
Other clothing	24	100.0	103.4	105.3	108.9	111.1	112.0	112.9	114.9	117.3	120.8	122.5	123.9	124.8
Footwear	18	100.0	100.9	102.5	103.9	105.7	107.2	107.9	107.4	108.5	109.4	110.5	111.7	113.4
CLOTHING & FOOTWEAR	91	100.0	102.6	104.2	106.7	108.3	109.0	109.7	110.9	112.9	115.1	116.3	117.2	118.6
Chemists' goods	12	100.0	100.9	101.5	103.4	105.0	105.3	105.6	105.8	107.9	109.7	111.3	112.4	113.9
Personal services	7	100.0	101.4	103.7	106.4	108.2	111.3	113.1	114.8	116.1	118.9	119.8	120.8	121.5

Index: January 1974 = 100

	Weight *	Jan	Feb	Mar	Apr	May	Jun	Jul	Aug	Sep	Oct	Nov	Dec	Next Jan
Purchase of motor vehicles	51	100.0	99.4	00.6	100.9	102.3	104.1	105.9	107.1	107.9	109.1	113.7	117.2	120.2
Maintenance of motor vcles	13	100.0	100.4	100.8	101.2	108.7	109.4	110.0	114.6	115.8	117.6	119.8	121.0	121.9
Petrol & oil	32	100.0	118.8	119.2	130.6	130.8	130.7	130.7	128.6	128.6	128.6	128.6	140.0	172.1
Vehicle tax & insurance	15	100.0	100.0	100.0	100.0	100.0	100.0	100.0	100.0	100.0	106.4	106.4	106.4	106.4
MOTORING EXPENDITURE	111	100.0	105.2	105.4	109.4	111.2	111.8	112.8	113.2	113.7	115.4	117.7	125.0	133.5
Rail fares	6	100.0	100.0	100.0	100.0	100.0	100.0	108.4	108.4	108.4	108.4	108.4	108.4	108.4
Bus & coach fares	15	100.0	100.4	102.1	106.0	107.4	108.8	108.8	109.9	113.3	114.0	115.0	116.3	116.1
Other travel costs	3	100.0	100.0	100.0	110.3	110.3	110.3	117.2	117.8	117.8	120.6	120.6	120.6	126.8
FARES & OTHER TRAVEL COSTS	24	100.0	100.3	101.3	105.1	105.9	106.8	109.8	110.5	112.6	113.4	114.0	114.8	115.5
Audio-visual equipment	8	100.0	100.0	100.0	102.8	102.8	102.8	102.5	101.1	101.1	104.6	106.1	107.6	106.2
Records, toys, photo & sports goods & personal articles	18	100.0	100.1	100.7	104.9	105.9	108.6	110.5	111.1	111.8	114.4	114.4	114.4	118.8
Books & newspapers	15	100.0	104.3	106.2	108.8	109.9	112.5	118.6	118.8	121.3	132.2	134.8	135.0	136.9
Gardening products	4	100.0	100.0	100.0	100.0	100.0	100.0	100.0	100.0	110.0	110.0	110.0	110.0	110.0
TV licences & rentals	11	100.0	100.0	100.0	100.0	103.3	103.3	103.3	102.5	102.5	102.5	102.5	102.5	102.5
Entertainment & recreation	10	100.0	100.3	100.3	102.2	103.2	103.5	104.0	104.4	105.0	106.5	109.8	110.4	111.4
LEISURE SERVICES	21	100.0	100.1	100.1	101.0	103.3	103.4	103.6	103.4	103.7	104.4	106.0	106.3	106.7

* Applied to change since January 1974
§ Variable from month to month
# Includes unpublished components for dwelling insurance & ground rent

	Weight *	Jan	Feb	Mar	Apr	May	Jun	Jul	Aug	Sep	Oct	Nov	Dec	Next Jan
Bread	12	108.3	116.8	118.9	119.2	123.1	123.3	123.4	123.3	123.2	123.4	122.1	128.4	129.3
Cereals	6	134.8	137.4	140.0	142.1	144.4	148.3	149.9	151.1	151.4	151.8	150.8	152.8	153.1
Biscuits & cakes	15	133.4	135.5	137.1	144.2	143.6	144.5	147.3	147.6	147.4	147.1	147.1	147.4	149.6
Beef	15	102.7	103.9	113.5	119.1	120.0	121.5	118.6	116.9	119.6	118.7	121.0	123.7	131.7
Lamb	7	99.5	99.7	105.5	109.8	111.4	112.8	109.8	107.7	106.9	107.3	109.6	112.8	117.1
of which Home-killed lamb	3.5	103.7	106.7	113.3	118.4	122.8	122.6	116.2	112.7	112.5	111.5	116.2	118.7	123.3
Pork	7	111.3	110.7	113.4	117.6	121.1	123.3	123.2	123.2	126.7	132.3	135.9	139.1	141.1
Bacon	8	115.8	114.5	116.3	117.3	118.7	120.6	121.7	123.6	123.0	128.9	133.5	136.1	141.8
Poultry & other meat	25	105.3	107.0	108.5	114.7	116.5	119.0	119.2	119.8	121.3	121.5	122.0	123.5	124.7
Fish	7	104.5	102.7	103.2	105.9	107.2	106.7	107.4	108.0	111.0	113.6	117.2	121.5	124.5
of which Fresh/smoked fish	3.57	104.4	98.9	99.5	104.4	104.3	103.0	103.4	104.1	106.9	110.6	111.7	117.2	121.4
Butter	5	118.4	121.5	130.9	133.4	134.0	134.8	135.7	137.5	140.4	146.0	149.9	152.3	158.0
Oils & fats	4	149.4	151.4	151.7	154.1	151.0	150.5	143.9	143.7	142.2	141.1	140.8	143.9	144.0
Cheese	5	121.7	122.6	122.3	125.3	129.1	130.4	130.3	131.7	134.7	139.3	141.0	143.5	145.6
Eggs	6	69.8	75.6	80.4	88.4	86.4	78.5	68.4	76.6	85.1	84.2	86.7	92.3	79.2
Milk, fresh	14	90.8	90.8	108.9	108.9	108.9	108.9	108.9	127.0	127.0	146.0	154.2	154.2	154.2
Milk products	3	131.8	133.5	133.4	146.5	147.3	151.2	152.2	153.0	155.3	159.4	160.9	163.2	165.2
Tea	3	108.5	113.7	117.2	119.1	120.6	119.7	120.0	123.0	125.1	125.7	125.1	125.9	125.6
Coffee & other hot drinks	3	125.7	127.1	127.5	128.6	128.3	129.1	128.7	128.6	128.9	130.3	132.1	132.5	138.5
Soft drinks	5	136.4	145.5	154.6	165.2	167.2	170.2	172.7	173.7	175.3	175.9	175.7	173.0	177.3
Sugar & preserves	9	241.4	249.9	249.2	249.9	249.8	248.9	247.5	233.8	224.6	207.4	207.8	207.8	207.6
Sweets & chocolates	17	152.0	161.3	164.7	167.2	169.0	170.5	171.9	173.5	173.5	173.4	172.8	173.3	175.2
Potatoes	9	138.2	137.0	136.4	144.6	154.2	204.1	249.0	232.8	235.9	247.9	257.1	273.1	326.5
of which Unproc'd potatoes	6	133.4	130.3	129.4	137.9	150.5	156.0	286.2	262.8	266.0	273.2	283.8	305.7	383.0
Other vegetables	15	125.0	128.9	138.6	150.8	156.4	164.0	148.5	125.8	136.5	146.9	143.5	149.2	157.5
of which Fresh vegetables	§	120.5	124.9	139.3	157.5	163.2	173.4	147.7	116.3	129.0	144.9	138.0	146.9	158.8
Fruit	13	126.1	128.4	131.3	137.1	142.7	147.6	152.7	153.0	138.5	132.1	133.4	134.4	142.0
of which Fresh fruit	§	124.3	127.3	132.0	140.8	149.5	156.0	160.5	164.3	141.6	134.2	138.0	142.2	146.4
Other foods (excl. petfood)	14	134.4	142.5	145.9	150.1	152.7	154.9	157.2	157.8	159.3	160.7	161.1	161.3	163.5
FOOD (excluding petfood)	227	118.2	121.2	126.0	130.7	132.8	136.0	136.4	136.3	137.3	138.4	141.7	144.4	148.5
Canteen meals	15	112.7	114.2	115.8	125.3	127.2	129.5	132.3	132.9	136.2	137.2	137.6	139.1	141.6
Other meals & snacks	33	121.0	122.9	124.5	128.7	130.6	133.0	136.3	137.7	140.0	141.8	143.6	145.0	147.7
CATERING	48	118.7	120.5	122.1	128.0	129.9	132.3	135.4	136.6	139.2	140.8	142.1	143.6	146.2
Beer	48	120.0	122.0	124.0	125.5	138.2	141.4	144.4	146.8	147.0	147.0	147.0	148.8	151.1
Wines & spirits	34	115.2	115.5	115.8	117.3	135.2	136.6	137.7	138.2	138.8	139.9	140.4	142.8	145.4
ALCOHOLIC DRINK	82	118.2	119.5	120.7	122.3	137.3	139.7	141.8	143.5	143.8	144.3	144.5	146.6	149.0
Cigarettes	42	123.5	123.5	125.0	125.2	152.3	157.7	158.0	158.1	159.7	159.9	159.9	161.4	161.8
Other tobacco	4	128.8	128.8	130.1	130.6	155.6	165.5	165.6	166.2	168.2	168.6	168.6	170.5	171.2
TOBACCO	46	124.0	124.0	125.5	125.7	152.6	158.4	158.7	158.8	160.5	160.7	160.7	162.2	162.6
Rent	30	103.2	103.2	103.2	110.5	110.8	112.0	112.1	112.5	112.7	116.9	117.6	117.2	117.8
Mortgage interest payments	25	103.2	104.1	105.2	103.1	104.1	105.2	106.3	107.3	108.5	109.6	110.6	111.7	112.8
Rates & water charges	28	112.0	112.0	112.0	154.8	154.8	159.1	159.1	159.1	158.8	158.8	158.8	158.8	158.8
Repair/maintenance charges	9	121.0	122.8	124.6	139.2	141.6	144.8	147.3	149.7	152.1	156.5	157.1	158.5	159.7
Do-it-yourself materials	14	141.6	144.7	147.3	150.2	153.4	154.6	155.3	162.6	163.0	164.5	166.2	167.1	167.1
HOUSING #	108	110.3	111.1	111.8	125.8	126.6	128.7	129.3	130.5	131.1	133.1	133.8	134.2	134.8
Coal & solid fuels	11	125.1	125.8	126.4	139.4	140.0	140.7	142.1	142.7	143.3	156.9	157.5	158.1	158.6
Electricity	25	131.9	134.8	137.2	144.9	160.7	177.1	184.0	184.0	185.2	185.4	185.7	185.9	186.1
Gas	12	106.7	112.3	116.3	118.4	118.5	118.6	118.6	118.7	118.7	122.6	130.5	138.3	144.3
Oil & other fuel	5	148.6	148.9	148.9	149.0	149.0	149.0	149.0	149.0	149.0	149.2	149.2	182.0	184.3
FUEL & LIGHT	53	124.9	127.8	130.0	136.7	144.0	151.4	154.9	155.0	155.6	159.6	161.9	166.8	168.7
Furniture	15	117.7	118.9	120.1	124.9	127.2	129.6	129.1	130.3	131.5	134.1	135.2	136.4	136.8
Furnishings	19	121.7	122.9	123.8	126.1	127.0	127.8	130.7	132.0	133.8	135.3	137.0	138.3	137.7
Electrical appliances	16	119.7	122.1	124.5	126.3	140.6	142.4	143.2	143.8	144.4	148.9	150.7	152.5	149.3
Other household equipment	10	121.1	123.0	126.0	128.2	131.4	133.1	135.5	137.1	139.0	141.2	143.1	144.1	146.2
Household consumables	16	135.1	140.2	141.2	146.3	148.7	150.5	155.8	158.2	160.7	162.7	163.5	164.0	166.3
Pet care	5	124.6	125.8	127.6	128.9	130.3	133.6	133.2	135.9	136.2	136.7	137.7	137.3	137.6
HOUSEHOLD GOODS	81	123.1	125.4	127.0	130.1	134.7	136.4	138.3	139.8	141.3	143.7	145.2	146.2	146.2
Postage	3	119.1	119.1	179.2	179.2	179.2	179.2	179.2	179.2	179.2	220.6	220.6	220.6	220.6
Telephone charges etc	8	114.1	114.1	114.1	114.1	138.9	145.0	150.8	150.8	150.8	193.9	193.9	193.9	193.9
Domestic services	7	131.0	133.8	136.8	140.7	142.8	145.2	148.5	149.4	152.0	154.7	157.5	160.2	164.0
Fees & subscriptions	7	121.2	122.0	122.5	134.2	134.9	135.6	136.5	136.8	137.3	140.5	140.8	141.3	146.7
HOUSEHOLD SERVICES	25	121.7	122.7	130.9	135.2	144.4	147.4	150.5	150.8	151.6	172.9	173.7	174.7	177.1
Men's outerwear	16	118.3	120.2	123.5	124.5	125.7	127.3	128.7	130.7	131.2	131.9	133.1	134.3	134.9
Women's outerwear	23	116.2	119.2	119.7	118.4	118.6	121.3	122.8	125.6	127.9	128.0	128.2	127.3	126.2
Children's outerwear	10	119.1	121.1	123.0	125.2	126.8	127.5	123.6	127.9	131.9	131.8	133.9	135.5	133.7
Other clothing	23	124.8	127.8	127.5	128.1	129.5	129.2	130.3	130.9	132.3	132.8	133.3	134.9	135.9
Footwear	17	113.4	115.0	118.3	119.3	119.6	121.4	121.7	122.7	123.3	123.8	125.3	126.9	127.9
CLOTHING & FOOTWEAR	89	118.6	121.0	122.5	123.0	123.8	125.1	125.7	127.6	129.3	129.6	130.5	131.4	131.5
Chemists' goods	12	113.9	117.0	119.3	124.0	127.0	128.3	130.6	132.1	132.9	135.0	134.7	135.2	138.4
Personal services	6	121.5	123.6	127.2	130.0	132.3	135.2	141.1	143.0	145.7	147.1	148.5	149.3	151.6

Index: January 1974 = 100

Index: January 1974 = 100

	Weight *	Jan	Feb	Mar	Apr	May	Jun	Jul	Aug	Sep	Oct	Nov	Dec	Next Jan
Purchase of motor vehicles	52	120.2	122.6	124.5	126.3	128.7	130.8	133.3	137.9	140.6	141.6	143.2	143.3	143.2
Maintenance of motor vcles	14	121.9	128.2	128.2	130.9	131.5	132.3	132.9	137.9	139.0	140.8	144.0	144.8	145.8
Petrol & oil	47	172.1	172.4	172.6	172.4	172.3	172.4	172.3	172.3	171.8	170.7	171.4	170.8	180.7
Vehicle tax & insurance	14	106.4	106.4	109.3	119.2	146.1	146.6	146.6	146.6	146.6	147.4	149.4	149.4	154.6
MOTORING EXPENDITURE	127	133.5	135.4	136.8	139.2	144.1	145.2	146.4	149.1	150.3	150.8	152.4	154.7	155.9
Rail fares	5	108.4	117.5	117.5	129.9	129.9	144.1	144.1	144.1	158.7	158.7	171.6	171.6	171.6
Bus & coach fares	13	116.1	119.2	127.4	135.3	139.4	144.8	146.5	146.9	147.4	150.5	158.2	164.0	164.7
Other travel costs	4	126.8	126.8	126.8	137.1	137.1	137.1	143.0	143.0	143.0	152.9	155.2	157.5	153.6
FARES & OTHER TRAVEL COSTS	22	115.5	119.6	124.3	133.6	136.1	142.7	144.7	144.9	148.8	152.2	160.3	164.1	163.8
Audio-visual equipment	10	106.2	106.7	107.3	109.5	129.5	131.1	129.9	129.9	129.9	131.3	131.3	131.3	131.2
Records, toys, photo & sports goods & personal articles	22	118.8	119.1	120.5	124.6	126.0	127.6	131.9	132.3	133.2	139.1	139.8	139.3	141.8
Books & newspapers	17	136.9	141.2	146.7	151.4	152.5	153.6	157.3	157.9	158.4	161.0	163.0	164.0	169.9
Gardening products	4	110.0	110.0	110.0	110.0	110.0	110.0	110.0	110.0	110.0	110.0	110.0	129.3	129.3
TV licences & rentals	12	102.5	102.5	102.5	111.2	129.2	129.2	129.2	117.1	125.3	130.7	135.5	117.8	118.2
Entertainment & recreation	9	111.4	112.2	112.7	117.4	118.9	122.2	124.3	125.3	130.7	135.5	139.0	140.7	141.1
LEISURE SERVICES	21	106.7	107.1	107.3	114.4	125.7	127.0	127.9	121.1	123.5	125.6	127.2	128.0	128.3

* Applied to change since January 1975
§ Variable from month to month
# Includes unpublished components for dwelling insurance & ground rent

Index: January 1974 = 100

	Weight *	Jan	Feb	Mar	Apr	May	Jun	Jul	Aug	Sep	Oct	Nov	Dec	Next Jan
Bread	11	129.3	129.7	129.6	135.3	136.1	136.0	136.5	143.8	144.8	151.6	153.2	153.7	159.3
Cereals	5	153.1	154.6	154.7	157.3	159.5	159.4	160.7	163.2	164.7	166.2	167.3	175.3	179.1
Biscuits & cakes	12	149.6	151.0	151.9	155.5	155.6	155.2	158.4	159.0	158.9	163.7	165.3	166.9	172.7
Beef	18	131.7	132.7	133.2	136.2	139.6	146.6	148.1	153.0	157.0	164.1	164.0	164.9	167.6
Lamb	7	117.1	118.3	118.3	126.7	134.6	136.7	134.5	136.0	139.7	147.7	152.0	152.9	157.7
of which Home-killed lamb	3.5	123.3	125.2	127.5	139.7	150.0	149.8	142.6	141.9	144.9	154.2	157.0	155.4	162.0
Pork	6	141.1	140.4	140.6	140.2	141.2	141.6	139.8	140.9	142.9	147.7	149.3	147.4	150.0
Bacon	8	141.8	144.7	143.1	142.5	142.0	141.5	139.4	141.5	145.1	150.2	150.4	153.7	150.9
Poultry & other meat	22	124.7	125.7	127.5	128.9	131.0	133.5	134.9	138.1	140.0	142.6	142.0	146.0	147.7
Fish	7	124.5	125.3	125.8	128.7	128.9	130.0	130.2	133.0	135.8	143.0	146.2	151.2	154.7
of which Fresh/smoked fish	3.5	121.4	119.1	119.7	123.6	123.5	124.3	123.7	127.7	131.7	136.9	141.4	149.3	151.9
Butter	5	158.0	160.1	163.2	170.9	182.8	192.9	199.2	203.8	209.2	218.0	228.7	233.5	251.9
Oils & fats	4	144.0	145.3	145.0	144.3	141.6	143.1	144.0	147.2	148.9	152.5	154.3	164.0	166.5
Cheese	5	145.6	147.3	147.1	148.3	148.4	149.0	149.9	153.9	158.2	161.5	166.0	168.5	179.1
Eggs	5	79.2	89.7	92.4	99.4	94.9	91.3	84.7	97.8	102.7	103.7	105.5	117.7	106.6
Milk, fresh	19	154.2	154.2	154.2	154.2	154.2	154.2	154.2	154.2	172.2	172.2	172.2	172.2	190.5
Milk products	3	165.2	168.0	168.0	168.3	168.3	168.0	169.2	179.4	180.8	184.4	182.0	186.7	189.6
Tea	3	125.6	126.2	125.5	126.1	126.0	125.8	126.3	129.1	142.1	165.7	191.9	196.9	207.5
Coffee & other hot drinks	2	138.5	153.5	157.0	158.8	160.8	165.5	170.6	177.6	183.6	190.7	200.2	208.4	225.5
Soft drinks	5	177.3	177.5	177.3	175.6	177.9	176.8	179.1	181.6	182.7	184.6	185.0	185.0	190.9
Sugar & preserves	6	207.6	208.1	207.8	208.0	208.4	208.5	208.7	212.2	211.6	214.0	217.0	217.7	219.6
Sweets & chocolates	13	175.2	178.8	179.9	180.4	181.1	183.0	184.1	185.8	189.8	193.1	201.0	201.8	205.5
Potatoes	16	326.5	382.3	396.7	408.3	396.0	333.7	222.9	305.5	367.0	398.7	398.4	392.2	425.4
of which Unproc'd potatoes	12.5	383.0	462.9	484.5	494.8	476.3	384.4	218.1	342.1	434.5	464.8	464.3	455.0	500.9
Other vegetables	15	157.5	163.5	172.8	181.3	171.6	177.6	170.2	162.0	169.2	169.3	184.3	201.3	226.7
of which Fresh vegetables	§	158.8	167.6	182.8	197.1	180.5	188.4	193.8	162.6	172.3	169.9	193.6	220.8	260.0
Fruit	11	142.0	143.1	144.9	146.9	150.4	151.9	153.9	151.7	150.0	151.1	159.9	163.9	169.4
of which Fresh fruit	§	146.4	147.5	150.3	153.7	158.5	159.8	161.6	156.9	152.8	152.5	163.7	165.9	169.0
Other foods (excl. petfood)	15	163.5	165.7	165.9	166.5	167.8	167.9	171.3	173.6	176.5	179.6	181.3	183.9	196.1
FOOD (excluding petfood)	223	148.5	152.4	154.1	157.1	157.4	157.0	153.6	158.7	164.8	169.7	173.1	176.5	184.2
Canteen meals	13.5	141.6	143.1	144.7	148.5	150.5	152.4	153.3	154.7	155.6	156.7	157.8	158.6	162.8
Other meals & snacks	33.5	147.7	150.0	151.1	154.6	155.9	157.5	159.5	161.6	163.1	167.2	170.4	173.0	175.8
CATERING	47	146.2	148.3	149.5	153.1	154.6	156.3	158.0	159.9	161.2	164.4	167.0	169.1	172.3
Beer	46	151.1	154.3	156.1	158.7	161.7	163.2	167.7	169.2	170.7	171.2	173.5	175.4	183.0
Wines & spirits	35	145.4	145.7	145.7	147.9	154.0	154.4	154.7	154.7	154.7	155.0	155.0	155.0	161.0
ALCOHOLIC DRINK	81	149.0	150.9	151.9	154.3	158.7	159.7	162.4	163.3	164.1	164.5	165.8	166.9	173.7
Cigarettes	42	161.8	162.0	162.0	162.0	170.1	174.6	174.6	174.6	174.6	174.3	177.3	179.0	192.4
Other tobacco	4	171.2	171.2	171.2	171.0.	178.0	182.3	182.3	182.8	182.8	182.8	185.4	186.8	202.0
TOBACCO	46	162.6	162.8	162.8	162.8	170.8	175.3	175.3	175.3	175.3	175.0	178.1	179.7	193.2
Rent	29	117.8	118.3	118.6	126.8	126.8	127.8	128.9	129.5	131.5	134.8	134.2	134.8	135.6
Mortgage interest payments	24	112.8	113.9	114.9	116.0	111.9	112.9	114.0	115.2	116.2	117.3	118.5	139.5	140.7
Rates	33	158.8	160.7	160.7	173.0	173.0	172.3	172.3	171.5	171.5	171.5	171.5	171.5	171.5
Water charges	2	158.8	158.8	158.8	188.7	188.7	188.7	188.7	188.7	188.7	188.7	188.7	188.7	188.7
Repair/maintenance charges	8	159.7	161.3	162.9	175.2	176.5	177.6	176.9	176.9	176.9	189.9	189.4	190.0	190.0
Do-it-yourself materials	14	167.1	167.8	167.8	169.8	170.4	170.7	171.4	175.3	175.6	176.3	179.0	180.3	179.6
HOUSING #	112	134.8	135.8	136.3	143.5	142.6	143.1	143.8	144.5	145.4	147.5	147.9	153.6	154.1
Coal & solid fuels	10	158.6	158.6	158.6	174.6	174.6	174.6	175.1	175.1	175.1	191.7	191.7	191.7	192.3
Electricity	27	186.1	187.5	188.4	192.4	204.8	213.2	217.3	218.2	218.7	219.0	219.9	220.4	220.7
Gas	15	144.3	144.3	144.3	144.4	144.5	144.6	144.6	144.6	144.6	147.0	153.1	158.0	160.4
Oil & other fuel	4	184.3	184.5	184.5	184.5	184.5	184.5	184.5	199.0	199.4	199.4	220.1	220.8	236.8
FUEL & LIGHT	56	168.7	169.4	169.7	174.6	180.0	183.8	185.6	187.0	187.3	191.3	194.9	196.7	198.8
Furniture	14	136.8	136.8	137.5	140.4	141.0	141.7	141.5	141.5	141.5	147.6	148.3	149.0	153.6
Furnishings	18	137.7	138.0	138.9	142.0	142.6	143.1	145.6	146.6	147.2	152.7	154.1	155.0	160.5
Electrical appliances	20	149.3	149.3	150.0	144.4	144.4	144.4	146.5	146.5	146.5	156.0	156.8	157.5	163.5
Other household equipment	10	146.2	148.5	150.1	153.4	154.5	155.5	157.2	160.0	162.4	165.0	166.5	167.8	169.9
Household consumables	15	166.3	171.4	172.5	173.4	175.0	176.6	177.3	182.1	182.8	186.8	187.8	190.3	194.1
Pet care	5	137.6	139.8	139.1	140.4	141.4	141.1	142.0	143.5	147.6	150.9	156.6	158.6	137.6
HOUSEHOLD GOODS	82	146.2	147.6	148.4	148.9	149.6	150.2	151.6	153.1	153.9	159.7	161.1	162.3	165.3
Postage	4	220.6	220.6	220.6	220.6	220.6	227.2	227.2	227.2	227.2	227.2	227.2	227.2	227.2
Telephone charges etc	12	193.9	193.9	193.9	193.9	193.9	193.9	193.9	193.9	193.9	193.9	193.9	193.9	193.1
Domestic services	6	164.0	166.9	168.7	171.5	173.8	175.7	177.1	179.9	180.9	184.0	185.1	187.8	191.5
Fees & subscriptions	7	146.7	147.4	148.6	151.8	152.4	152.7	154.6	155.4	155.2	159.3	159.8	159.9	164.0
HOUSEHOLD SERVICES	29	177.1	177.9	178.7	180.3	180.9	182.1	183.1	183.9	184.1	186.0	186.3	187.0	188.7
Men's outerwear	16	134.9	137.7	139.1	140.5	141.2	142.4	142.8	144.3	146.0	147.9	149.3	150.9	152.5
Women's outerwear	24	126.2	130.6	131.0	131.2	131.4	130.5	131.3	133.0	135.8	138.4	139.2	140.0	141.9
Children's outerwear	9	133.7	137.5	143.1	144.7	145.3	145.6	143.7	149.5	150.3	152.4	154.4	154.9	154.4
Other clothing	20	135.9	138.8	139.3	140.5	141.3	141.6	142.9	144.9	146.3	148.9	150.5	151.3	153.8
Footwear	15	127.9	130.8	130.4	130.1	131.5	133.0	134.3	135.8	137.8	138.7	140.3	141.1	142.9
CLOTHING & FOOTWEAR	84	131.5	134.9	135.9	136.6	137.3	137.7	138.3	140.5	142.4	144.5	145.9	146.8	148.5
Chemists' goods	13	138.4	140.1	140.5	143.8	143.2	142.3	147.5	148.2	149.0	151.0	153.2	155.8	159.4
Personal services	6	151.6	153.7	156.0	158.4	160.4	162.1	165.1	168.1	170.4	171.8	174.2	175.9	179.6

	Weight *	Jan	Feb	Mar	Apr	May	Jun	Jul	Aug	Sep	Oct	Nov	Dec	Next Jan
Purchase of motor vehicles	46	140.2	143.9	145.8	148.6	150.9	153.7	156.1	159.0	161.7	163.8	165.7	168.0	170.0
Maintenance of motor vcles	14	145.8	148.7	149.2	151.0	155.4	155.4	155.4	161.4	161.4	161.4	168.8	168.8	174.2
Petrol & oil	40	180.7	177.6	175.6	178.2	182.5	183.0	183.4	184.9	185.0	185.0	193.3	193.5	193.7
Vehicle tax & insurance	16	154.6	154.6	154.6	158.3	158.3	158.3	158.4	158.4	158.4	158.6	158.6	158.6	158.6
MOTORING EXPENDITURE	116	155.9	155.7	156.0	158.7	161.6	162.9	164.1	166.5	167.8	168.7	173.0	174.0	175.6
Rail fares	8	171.6	171.6	171.6	186.5	186.5	186.5	186.5	197.9	197.9	197.9	197.9	197.9	215.2
Bus & coach fares	14	164.7	164.9	167.7	172.4	180.0	180.3	187.9	187.8	188.3	189.4	190.9	192.4	194.5
Other travel costs	2	153.6	153.6	153.6	157.6	157.6	157.6	160.1	160.1	160.1	172.6	172.6	172.6	175.4
FARES & OTHER TRAVEL COSTS	24	163.8	163.9	165.6	173.5	177.9	178.1	182.7	186.2	186.5	188.2	189.1	189.9	196.9
Audio-visual equipment	13	131.2	131.2	131.2	123.2	123.2	123.2	122.4	122.4	122.4	127.7	128.3	129.0	135.5
Records, toys, photo & sports goods & personal articles	26	141.8	142.2	142.4	149.4	149.9	149.9	153.3	153.7	153.7	158.8	159.0	159.0	166.2
Books & newspapers	16	169.9	172.4	172.8	176.0	176.7	176.9	178.2	178.9	179.6	183.3	184.3	184.5	190.9
Gardening products	4	129.3	129.3	129.3	129.3	129.3	129.3	129.3	129.3	129.3	129.3	145.2	150.9	150.9
TV licences & rentals	13	118.2	118.4	118.7	116.8	123.4	123.5	123.5	123.5	123.6	123.8	123.8	123.9	123.9
Entertainment & recreation	9	141.1	142.4	143.6	143.8	143.6	144.2	144.2	144.5	146.7	150.7	153.4	153.8	158.7
LEISURE SERVICES	22	128.3	128.9	129.5	128.4	132.6	132.9	132.9	133.0	133.9	135.4	136.4	136.7	138.5

Index: January 1974 = 100

* Applied to change since January 1976
§ Variable from month to month
# Includes unpublished components for dwelling insurance & ground rent

Index: January 1974 = 100

	Weight *	Jan	Feb	Mar	Apr	May	Jun	Jul	Aug	Sep	Oct	Nov	Dec	Next Jan
Bread	13	159.3	159.1	163.3	163.6	168.7	168.3	168.2	173.0	174.2	176.3	176.4	187.2	188.7
Cereals	4	179.1	182.9	186.1	189.8	196.1	199.1	201.5	204.6	206.2	205.2	206.4	208.8	211.2
Biscuits & cakes	12	172.7	173.3	173.6	179.1	182.3	182.9	190.9	193.0	195.1	199.1	199.2	200.1	200.7
Beef	19	167.6	165.7	163.8	163.0	165.1	168.8	171.3	171.8	172.4	172.0	171.2	171.7	174.1
Lamb	8	157.7	158.5	158.2	161.0	162.8	161.3	157.1	156.2	158.9	163.3	163.9	164.9	167.8
of which Home-killed lamb	3.92	162.0	164.3	168.8	178.8	182.5	177.6	167.0	166.1	170.7	173.6	173.7	173.9	179.0
Pork	5	150.0	148.5	145.9	146.2	146.4	148.5	150.7	151.2	152.9	158.2	159.9	160.3	160.9
Bacon	7	150.9	147.8	144.0	142.9	145.3	146.6	149.9	153.0	155.2	155.9	152.7	154.4	156.7
Poultry & other meat	24	147.7	148.7	149.8	151.5	152.2	152.2	152.1	153.0	153.9	153.9	154.1	154.7	154.4
Fish	8	154.7	154.2	159.0	165.7	166.8	167.6	168.5	170.6	173.3	175.2	180.2	181.0	186.5
of which Fresh/smoked fish	3.84	151.9	150.2	151.5	157.6	158.3	159.8	160.9	165.9	171.1	172.6	178.4	180.6	185.1
Butter	8	251.9	255.3	257.3	256.1	221.8	220.1	223.3	226.2	233.9	238.9	243.6	246.3	247.4
Oils & fats	4	166.5	169.3	171.8	177.8	183.8	188.0	192.1	195.1	197.4	196.0	193.6	194.3	193.3
Cheese	5	179.1	183.9	186.5	189.7	191.0	189.2	190.7	196.7	201.6	207.0	210.2	210.4	213.2
Eggs	6	106.6	113.8	114.0	109.3	107.5	95.7	104.0	109.4	111.8	108.2	105.5	118.2	118.9
Milk, fresh	20	190.5	190.5	190.5	190.5	190.5	208.7	208.7	208.7	208.7	208.7	208.7	208.7	226.8
Milk products	3	189.6	191.7	200.5	196.3	197.2	195.8	195.2	205.8	207.6	212.3	212.6	216.9	216.6
Tea	4	207.5	214.3	218.2	237.8	295.1	342.5	367.3	353.3	354.8	352.5	340.9	331.5	329.9
Coffee & other hot drinks	4	225.5	242.1	278.2	295.7	307.2	326.3	357.9	375.1	381.1	392.0	412.4	423.5	364.0
Soft drinks	6	190.9	191.7	193.2	194.9	196.7	193.5	196.1	197.5	197.9	199.4	199.6	196.8	202.2
Sugar & preserves	6	219.6	220.0	221.3	222.1	222.3	221.9	224.0	229.1	231.6	233.6	234.9	235.1	234.8
Sweets & chocolates	14	205.5	212.0	216.5	219.6	222.2	223.6	227.7	234.5	237.6	240.0	242.0	242.8	245.6
Potatoes	16	425.4	421.8	404.3	362.9	297.6	323.6	250.8	216.1	226.0	211.5	210.0	210.4	208.6
of which Unproc'd potatoes	12	500.9	495.1	450.8	384.5	282.0	322.9	208.6	163.6	179.1	173.6	171.5	171.9	174.3
Other vegetables	19	226.7	227.6	236.2	268.8	267.2	264.1	215.1	186.3	180.2	167.4	173.7	180.4	174.3
of which Fresh vegetables	§	260.0	261.2	271.9	327.9	322.9	316.6	232.9	186.9	173.8	151.8	157.6	162.5	159.1
Fruit	12	169.4	172.7	177.6	186.4	194.6	212.2	228.4	241.1	225.5	221.4	217.7	214.1	210.2
of which Fresh fruit	§	169.0	171.1	174.4	186.4	197.9	222.6	245.5	266.5	236.5	229.6	222.6	217.2	213.6
Other foods (excl. petfood)	15	196.1	198.6	204.6	209.2	214.5	217.1	220.3	222.0	221.6	221.9	219.3	219.7	210.0
FOOD (excluding petfood)	242	184.2	185.5	187.6	190.8	191.0	195.0	193.2	193.0	193.5	193.2	193.7	195.6	196.1
Canteen meals	12	162.8	164.2	165.9	167.2	169.4	170.7	172.6	173.9	190.0	189.8	189.8	190.4	191.5
Other meals & snacks	33	175.8	177.3	180.4	183.1	186.7	188.9	191.5	194.2	196.3	198.0	200.1	200.7	202.4
CATERING	45	172.3	173.8	176.5	178.8	182.0	184.0	186.4	188.7	194.7	195.9	197.4	198.0	199.5
Beer	51	183.0	185.2	189.4	191.4	195.3	195.3	195.8	197.6	199.5	200.4	200.4	200.4	201.3
Wines & spirits	32	161.0	164.4	165.5	167.1	168.2	168.6	169.2	169.2	170.8	171.6	171.6	171.6	171.8
ALCOHOLIC DRINK	83	173.7	176.4	179.3	181.2	183.9	184.0	184.6	185.7	187.4	188.3	188.3	188.3	188.9
Cigarettes	42	192.4	193.4	192.8	205.7	205.7	215.5	215.5	217.0	217.0	217.6	217.6	217.6	222.2
Other tobacco	4	202.0	203.6	203.4	215.1	215.1	222.6	222.6	223.4	223.4	224.2	224.2	224.2	228.3
TOBACCO	46	193.2	194.3	193.7	206.5	206.5	216.1	216.1	217.6	217.6	218.2	218.2	218.2	222.8
Rent	31	135.6	135.9	136.0	146.3	146.9	147.8	148.7	149.3	149.5	151.1	151.8	152.4	152.9
Mortgage interest payments	27	140.7	141.9	143.3	144.5	136.9	135.0	129.5	131.2	132.5	122.8	121.8	122.9	124.1
Rates	30	171.5	171.5	171.5	194.1	193.1	193.1	192.8	192.8	192.8	192.8	192.8	192.8	192.8
Water charges	2	188.7	188.7	188.7	212.9	212.9	212.9	212.9	212.9	212.9	212.9	212.9	212.9	212.9
Repair/maintenance charges	8	190.0	190.0	190.0	208.4	207.7	208.2	211.9	213.8	213.8	218.9	218.1	218.5	218.5
Do-it-yourself materials	12	179.6	180.0	187.7	189.1	190.4	191.6	193.1	195.0	197.0	198.8	199.0	199.6	200.1
HOUSING #	112	154.1	154.6	155.7	166.3	164.3	164.3	163.3	164.3	164.8	163.3	163.3	163.8	164.3
Coal & solid fuels	10	192.3	192.3	192.3	201.2	201.7	201.7	201.4	201.4	201.4	218.4	221.0	221.0	221.0
Electricity	28	220.7	219.0	220.5	224.0	235.4	241.3	244.1	245.5	246.4	246.8	245.6	244.8	244.8
Gas	15	160.4	160.3	160.4	163.9	169.5	174.8	177.4	177.4	177.4	177.4	176.1	176.1	176.0
Oil & other fuel	5	236.8	236.8	236.8	236.8	244.4	244.4	244.4	244.6	244.6	244.6	244.6	244.6	244.6
FUEL & LIGHT	58	198.8	198.0	198.7	202.9	210.4	214.5	216.6	217.3	217.5	220.8	220.3	220.0	219.9
Furniture	13	153.6	157.1	159.0	161.3	162.8	163.6	163.4	165.7	167.7	169.3	170.3	171.3	171.4
Furnishings	15	160.5	163.4	167.5	168.5	170.9	172.1	173.6	176.4	178.0	179.5	180.8	181.8	182.2
Electrical appliances	15	163.5	167.4	168.2	170.5	172.7	173.5	174.6	177.7	179.4	180.7	183.0	183.9	185.1
Other household equipment	10	169.9	171.9	174.3	176.1	177.6	178.4	179.8	182.8	184.4	187.4	189.8	191.2	192.8
Household consumables	14	194.1	197.5	199.9	205.3	209.4	210.7	212.9	215.7	216.9	223.0	222.6	223.0	224.3
Pet care	5	137.6	139.8	139.1	140.4	141.4	141.1	142.0	143.5	147.6	150.9	156.6	158.6	187.0
HOUSEHOLD GOODS	72	165.3	168.5	170.5	173.0	175.1	176.1	177.3	180.0	181.8	184.4	186.1	187.1	190.3
Postage	3	227.2	227.2	227.2	227.2	227.2	247.6	247.6	247.6	247.6	247.6	247.6	247.6	247.6
Telephone charges etc	10	193.1	193.1	193.1	193.1	193.1	193.1	180.2	158.5	141.3	153.1	170.3	187.5	191.7
Domestic services	5	191.5	194.2	196.1	198.2	200.6	202.3	203.2	204.2	207.3	209.4	211.0	212.8	215.5
Fees & subscriptions	7	164.0	165.3	165.5	171.5	172.9	172.5	182.7	183.2	183.5	193.4	194.2	194.8	199.4
HOUSEHOLD SERVICES	25	188.7	189.6	190.1	192.5	193.4	195.6	194.0	186.0	180.0	188.1	195.4	202.7	206.4
Men's outerwear	16	152.5	155.7	157.3	157.4	158.7	159.5	159.8	162.6	163.5	165.0	166.8	167.2	167.9
Women's outerwear	23	141.9	142.3	144.7	142.4	141.6	142.5	147.0	152.0	153.2	153.0	154.1	153.9	146.9
Children's outerwear	9	154.4	156.7	158.3	158.9	159.6	161.0	161.9	168.6	169.2	170.6	170.6	171.0	174.1
Other clothing	18	153.8	158.5	159.3	161.7	163.1	164.7	165.6	169.4	170.3	171.8	173.2	173.6	174.1
Footwear	16	142.9	146.1	150.9	153.5	155.2	156.0	156.6	154.0	157.0	161.0	161.7	162.8	164.5
CLOTHING & FOOTWEAR	82	148.5	151.1	153.4	153.8	154.6	155.7	157.4	160.4	161.8	163.3	164.4	164.7	163.6
Chemists' goods	12	159.4	160.9	164.6	167.1	169.0	170.2	172.9	172.8	175.2	176.9	177.2	177.0	177.8
Personal services	7	179.6	182.3	183.7	187.5	190.2	192.2	193.4	195.4	197.9	199.7	202.8	205.3	207.4

Index: January 1974 = 100

	Weight *	Jan	Feb	Mar	Apr	May	Jun	Jul	Aug	Sep	Oct	Nov	Dec	Next Jan
Purchase of motor vehicles	50	170.0	171.9	174.3	176.5	179.0	181.4	184.3	186.0	188.0	189.9	192.4	194.7	197.0
Maintenance of motor vcles	14	174.2	182.9	182.9	183.6	190.4	193.4	193.4	201.0	201.0	201.0	204.7	204.7	205.9
Petrol & oil	38	193.7	193.9	193.9	206.1	209.4	209.4	206.9	191.4	190.6	189.6	188.7	188.3	187.5
Vehicle tax & insurance	14	158.6	161.9	161.9	183.8	183.8	183.8	183.8	187.7	188.8	188.8	188.8	188.8	189.0
MOTORING EXPENDITURE	116	175.6	178.0	179.1	186.7	190.0	191.0	191.6	189.2	190.0	190.6	191.9	192.8	193.7
Rail fares	7	215.2	215.2	215.2	215.2	215.2	215.2	215.4	222.9	222.9	222.9	222.9	222.9	246.6
Bus & coach fares	14	194.5	197.8	198.8	201.9	203.8	204.6	206.6	214.9	215.1	216.5	218.8	219.2	223.9
Other travel costs	2	175.4	181.2	183.0	185.7	188.2	189.4	191.4	193.3	195.9	197.5	198.9	200.0	200.0
FARES & OTHER TRAVEL COSTS	23	196.9	199.6	200.4	202.5	204.0	204.6	206.0	213.5	213.9	214.8	216.4	216.8	226.2
Audio-visual equipment	10	135.5	137.8	138.3	139.0	138.9	138.8	138.9	138.9	140.1	140.6	141.7	141.6	141.2
Records, toys, photo & sports goods & personal articles	25	166.2	168.3	170.4	171.7	171.9	172.1	172.8	174.1	176.1	178.4	177.0	177.3	177.7
Books & newspapers	15	190.9	194.5	197.0	208.8	209.5	209.9	214.4	214.8	215.7	219.9	220.4	221.0	224.0
Gardening products	5	150.9	150.9	150.9	160.3	160.3	160.3	160.3	160.3	160.3	160.3	181.1	185.6	185.6
TV licences & rentals	13	123.9	124.0	124.0	124.1	124.1	124.1	124.3	138.1	138.1	138.3	138.4	138.5	138.5
Entertainment & recreation	9	158.7	159.2	159.7	162.4	169.2	170.3	170.6	171.4	177.0	177.1	179.0	179.5	184.1
LEISURE SERVICES	22	138.5	138.7	138.9	140.0	142.4	142.8	143.0	152.4	154.4	154.6	155.3	155.6	157.2

* Applied to change since January 1977
§ Variable from month to month
# Includes unpublished components for dwelling insurance & ground rent

| | Index: January 1974 = 100 | | | | | | | | | | | | |
	Weight *	Jan	Feb	Mar	Apr	May	Jun	Jul	Aug	Sep	Oct	Nov	Dec	Next Jan
Bread	13	188.7	188.5	189.0	200.6	200.9	201.2	201.9	204.4	204.5	204.7	205.6	211.8	214.0
Cereals	5	211.2	213.3	215.0	217.3	219.7	220.9	222.5	223.3	225.0	226.3	229.1	231.7	232.6
Biscuits & cakes	13	200.7	203.3	204.4	208.3	208.7	208.7	209.8	209.9	210.0	211.4	211.9	213.5	216.5
Beef	16	174.1	177.1	179.7	185.6	191.0	195.9	199.6	200.5	202.4	202.4	202.6	203.2	212.0
Lamb	7	167.8	168.6	167.4	172.3	185.3	189.8	191.9	192.2	193.8	195.3	195.4	194.3	198.8
of which Home-killed lamb	3.5	179.0	180.4	182.8	189.1	208.9	211.7	207.3	204.5	205.9	203.9	202.8	203.1	209.0
Pork	6	160.9	161.2	163.0	164.3	168.7	169.5	170.4	171.5	172.9	177.0	177.8	179.0	181.6
Bacon	7	156.7	156.9	158.2	159.0	161.2	162.7	164.1	165.4	165.7	166.9	167.0	169.4	172.7
Poultry & other meat	22	154.4	155.4	157.0	158.6	160.4	162.2	164.7	166.3	167.1	167.0	168.0	169.2	171.0
Fish	8	186.5	185.4	184.4	186.2	187.1	187.8	189.3	189.2	191.3	193.1	193.7	197.4	203.4
of which Fresh/smoked fish	3.76	185.1	182.5	180.2	183.7	184.1	185.4	187.7	187.5	190.4	194.0	195.4	203.2	211.1
Butter	6	247.4	248.6	251.7	256.0	258.6	267.2	282.8	291.1	297.1	301.6	298.2	296.3	316.7
Oils & fats	5	193.3	190.8	186.4	184.2	186.3	186.9	186.3	189.2	189.9	189.6	188.4	188.2	191.5
Cheese	6	213.2	214.1	213.1	214.6	213.7	215.0	214.5	218.0	220.1	223.6	227.0	230.1	237.1
Eggs	6	118.9	113.7	116.4	112.9	111.7	105.4	105.9	104.1	100.8	101.1	103.4	117.7	127.1
Milk, fresh	21	226.8	226.8	226.8	226.8	226.8	226.8	226.8	226.8	226.8	225.3	241.6	243.4	243.4
Milk products	3	216.6	219.1	219.2	225.5	227.3	234.6	234.1	235.5	236.8	241.0	242.6	243.2	244.1
Tea	6	329.9	330.1	310.3	297.8	296.0	296.3	295.1	291.1	289.4	274.7	271.2	267.4	269.0
Coffee & other hot drinks	4	364.0	360.2	357.9	351.1	351.9	353.0	346.3	343.6	343.1	324.9	323.2	322.2	323.0
Soft drinks	5	202.2	205.2	205.7	205.7	204.2	204.9	210.1	212.5	212.6	214.9	211.1	216.9
Sugar & preserves	6	234.8	237.3	239.5	240.3	241.4	242.1	246.0	253.3	257.1	258.9	260.5	260.4	263.1
Sweets & chocolates	15	245.6	249.2	250.9	253.2	256.8	257.0	260.1	263.5	268.1	268.8	269.2	269.8	274.2
Potatoes	7	208.6	210.6	216.3	232.4	234.8	274.4	197.9	197.8	204.8	211.9	212.1	217.8	273.4
of which Unproc'd potatoes	6	174.3	177.0	184.8	206.9	210.2	263.6	157.7	157.6	167.0	176.5	176.8	184.5	258.7
Other vegetables	12	174.3	181.1	189.8	199.3	194.0	206.1	196.0	180.3	183.0	177.1	185.1	196.8	224.1
of which Fresh vegetables	§	159.1	171.6	185.9	202.5	191.0	208.7	188.6	164.5	168.2	160.1	169.9	190.4	240.3
Fruit	13	210.2	207.9	206.5	209.2	212.0	222.4	231.7	227.9	207.3	191.6	191.8	196.9	204.2
of which Fresh fruit	§	213.6	210.1	208.3	212.5	217.3	233.2	247.0	243.9	211.1	187.6	187.1	194.0	205.0
Other foods (excl. petfood)	15	210.0	212.0	212.6	216.5	217.5	218.9	220.8	222.7	222.5	224.9	225.1	224.1	226.7
FOOD (excluding petfood)	233	196.1	197.3	198.4	201.6	203.2	206.7	206.1	206.2	206.3	205.6	207.9	210.5	217.7
Canteen meals	17	191.5	192.9	193.8	194.1	194.9	195.7	196.4	198.0	196.9	198.6	200.3	200.3	203.0
Other meals & snacks	34	202.4	203.3	204.5	207.7	209.5	211.1	214.0	216.6	217.6	219.4	221.4	222.4	225.5
CATERING	51	199.5	200.6	201.7	203.9	205.4	206.7	208.9	211.1	211.4	213.2	215.1	215.7	218.7
Beer	52	201.3	204.9	210.0	212.5	212.5	212.5	212.9	212.9	212.9	213.4	213.4	213.4	213.4
Wines & spirits	33	171.8	171.8	174.0	174.7	174.7	174.7	176.4	176.4	176.4	177.8	177.8	177.8	178.9
ALCOHOLIC DRINK	85	188.9	191.0	194.8	196.6	196.6	196.6	197.5	197.5	197.5	198.4	198.4	198.4	198.9
Cigarettes	44	222.2	222.2	222.2	223.6	223.6	223.6	223.6	226.5	228.7	230.4	230.4	230.4	230.9
Other tobacco	4	228.3	228.3	228.3	229.7	229.7	229.7	229.7	232.2	234.5	237.2	237.2	237.2	237.8
TOBACCO	48	222.8	222.8	222.8	224.2	224.2	224.2	224.2	227.0	229.2	231.1	231.1	231.1	231.5
Rent	32	152.9	153.6	154.0	160.1	160.6	162.8	163.4	163.6	164.4	165.6	166.8	167.6	167.2
Mortgage interest payments	23	124.1	114.0	113.0	114.8	115.9	116.9	123.2	135.9	137.3	139.6	141.1	154.3	172.2
Rates	31.6	192.8	192.8	192.8	212.9	212.2	212.2	212.2	212.2	212.2	212.2	212.2	212.2	212.2
Water charges	2.4	212.9	212.9	212.9	229.6	229.6	229.6	229.6	229.6	229.6	229.6	229.6	229.6	229.6
Repair/maintenance charges	8	218.5	218.6	220.7	233.8	234.0	234.2	234.2	236.0	236.0	248.6	248.4	248.4	248.4
Do-it-yourself materials	14	200.1	201.9	204.3	205.7	206.5	208.1	209.0	209.6	210.6	212.4	213.3	214.9	215.2
HOUSING #	113	164.3	162.1	162.3	170.6	171.0	172.1	174.1	177.8	178.6	180.5	181.4	185.4	190.3
Coal & solid fuels	11	221.0	221.0	221.0	221.0	222.4	222.4	223.4	223.4	223.4	223.4	246.5	246.5	247.9
Electricity	29	244.8	247.5	249.7	253.3	259.1	264.9	268.5	268.5	268.4	267.6	265.8	263.6	263.6
Gas	16	176.0	176.0	176.0	176.0	176.0	176.1	176.1	176.1	176.1	176.1	176.2	176.2	176.3
Oil & other fuel	4	244.6	244.6	244.6	244.6	244.6	244.6	244.6	244.6	244.6	244.6	244.6	244.6	244.6
FUEL & LIGHT	60	219.9	221.1	222.0	223.6	226.4	228.9	230.6	230.6	230.6	230.3	233.7	232.8	233.1
Furniture	14	171.4	173.5	174.9	176.4	177.7	177.3	178.0	181.7	182.8	184.5	185.1	185.9	184.7
Furnishings	15	182.2	184.9	187.7	188.5	189.6	190.4	189.9	192.7	195.5	196.4	197.2	199.1	197.4
Electrical appliances	17	185.1	186.1	187.9	189.8	190.5	191.2	191.5	192.4	192.6	193.5	195.5	196.3	196.3
Other household equipment	10	192.8	195.3	197.4	199.0	200.0	201.2	202.4	203.6	204.4	206.6	207.4	209.4	208.2
Household consumables	14	224.3	224.9	226.8	227.4	229.9	231.0	231.3	233.0	232.7	234.9	235.7	237.3	241.1
Pet care	6	187.0	193.7	194.6	197.1	195.6	198.4	198.1	199.9	198.8	199.5	200.7	200.9	200.5
HOUSEHOLD GOODS	76	190.3	192.4	194.3	195.7	196.8	197.6	197.9	200.0	200.8	202.2	203.3	204.6	204.4
Postage	3	247.6	247.6	247.6	247.6	247.6	247.6	247.6	247.6	247.6	247.6	247.6	247.6	247.6
Telephone charges etc	11	191.7	191.7	191.7	191.7	191.7	191.7	191.7	191.7	191.7	191.7	191.7	191.7	191.7
Domestic services	5	215.5	218.2	219.7	221.5	224.1	225.6	227.6	229.5	232.8	236.5	238.2	240.0	242.3
Fees & subscriptions	7	199.4	202.6	208.5	214.7	213.8	214.4	215.1	216.3	218.4	220.2	222.5	223.9	227.3
HOUSEHOLD SERVICES	26	206.4	207.8	209.7	211.7	211.9	212.4	213.0	213.6	214.9	216.0	217.0	217.7	219.0
Men's outerwear	13	167.9	172.1	172.9	173.9	175.7	177.1	178.0	179.4	180.4	184.6	185.8	186.2	186.1
Women's outerwear	22	146.9	151.7	152.2	153.3	153.3	153.1	153.4	153.5	156.1	155.3	155.0	154.8	153.8
Children's outerwear	10	174.1	177.1	176.4	178.6	178.9	180.6	177.3	182.1	182.6	182.4	183.5	183.9	182.8
Other clothing	18	174.1	177.6	180.2	180.7	181.8	181.9	184.4	186.7	187.5	190.2	189.9	192.0	193.0
Footwear	17	164.5	165.4	166.2	167.7	168.2	168.5	170.0	171.5	172.8	174.4	175.1	176.0	176.3
CLOTHING & FOOTWEAR	80	163.6	167.1	167.9	169.1	169.8	170.3	170.9	172.5	174.0	175.3	175.6	176.3	176.1
Chemists' goods	12	177.8	178.8	178.5	180.4	181.8	181.8	184.2	186.2	186.9	189.0	188.8	189.2	188.6
Personal services	7	207.4	210.5	212.6	215.6	216.8	219.9	221.5	223.0	225.5	228.2	229.3	232.5	239.7

Index: January 1974 = 100

	Weight *	Jan	Feb	Mar	Apr	May	Jun	Jul	Aug	Sep	Oct	Nov	Dec	Next Jan
Purchase of motor vehicles	51	197.0	199.3	201.6	204.2	207.2	210.2	212.4	215.3	218.3	220.9	223.4	226.0	228.8
Maintenance of motor vcles	15	205.9	213.6	213.6	213.6	217.3	217.3	217.3	222.4	222.4	222.4	225.0	225.7	226.4
Petrol & oil	34	187.5	188.1	187.5	186.1	185.6	185.8	186.0	186.0	185.8	185.9	190.3	191.3	192.7
Vehicle tax & insurance	16	189.0	191.7	191.7	195.5	195.5	196.9	197.9	197.9	197.9	197.9	197.9	197.9	198.2
MOTORING EXPENDITURE	116	193.7	196.3	197.0	198.3	199.9	201.4	202.6	204.4	205.7	206.8	209.6	211.0	212.9
Rail fares	7	246.6	246.6	246.6	246.6	246.6	246.6	252.9	252.9	252.9	252.9	252.9	252.9	271.8
Bus & coach fares	14	223.9	226.5	226.7	231.6	232.4	234.6	238.6	239.5	241.0	241.2	242.9	244.2	249.9
Other travel costs	3	200.0	203.8	205.8	205.7	207.3	208.3	207.7	208.6	209.9	211.0	211.9	212.4	211.9
FARES & OTHER TRAVEL COSTS	24	226.2	228.3	228.7	231.6	232.3	233.7	237.6	238.3	239.4	239.7	240.8	241.6	250.0
Audio-visual equipment	8	141.2	142.4	142.9	143.4	143.5	145.0	143.8	145.3	145.5	144.8	145.4	146.1	145.6
Records, toys, photo & sports goods & personal articles	22	177.7	179.7	181.0	182.6	183.3	184.3	187.8	188.4	190.0	191.9	192.1	192.9	196.1
Books & newspapers	17	224.0	224.7	224.8	229.0	230.4	230.4	234.7	235.7	238.5	242.8	243.1	243.1	243.7
Gardening products	5	185.6	185.6	185.6	198.0	198.0	198.0	198.0	198.0	198.0	198.0	209.7	212.4	212.4
TV licences & rentals	14	138.5	138.6	138.6	138.7	138.8	138.8	138.9	139.0	139.0	139.1	139.2	146.0	146.1
Entertainment & recreation	9	184.1	184.9	185.7	185.7	187.8	187.8	188.8	189.1	195.7	196.6	198.2	198.4	208.4
LEISURE SERVICES	23	157.2	157.6	157.8	157.9	158.6	158.6	159.0	159.2	161.4	161.8	162.4	167.2	170.5

* Applied to change since January 1978
§ Variable from month to month
# Includes unpublished components for dwelling insurance & ground rent

Index: January 1974 = 100

	Weight*	Jan	Feb	Mar	Apr	May	Jun	Jul	Aug	Sep	Oct	Nov	Dec	Next Jan
Bread	13	214.0	213.9	214.4	214.4	215.6	225.1	226.3	226.9	227.8	230.4	231.6	245.6	248.3
Cereals	5	232.6	232.9	235.4	237.9	239.9	242.4	244.4	248.5	252.2	256.7	265.5	265.8	267.8
Biscuits & cakes	12	216.5	219.2	219.6	220.5	220.8	221.4	229.4	233.0	233.8	239.5	239.8	243.0	258.8
Beef	18	212.0	212.2	212.1	211.7	216.6	228.7	234.1	234.4	234.8	233.7	234.0	234.8	240.1
Lamb	8	198.8	199.4	198.5	201.8	212.7	219.9	213.7	206.8	201.4	197.8	197.3	196.1	200.7
of which Home-killed lamb	4	209.0	210.4	214.2	223.8	243.4	255.2	242.1	227.5	218.1	211.1	210.0	206.7	215.2
Pork	6	181.6	181.3	180.3	180.1	180.0	181.0	181.1	182.1	184.1	191.1	195.0	198.8	199.6
Bacon	8	172.7	174.3	174.2	172.6	174.1	175.8	178.8	181.5	182.5	184.0	186.6	188.8	192.0
Poultry & other meat	22	171.0	172.2	173.2	174.2	176.6	180.3	184.2	186.3	187.9	189.8	190.1	193.1	194.4
Fish	8	203.4	200.4	202.1	200.9	203.8	204.5	205.4	207.0	208.5	210.4	211.9	212.5	216.8
of which Fresh/smoked fish	3.92	211.1	204.4	207.8	205.8	207.1	208.2	208.6	208.7	211.6	214.6	217.7	219.1	222.2
Butter	6	316.7	324.6	330.6	332.5	336.0	337.2	318.8	326.9	319.1	327.1	332.2	335.1	341.7
Oils & fats	4	191.5	191.9	190.6	193.4	195.2	197.9	201.5	202.3	199.3	197.5	198.3	195.8	199.8
Cheese	6	237.1	241.4	245.4	249.5	252.6	255.1	258.4	260.3	265.7	268.7	271.8	274.3	277.3
Eggs	6	127.1	137.0	130.0	128.2	120.5	120.1	119.6	120.5	128.3	130.4	131.3	141.5	143.3
Milk, fresh	20	243.4	243.4	243.4	243.4	243.4	267.7	270.3	270.3	270.3	270.3	270.3	270.3	270.3
Milk products	3	244.1	250.7	251.1	251.9	255.9	258.2	260.0	269.8	278.8	283.9	285.5	285.3	293.7
Tea	4	269.0	278.9	280.4	278.5	279.9	277.1	273.6	272.9	276.5	275.1	277.1	275.3	278.9
Coffee & other hot drinks	3	323.0	320.9	321.3	317.6	318.6	319.2	317.2	317.4	325.2	336.7	340.3	338.7	343.6
Soft drinks	4	216.9	219.9	219.9	223.2	223.8	223.9	238.7	239.5	246.1	253.1	255.4	251.9	260.7
Sugar & preserves	5	263.1	264.9	264.4	264.6	270.7	273.0	276.2	283.3	286.4	288.3	290.1	290.4	293.9
Sweets & chocolates	17	274.2	274.1	274.6	277.1	288.8	293.5	318.5	321.8	323.4	326.9	328.5	328.6	331.8
Potatoes	9	273.4	267.1	272.3	269.3	271.9	313.0	274.8	285.1	305.1	310.2	314.4	317.9	323.9
of which Unproc'd potatoes	5.4	258.7	248.8	256.9	252.2	254.2	319.1	233.0	249.2	279.6	287.6	294.3	299.8	305.8
Other vegetables	15	224.1	223.8	241.4	255.2	252.5	244.6	217.5	200.6	192.5	196.5	211.0	217.0	234.2
of which Fresh vegetables	§	240.3	239.5	270.8	296.6	286.2	271.3	225.8	197.6	181.5	188.7	206.2	212.1	240.3
Fruit	10	204.2	204.4	205.3	207.9	214.6	219.8	226.3	225.2	213.4	210.3	211.6	216.7	221.0
of which Fresh fruit	§	205.0	204.0	205.0	209.7	219.9	226.9	235.4	234.6	214.9	208.8	211.4	214.9	223.1
Other foods (excl. petfood)	14	226.7	229.0	229.4	231.8	235.3	237.7	242.8	244.8	244.7	249.5	251.2	253.1	257.5
FOOD (excluding petfood)	226	217.7	218.9	220.4	221.9	224.4	230.6	231.4	231.9	232.6	234.9	237.1	240.0	245.0
Canteen meals	16	203.0	203.9	204.2	205.8	207.0	207.2	211.5	212.9	231.2	232.8	235.3	236.4	240.9
Other meals & snacks	35	225.5	227.1	229.4	234.1	236.4	241.8	262.3	265.1	266.7	271.5	273.2	276.0	280.0
CATERING	51	218.7	220.1	221.7	225.4	227.3	231.0	246.1	248.4	255.7	259.4	261.4	263.6	267.8
Beer	48	213.4	215.5	218.9	223.2	226.7	227.8	242.3	245.4	248.8	252.2	254.3	255.4	268.0
Wines & spirits	29	178.9	178.9	183.2	183.9	185.0	185.0	199.7	199.7	200.6	202.0	202.9	203.8	204.8
ALCOHOLIC DRINK	77	198.9	200.1	203.9	206.7	209.2	209.8	224.4	226.2	228.5	231.1	232.7	233.7	241.4
Cigarettes	40	230.9	230.9	230.9	231.3	231.3	231.3	257.3	257.3	264.8	267.5	267.5	267.5	269.9
Other tobacco	4	237.8	237.8	237.8	237.8	237.8	237.8	249.7	249.7	264.0	267.1	267.1	267.1	267.1
TOBACCO	44	231.5	231.5	231.5	231.9	231.9	231.9	256.7	256.7	264.8	267.5	267.5	267.5	269.7
Rent	32	167.2	167.9	168.3	173.1	176.4	178.2	179.1	179.2	179.5	184.3	185.5	185.6	186.0
Mortgage interest payments	31	172.2	174.1	177.6	179.6	181.6	193.4	195.7	198.5	201.1	203.7	206.4	209.0	260.8
Rates	27.88	212.2	212.2	212.2	250.4	250.1	250.1	250.1	250.1	250.1	250.1	250.1	250.1	250.3
Water charges	6.12	229.6	229.6	229.6	250.2	250.2	250.2	250.2	250.2	250.2	250.2	250.2	250.2	250.2
Repair/maintenance charges	8	248.4	248.4	248.4	269.7	271.7	273.3	285.7	285.7	288.2	292.0	293.6	293.6	293.6
Do-it-yourself materials	12	215.2	217.8	219.2	222.2	224.5	226.4	239.4	243.5	246.6	249.2	252.3	253.0	255.5
HOUSING #	120	190.3	191.4	192.7	205.0	206.9	211.2	214.0	215.4	216.7	219.5	221.1	222.1	237.4
Coal & solid fuels	10	247.9	248.4	248.4	249.6	251.9	251.9	270.6	270.6	270.6	270.6	300.4	300.4	301.7
Electricity	29	263.6	265.3	267.5	268.6	269.6	272.3	279.8	285.7	293.9	301.6	309.0	314.2	314.2
Gas	16	176.3	176.4	176.4	176.4	176.4	177.4	182.7	187.0	190.2	190.2	190.2	190.3	190.4
Oil & other fuel	4	244.6	252.7	267.2	270.6	270.6	297.0	331.2	353.8	356.7	358.1	358.4	358.6	374.7
FUEL & LIGHT	59	233.1	234.4	236.3	237.2	238.0	241.3	251.6	257.2	262.1	265.5	273.5	275.8	277.1
Furniture	14	184.7	188.1	189.7	191.3	192.8	193.6	205.2	208.6	211.4	212.8	215.6	217.4	216.9
Furnishings	14	197.4	200.5	204.5	205.6	207.0	209.2	224.1	225.6	228.5	231.4	233.2	234.2	234.2
Electrical appliances	16	196.3	198.6	200.2	201.6	203.2	204.8	213.3	215.6	218.2	220.3	222.5	224.1	225.2
Other household equipment	10	208.2	216.5	217.0	219.6	221.3	225.3	239.6	240.8	242.9	247.9	249.8	252.7	253.7
Household consumables	15	241.1	243.7	245.5	249.9	250.7	252.9	272.5	277.0	282.1	288.0	289.2	293.0	301.1
Pet care	6	200.5	201.6	203.3	203.1	199.6	200.9	216.1	220.2	223.5	222.6	222.7	225.8	228.3
HOUSEHOLD GOODS	75	204.4	207.8	209.7	211.7	212.7	214.6	228.2	231.0	234.1	237.0	238.9	241.0	242.9
Postage	2	247.6	247.6	247.6	247.6	247.6	247.6	247.6	253.3	284.3	284.3	284.3	284.3	284.3
Telephone charges etc	11	191.7	191.7	191.7	191.7	191.7	191.7	191.8	191.8	194.3	196.9	201.4	202.8	232.3
Domestic services	5	242.3	245.7	249.3	252.2	255.6	259.3	272.0	275.1	278.6	282.5	286.9	288.5	291.8
Fees & subscriptions	9	227.3	229.2	233.1	237.8	239.1	243.3	250.8	255.0	259.0	262.8	269.4	270.9	279.6
HOUSEHOLD SERVICES	27	219.0	220.3	222.1	224.0	225.1	227.0	231.6	233.8	239.0	242.0	246.9	248.3	265.4
Men's outerwear	13	186.1	188.6	189.5	191.8	193.7	195.3	205.5	206.7	207.9	212.6	214.0	214.1	214.2
Women's outerwear	24	153.8	155.3	155.9	155.0	154.3	156.7	162.4	159.9	159.7	160.1	159.8	159.7	159.5
Children's outerwear	10	182.8	186.5	188.2	190.6	191.5	192.6	194.7	195.1	195.1	195.6	195.8	196.2	197.3
Other clothing	18	193.0	197.0	199.4	200.3	202.1	203.9	215.3	217.8	219.1	222.0	223.3	224.2	226.1
Footwear	17	176.3	178.0	180.6	181.5	182.6	185.3	195.7	199.4	201.3	203.1	205.7	207.3	207.7
CLOTHING & FOOTWEAR	82	176.1	178.6	180.1	180.8	181.6	183.7	191.8	192.4	193.2	195.0	196.0	196.5	197.1
Chemists' goods	12	188.6	189.1	190.7	195.9	198.5	199.9	223.7	226.3	230.0	232.4	232.5	236.4	238.7
Personal services	7	239.7	242.6	244.2	246.6	249.7	253.2	270.9	273.7	275.7	278.0	279.5	283.6	295.0

	Weight*	Jan	Feb	Mar	Apr	May	Jun	Jul	Aug	Sep	Oct	Nov	Dec	Next Jan
						Index: January 1974 = 100								
Purchase of motor vehicles	57	228.8	230.9	232.3	234.2	235.7	237.8	242.7	247.4	250.0	253.1	255.9	254.7	255.3
Maintenance of motor vcles	16	220.4	206.2	236.2	236.2	244.2	244.2	258.9	269.3	269.3	269.3	279.6	279.6	281.2
Petrol & oil	33	192.7	195.3	200.9	210.6	214.6	235.5	285.1	285.1	284.5	283.2	281.0	283.5	288.9
Vehicle tax & insurance	16	198.2	202.0	202.0	206.2	206.2	206.2	209.1	211.6	211.6	211.8	213.7	213.7	217.6
MOTORING EXPENDITURE	122	212.9	216.3	218.6	222.8	225.7	232.9	252.0	255.6	256.6	257.6	260.0	259.9	262.5
Rail fares	7	271.8	271.8	271.8	271.8	271.8	271.8	276.1	276.1	283.1	283.1	283.1	283.1	327.0
Bus & coach fares	12	249.9	252.0	252.4	252.9	254.8	256.3	262.6	265.3	279.3	281.5	283.0	283.8	298.7
Other travel costs	2	211.9	214.8	216.2	217.2	218.3	219.2	233.2	238.0	242.0	246.3	249.7	249.6	251.3
FARES & OTHER TRAVEL COSTS	21	250.0	251.5	251.9	252.3	253.6	254.5	261.0	263.1	273.6	275.4	276.6	277.0	299.2
Audio-visual equipment	10	145.6	145.4	144.8	145.3	145.9	146.5	150.0	150.1	149.9	149.9	150.8	151.1	149.6
Records, toys, photo & sports goods & personal articles	24	196.1	199.0	200.5	206.4	208.4	210.1	225.1	226.7	227.7	228.6	229.2	229.9	229.9
Books & newspapers	15	243.7	246.6	248.1	253.3	253.8	254.6	259.7	259.8	261.2	274.5	275.9	277.7	280.6
Gardening products	4	212.4	212.4	212.4	218.5	218.5	219.8	219.8	219.8	219.8	219.3	231.2	236.6	236.6
TV licences & rentals	13	146.1	146.2	146.2	146.3	146.4	146.4	154.6	154.6	154.6	154.6	154.6	169.0	173.4
Entertainment & recreation	12	208.4	208.7	209.0	211.0	212.1	212.4	228.5	228.8	234.3	237.0	237.9	238.5	266.6
LEISURE SERVICES	25	170.5	170.7	170.8	171.7	172.2	172.3	183.6	183.7	185.9	186.9	187.3	196.3	210.0

* Applied to change since January 1979
§ Variable from month to month
\# Includes unpublished components for dwelling insurance & ground rent

Index: January 1974 = 100

	Weight *	Jan	Feb	Mar	Apr	May	Jun	Jul	Aug	Sep	Oct	Nov	Dec	Next Jan
Bread	12	248.3	249.2	249.4	249.4	262.6	264.6	265.5	265.9	265.7	265.9	265.9	273.5	275.5
Cereals	4	267.8	268.1	269.6	271.3	279.8	284.0	286.6	289.3	290.4	291.5	293.9	297.5	300.5
Biscuits & cakes	12	258.8	260.5	262.8	263.2	265.6	268.8	273.3	272.0	273.0	273.6	277.4	278.2	281.2
Beef	17	240.1	241.2	243.0	250.9	253.9	254.2	254.1	252.6	250.9	249.1	248.4	254.2	257.4
Lamb	6	200.7	199.6	206.9	217.6	222.8	233.2	221.4	215.5	209.1	210.1	197.1	206.2	211.1
of which Home-killed lamb	3	215.2	214.9	225.9	239.5	243.4	244.5	238.3	226.6	215.9	223.0	201.3	218.4	227.7
Pork	6	199.6	198.5	196.0	198.7	199.5	200.7	201.0	200.6	199.8	200.7	202.2	204.2	204.0
Bacon	7	192.0	193.6	192.8	193.5	194.0	196.2	197.1	198.0	197.2	197.2	198.0	199.3	201.0
Poultry & other meat	21	194.4	196.7	198.2	200.2	201.9	203.5	205.3	205.6	205.6	205.2	204.7	205.3	204.1
Fish	7	216.8	215.9	218.5	219.7	219.7	220.2	220.4	220.3	221.3	223.9	223.0	226.2	228.4
of which Fresh/smoked fish	3.22	222.2	219.9	218.0	220.6	219.9	219.9	220.2	219.7	219.1	223.8	221.8	226.7	229.8
Butter	5	341.7	347.4	351.2	357.4	361.8	363.5	363.9	365.8	366.0	364.3	364.5	365.0	366.4
Oils & fats	4	199.8	201.7	202.2	201.6	203.6	202.0	203.4	203.4	201.7	201.5	199.6	201.3	202.9
Cheese	5	277.3	281.1	282.6	284.6	287.8	290.9	293.3	295.5	299.1	302.0	304.6	305.9	309.0
Eggs	5	143.3	143.4	143.5	143.9	145.5	144.8	142.1	141.5	141.2	141.8	149.5	153.8	154.2
Milk, fresh	17	270.3	270.3	297.3	297.3	297.3	297.3	297.3	306.3	306.4	306.4	306.4	306.4	333.3
Milk products	3	293.7	299.9	302.5	310.4	313.2	314.2	315.9	325.0	326.5	328.5	328.9	330.4	335.1
Tea	3	278.9	283.2	282.8	280.0	283.1	283.1	267.6	279.4	301.8	306.9	310.5	311.9	310.9
Coffee & other hot drinks	4	343.6	347.8	351.3	350.0	350.5	351.2	351.5	350.6	341.8	338.5	335.2	331.8	331.3
Soft drinks	5	260.7	267.7	271.2	279.0	281.3	282.6	285.5	286.1	289.8	293.0	293.7	289.3	299.6
Sugar & preserves	4	293.9	297.3	298.2	299.2	302.7	307.0	311.4	318.8	321.5	322.0	323.0	326.1	328.3
Sweets & chocolates	17	331.8	338.2	342.7	347.0	348.4	351.2	357.9	364.0	368.2	365.7	366.6	367.9	374.4
Potatoes	9	323.9	325.3	324.6	307.8	284.2	288.8	293.5	259.3	276.5	288.0	292.2	299.0	300.6
of which Unproc'd potatoes	6.48	305.8	307.7	305.3	283.3	252.4	257.1	252.6	207.9	229.7	244.1	249.5	257.1	259.2
Other vegetables	13	234.2	237.0	247.4	255.6	248.7	251.4	245.7	222.9	231.9	236.1	243.2	250.5	252.2
of which Fresh vegetables	§	240.3	245.8	257.9	270.2	255.8	260.5	249.5	214.8	226.9	232.1	241.3	250.7	251.4
Fruit	10	221.0	222.2	225.6	234.7	239.9	248.7	270.0	274.7	246.1	232.5	229.7	230.1	231.8
of which Fresh fruit	§	223.1	224.3	229.2	242.9	250.3	263.0	289.8	303.2	257.3	236.1	231.2	233.0	233.6
Other foods (excl. petfood)	13	257.5	259.2	263.7	271.7	275.9	279.6	283.4	284.7	285.1	290.0	291.4	291.7	295.8
FOOD (excluding petfood)	209	245.0	246.9	251.2	254.3	255.8	258.0	260.0	258.9	258.9	259.1	259.8	262.4	266.5
Restaurant meals	20	281.8	284.4	288.4	294.0	298.7	303.0	307.1	309.0	311.7	312.7	313.8	314.1	315.3
Canteen meals	9	240.9	256.5	258.1	266.1	277.3	279.6	280.9	282.7	289.4	290.1	292.5	293.5	301.1
Take-away meals & snacks	12	241.3	242.8	245.1	248.4	254.8	253.1	258.1	259.3	261.0	263.8	267.4	268.7	270.4
CATERING	41	267.8	273.3	276.3	281.9	288.9	290.9	294.8	296.5	299.9	301.5	303.7	304.6	307.5
Beer	49	268.0	270.7	274.2	287.8	288.6	291.1	291.9	292.1	305.3	305.5	305.5	305.5	310.9
Wines & spirits	33	204.8	208.6	211.0	220.1	221.4	221.4	227.5	227.5	227.5	232.0	232.0	232.0	232.6
ALCOHOLIC DRINK	82	241.4	244.7	247.7	259.4	260.4	261.7	265.1	265.2	272.3	274.6	274.6	274.6	277.7
Cigarettes	37	269.9	269.9	275.3	293.3	294.7	294.7	294.7	298.8	298.8	298.2	298.2	298.2	296.9
Other tobacco	3	267.1	267.1	273.3	287.9	289.3	289.3	289.3	293.4	293.4	293.6	293.6	293.6	293.6
TOBACCO	40	269.7	269.7	275.2	292.9	294.3	294.3	294.3	298.4	298.4	297.9	297.9	297.9	296.6
Rent	28	186.0	186.1	186.7	211.4	212.4	217.4	218.0	219.1	219.4	223.2	228.0	227.8	228.3
Mortgage interest payments	38	260.8	273.3	276.6	279.0	282.7	286.3	290.4	294.2	298.0	302.2	306.2	309.9	300.2
Rates	26.23	250.3	250.3	250.3	318.6	318.7	318.7	318.7	318.7	318.7	318.7	318.7	318.7	318.7
Water charges	4.77	250.2	250.2	250.2	309.7	309.7	309.7	309.7	309.7	309.7	309.7	309.7	309.7	309.7
Repair/maintenance charges	8	293.6	296.6	299.5	336.5	340.7	340.2	340.2	340.2	340.2	357.4	355.9	356.0	356.0
Do-it-yourself materials	16	255.5	259.4	265.7	268.6	274.3	278.1	282.6	285.5	287.6	288.7	290.3	290.0	290.7
HOUSING #	124	237.4	241.7	243.8	269.8	272.1	275.1	277.0	278.8	280.3	283.7	286.4	287.4	285.0
Coal & solid fuels	9	301.7	303.2	331.0	331.0	331.0	331.0	344.3	344.3	344.3	344.3	376.9	376.9	395.1
Electricity	29	314.2	314.3	314.3	323.3	340.8	361.7	369.4	372.6	387.9	399.7	407.7	407.7	407.7
Gas	16	190.4	190.6	190.6	195.5	205.1	217.1	221.9	221.9	221.9	225.1	233.3	239.8	243.1
Oil & other fuel	5	374.7	386.9	390.9	406.9	406.9	422.9	428.2	428.2	429.0	432.1	434.3	434.7	441.3
FUEL & LIGHT	59	277.1	278.2	282.3	289.1	300.5	315.3	322.8	324.1	330.8	337.4	348.8	351.4	355.7
Furniture	16	216.9	222.3	224.5	225.3	226.3	225.7	226.1	228.1	229.9	231.1	232.8	233.2	231.5
Furnishings	15	234.2	240.6	246.6	248.0	250.5	250.0	249.6	249.6	250.3	252.0	253.1	253.1	251.6
Electrical appliances	18	225.2	228.8	230.9	233.3	233.9	234.5	234.0	236.4	238.8	238.9	241.4	241.4	238.9
Other household equipment	11	253.7	258.6	262.1	267.2	268.5	270.4	275.8	277.7	279.8	285.8	287.3	288.0	287.7
Household consumables	16	301.1	305.0	309.0	312.4	313.7	317.4	322.2	322.9	326.5	329.0	329.7	331.7	333.6
Pet care	5	228.3	231.5	237.1	238.0	243.0	245.8	248.1	252.6	253.8	256.5	259.5	263.1	264.8
HOUSEHOLD GOODS	81	242.9	247.8	251.3	253.6	255.2	256.1	257.6	259.2	261.3	263.4	265.0	265.7	264.8
Postage	2	284.3	345.0	345.0	350.8	350.8	350.8	350.8	350.8	350.8	350.8	350.8	350.8	356.7
Telephone charges etc	12	232.3	238.2	241.9	242.3	242.3	242.3	242.3	242.3	242.3	242.3	285.0	292.7	299.9
Domestic services	5	291.8	296.7	301.8	308.1	313.2	316.2	320.8	324.2	326.0	329.2	332.5	333.4	338.0
Fees & subscriptions	10	279.6	281.9	287.4	293.3	295.4	296.3	310.2	311.3	315.9	319.0	322.7	323.8	327.1
HOUSEHOLD SERVICES	29	265.4	273.7	278.0	281.5	282.9	283.7	289.0	289.8	291.7	293.1	315.1	319.3	324.9
Men's outerwear	16	214.2	217.8	219.4	219.8	222.3	223.9	224.9	225.5	225.0	226.1	226.4	226.4	227.2
Women's outerwear	22	159.5	161.5	165.4	166.1	165.9	167.0	165.8	164.6	165.7	163.8	164.6	162.5	161.3
Children's outerwear	9	197.3	202.8	203.4	206.7	208.3	207.9	208.9	208.4	210.3	209.7	211.2	209.8	207.0
Other clothing	19	226.1	229.2	233.0	236.0	236.3	236.7	239.5	238.0	239.1	241.0	239.8	240.6	240.1
Footwear	18	207.7	209.1	213.9	214.7	216.3	218.8	220.8	222.6	225.0	225.3	226.3	226.2	226.1
CLOTHING & FOOTWEAR	84	197.1	199.8	203.1	204.6	205.5	206.7	207.5	207.3	208.4	208.4	208.8	208.1	207.5
Chemists' goods	12	238.7	247.5	248.9	252.2	257.3	259.7	265.6	268.3	270.5	272.6	273.6	278.8	279.4
Personal services	7	295.0	299.0	304.1	307.8	311.9	314.7	317.4	318.7	321.9	324.0	327.1	330.1	333.9

Index: January 1974 = 100

	Weight *	Jan	Feb	Mar	Apr	May	Jun	Jul	Aug	Sep	Oct	Nov	Dec	Next Jan
Purchase of motor vehicles	54	255.3	257.5	259.7	261.8	264.0	264.2	267.1	267.8	267.1	267.8	270.2	271.7	271.9
Maintenance of motor vcles	16	281.2	298.7	301.3	003.0	311.9	312.5	314.5	318.6	318.6	318.6	324.1	324.1	325.3
Petrol & oil	43	288.9	295.9	299.9	321.9	322.5	330.8	327.7	326.0	321.3	318.7	313.8	315.0	317.3
Vehicle tax & insurance	15	217.6	222.6	223.8	241.5	245.5	245.5	249.4	254.2	254.2	258.8	260.2	261.7	261.7
MOTORING EXPENDITURE	128	262.5	268.4	271.1	281.5	284.1	286.9	287.9	288.9	287.2	287.2	287.6	288.9	289.9
Rail fares	7	327.0	327.1	327.1	340.2	340.4	340.4	340.4	340.4	340.4	349.5	349.5	397.8	397.8
Bus & coach fares	13	298.7	310.7	325.5	330.8	332.3	335.8	337.2	338.3	342.5	352.1	356.0	357.5	357.5
Other travel costs	3	251.3	255.3	258.7	260.9	262.0	261.6	262.0	263.9	266.4	267.5	267.9	267.4	264.3
FARES & OTHER TRAVEL COSTS	23	299.2	306.7	315.5	322.6	323.7	325.5	326.4	327.3	330.1	338.3	340.5	354.8	354.3
Audio-visual equipment	9	149.6	150.0	150.4	150.5	150.6	149.5	148.8	149.4	148.7	149.7	150.2	150.1	149.3
Records, toys, photo & sports goods & personal articles	28	229.9	233.0	233.9	240.1	241.6	242.4	242.4	242.5	243.4	245.7	246.5	247.3	247.2
Books & newspapers	14	280.6	283.3	289.0	304.5	305.3	310.0	313.5	315.1	327.5	339.2	339.7	339.8	351.0
Gardening products	4	236.6	236.6	236.6	250.9	250.9	250.9	250.9	250.9	250.9	250.9	262.1	265.9	265.9
TV licences & rentals	13	173.4	173.4	173.4	176.2	176.2	176.2	175.3	175.3	175.3	175.3	175.3	175.3	177.0
Entertainment & recreation	13	266.6	267.0	267.4	279.2	282.3	283.3	287.1	287.9	291.1	292.5	299.7	300.2	326.4
LEISURE SERVICES	26	210.0	210.2	210.4	216.7	217.9	218.3	219.2	219.6	220.9	221.4	224.2	224.4	235.7

* Applied to change since January 1980
§ Variable from month to month
# Includes unpublished components for dwelling insurance & ground rent

Index: January 1974 = 100

	Weight *	Jan	Feb	Mar	Apr	May	Jun	Jul	Aug	Sep	Oct	Nov	Dec	Next Jan
Bread	12	275.5	276.4	..	275.9	276.5	284.5	285.9	286.8	286.5	287.2	287.2	290.2	292.0
Cereals	4	300.5	301.3	..	304.6	307.2	310.2	314.4	317.7	319.9	321.4	322.9	323.1	324.8
Biscuits & cakes	12	281.2	287.2	..	290.0	294.3	294.8	296.6	297.6	297.6	297.0	297.8	297.9	303.6
Beef	16	257.4	261.0	..	274.9	278.3	281.2	281.4	279.4	280.8	282.5	286.8	297.9	305.9
Lamb	6	211.1	219.2	..	234.0	248.6	253.6	242.0	226.9	230.3	239.1	245.3	252.0	261.6
of which Home-killed lamb	3	227.7	235.1	..	261.6	271.6	272.3	254.0	231.9	233.7	244.2	252.8	266.1	277.8
Pork	6	204.0	203.7	..	207.7	211.2	212.2	213.1	212.6	212.6	216.9	222.7	225.4	226.6
Bacon	6	201.0	200.1	..	200.2	204.2	205.3	205.3	207.0	209.7	217.5	226.7	229.5	231.9
Poultry & other meat	19	204.1	204.7	..	207.6	209.0	211.2	212.4	213.8	214.1	216.7	218.9	220.8	222.1
Fish	7	228.4	231.2	..	228.4	229.0	229.3	228.7	228.9	229.7	231.3	231.9	235.2	238.1
of which Fresh/smoked fish	3.29	229.8	230.4	..	224.2	226.1	226.3	225.1	224.8	224.9	227.7	228.0	229.3	234.6
Butter	5	366.4	368.2	..	368.0	370.9	374.1	380.4	389.2	397.8	405.9	409.4	409.6	411.4
Oils & fats	3	202.9	201.1	..	201.1	203.0	203.0	203.4	205.1	204.1	206.0	205.5	207.3	211.8
Cheese	5	309.0	309.5	..	308.6	310.9	318.3	323.4	328.6	335.5	341.5	346.2	345.9	345.9
Eggs	5	154.2	152.7	..	155.7	157.3	156.4	149.3	151.4	157.2	161.2	171.2	175.4	176.5
Milk, fresh	19	333.3	333.3	..	333.3	333.3	333.3	333.3	333.3	333.3	333.3	336.0	336.0	360.4
Milk products	3	335.1	336.1	..	342.7	346.0	344.3	346.3	347.8	348.6	351.5	355.4	354.1	355.6
Tea	3	310.9	312.3	..	311.2	309.5	308.6	306.2	306.5	306.5	304.9	303.3	300.1	300.0
Coffee & other hot drinks	3	331.3	331.7	..	325.6	325.8	327.1	324.5	324.4	324.0	319.2	317.1	316.0	318.2
Soft drinks	5	299.6	304.7	..	307.6	308.1	306.9	307.2	306.1	308.5	313.5	313.1	310.8	314.0
Sugar & preserves	4	328.3	329.0	..	329.0	330.4	331.5	333.1	340.4	346.0	352.7	355.2	356.6	358.2
Sweets & chocolates	16	374.4	378.6	..	380.8	383.2	383.2	384.5	385.4	386.0	385.3	386.7	384.0	383.5
Potatoes	7	300.6	302.5	..	302.7	302.1	327.6	340.7	337.1	366.2	387.9	388.7	392.7	425.9
of which Unproc'd potatoes	4.41	259.2	259.8	..	260.0	259.1	294.1	311.1	306.1	345.0	363.9	365.0	369.4	410.9
Other vegetables	13	252.2	256.2	..	286.2	289.1	299.7	286.0	248.0	249.0	257.8	261.0	279.7	308.8
of which Fresh vegetables	§	251.4	254.9	..	307.5	307.1	322.7	298.8	238.5	237.6	250.3	255.0	284.9	336.5
Fruit	10	231.8	234.0	..	243.2	246.0	250.1	252.0	250.7	255.6	256.3	259.3	256.2	268.4
of which Fresh fruit	§	233.6	236.4	..	250.6	254.6	259.4	260.5	261.2	270.4	276.2	284.7	283.0	289.7
Other foods (excl. petfood)	12	295.8	299.3	..	306.1	308.8	311.9	313.8	315.8	316.4	315.5	315.7	316.4	317.2
FOOD (excluding petfood)	201	266.5	268.7	278.5	274.2	276.8	280.1	279.8	277.4	279.8	283.0	285.9	289.0	296.9
Restaurant meals	20.6	315.3	316.4	319.7	320.9	322.5	324.5	328.7	329.1	330.5	330.6	331.7	335.3	335.8
Canteen meals	8.8	301.1	302.6	305.3	305.2	308.2	310.4	309.5	310.6	318.5	319.8	322.9	323.2	328.0
Take-away meals & snacks	12.6	270.4	272.5	..	275.3	278.8	280.2	281.7	282.3	282.9	286.5	288.8	288.8	290.1
CATERING	42	307.5	309.2	311.8	312.9	315.5	317.4	319.8	320.4	322.6	325.0	326.3	328.1	329.7
Beer	49	310.9	317.1	343.5	346.6	346.6	346.6	349.1	349.1	354.4	359.7	361.3	361.3	366.0
Wines & spirits	30	232.6	236.6	..	252.4	252.4	252.4	259.3	259.3	259.3	262.8	262.8	262.8	262.4
ALCOHOLIC DRINK	79	277.7	283.0	299.8	306.5	306.5	306.5	311.0	311.0	313.9	318.5	319.3	319.3	321.8
Cigarettes	33	296.9	308.5	..	363.2	363.2	363.2	363.2	376.1	385.4	390.6	390.6	390.6	393.2
Other tobacco	3	293.6	301.4	..	352.2	352.2	352.2	352.2	371.4	379.8	379.7	379.7	379.7	380.0
TOBACCO	36	296.6	307.9	315.2	362.2	362.2	362.2	362.2	375.7	384.9	389.7	389.7	389.7	392.1
Rent	30	228.3	228.7	229.3	298.2	303.6	304.3	304.4	304.4	304.6	309.4	311.9	312.0	312.3
Mortgage interest payments	42	300.2	297.5	300.0	288.9	285.0	288.3	291.4	294.7	298.1	301.3	334.8	352.5	356.1
Rates	28.37	318.7	318.7	318.7	382.7	393.2	393.2	393.2	393.2	393.2	425.1	425.1	425.1	413.0
Water charges	7.63	309.7	309.7	309.7	350.0	350.0	350.0	350.0	350.0	350.0	350.0	350.0	350.0	350.0
Repair/maintenance charges	8	356.0	356.0	356.0	389.6	390.0	390.4	390.5	390.5	390.5	404.3	407.9	407.9	407.9
Do-it-yourself materials	16	290.7	294.2	297.2	299.4	301.8	302.9	302.4	305.7	308.9	309.2	311.8	313.2	314.3
HOUSING #	135	285.0	284.7	285.9	317.7	320.4	321.7	322.6	324.0	325.5	334.5	345.6	351.0	350.0
Coal & solid fuels	9	395.1	398.8	398.8	398.8	374.8	374.8	374.8	398.9	398.9	398.9	429.0	429.0	429.9
Electricity	31	407.7	407.7	407.7	414.7	432.2	445.6	451.9	451.9	451.9	451.9	435.0	426.6	428.7
Gas	18	243.1	243.2	243.3	248.5	261.6	272.1	277.4	277.4	277.4	281.8	293.0	301.8	306.6
Oil & other fuel	4	441.3	465.4	465.9	470.3	476.6	487.6	487.6	499.0	503.0	527.9	542.9	542.9	549.5
FUEL & LIGHT	62	355.7	357.4	357.5	363.0	373.3	384.2	389.2	393.0	393.2	396.4	398.5	398.6	401.9
Furniture	16	231.5	236.4	237.8	238.2	238.8	237.3	236.4	238.0	240.1	240.5	241.7	241.4	239.3
Furnishings	14	251.6	254.5	255.2	256.2	256.7	256.6	255.5	257.0	261.9	259.1	257.8	257.4	256.5
Electrical appliances	15	238.9	243.0	244.2	246.5	246.9	247.5	246.7	248.2	250.3	250.3	252.5	252.0	249.8
Other household equipment	12	287.7	289.7	289.5	293.1	294.6	294.9	301.1	305.5	307.1	308.9	309.2	308.3	310.0
Household consumables	15	333.6	337.7	338.4	341.7	344.5	344.8	346.0	346.5	344.5	345.8	348.3	350.8	356.1
Pet care	6	264.8	267.1	..	266.6	265.9	267.9	265.2	266.1	264.2	264.4	261.5	261.7	261.6
HOUSEHOLD GOODS	78	264.8	268.5	269.2	271.1	271.9	271.9	272.2	273.9	275.6	275.6	276.3	276.3	276.2
Postage	2	356.7	410.6	410.6	411.0	411.0	411.0	411.0	411.0	411.0	411.0	411.0	411.0	411.0
Telephone charges etc	16	299.9	299.9	299.9	300.5	300.5	300.5	300.5	300.5	300.5	300.5	339.2	344.3	349.4
Domestic services	4	338.0	343.1	..	350.2	353.9	356.1	358.6	361.7	364.6	366.0	369.6	370.3	374.1
Fees & subscriptions	11	327.1	326.8	327.1	331.3	332.1	332.1	333.3	343.4	349.0	354.6	354.6	355.1	359.3
HOUSEHOLD SERVICES	33	324.9	328.4	..	331.0	331.6	331.9	332.6	336.4	338.6	340.6	361.4	364.3	368.7
Men's outerwear	14	227.2	230.8	230.9	231.5	230.9	230.9	231.4	232.2	233.2	232.7	229.7	229.5	227.4
Women's outerwear	24	161.3	160.0	160.4	159.9	160.6	159.7	158.7	162.0	161.1	163.0	163.4	163.1	158.9
Children's outerwear	9	207.0	210.8	208.9	208.7	208.7	208.8	210.7	213.0	214.0	217.3	218.0	218.2	216.5
Other clothing	17	240.1	241.1	242.3	242.8	242.3	241.1	242.5	242.7	245.3	246.5	245.7	245.9	245.1
Footwear	17	226.1	220.2	222.2	222.7	221.5	222.1	220.3	219.4	222.5	222.8	221.2	218.0	218.8
CLOTHING & FOOTWEAR	81	207.5	207.0	207.6	207.6	207.5	207.1	206.9	208.4	209.4	210.7	210.0	209.3	207.1
Chemists' goods	12	279.4	282.8	283.8	287.5	288.2	290.3	291.3	293.3	294.1	294.7	300.0	303.7	304.7
Personal services	7	333.9	340.1	..	346.9	349.9	353.2	354.9	356.7	359.1	359.6	362.9	366.1	368.0

	Weight *	Index: January 1974 = 100												Next
		Jan	Feb	Mar	Apr	May	Jun	Jul	Aug	Sep	Oct	Nov	Dec	Jan
Purchase of motor vehicles	56	271.9	273.2	271.4	274.3	278.0	280.9	284.1	286.6	285.5	286.0	288.7	289.5	288.5
Maintenance of motor vcles	15	325.3	337.2	337.2	337.2	339.0	339.5	339.5	344.2	344.2	344.2	346.2	346.2	347.6
Petrol & oil	40	317.3	324.9	..	370.8	368.0	372.5	378.0	405.9	405.1	403.6	405.7	399.8	392.0
Vehicle tax & insurance	17	261.7	264.7	282.7	282.7	283.2	283.2	287.2	287.8	287.8	288.1	288.2	288.2	288.2
MOTORING EXPENDITURE	128	289.9	294.2	307.8	310.5	311.7	314.4	318.1	327.8	327.0	326.9	329.0	327.6	325.1
Rail fares	8	397.8	397.8	397.8	397.8	397.8	397.8	397.8	397.8	397.8	371.7	371.7	386.0	386.2
Bus & coach fares	12	357.5	358.7	372.3	376.6	376.7	379.4	378.9	383.8	383.0	359.1	359.5	359.5	366.2
Other travel costs	4	264.3	269.9	271.6	271.4	272.6	271.3	271.2	271.1	271.5	272.2	272.2	272.6	268.9
FARES & OTHER TRAVEL COSTS	24	354.3	356.1	363.3	365.4	365.7	366.7	366.4	368.8	368.6	349.1	349.3	353.6	356.2
Audio-visual equipment	8	149.3	150.3	150.5	149.8	149.3	149.4	149.7	149.2	149.4	148.8	149.0	148.7	148.8
Records, toys, photo & sports goods & personal articles	27	247.2	247.9	248.4	247.7	249.3	245.0	244.3	245.0	245.6	248.5	248.4	248.5	248.7
Books & newspapers	17	351.0	352.7	354.1	360.8	358.0	358.5	369.3	373.8	386.6	392.7	396.7	396.8	407.2
Gardening products	4	265.9	265.9	265.9	265.9	265.7	265.7	265.7	265.7	265.7	265.7	257.9	258.7	258.7
TV licences & rentals	12	177.0	177.0	177.0	177.0	177.0	177.0	177.4	177.4	177.4	177.4	177.4	197.5	197.5
Entertainment & recreation	14	326.4	326.8	327.3	342.2	349.4	349.8	351.5	352.3	354.6	356.5	358.7	359.2	367.5
LEISURE SERVICES	26	235.7	235.9	236.1	241.9	244.7	244.9	245.7	246.1	246.9	247.7	248.6	261.1	264.3

* Applied to change since January 1981
§ Variable from month to month
# Includes unpublished components for dwelling insurance & ground rent
.. Not available

Index: January 1974 = 100

	Weight *	Jan	Feb	Mar	Apr	May	Jun	Jul	Aug	Sep	Oct	Nov	Dec	Next Jan
Bread	11	292.0	292.5	292.8	293.0	292.1	292.0	292.4	295.3	296.3	296.5	296.5	300.9	302.3
Cereals	4	324.8	329.0	330.6	331.3	334.2	335.6	337.6	340.4	341.3	342.1	342.6	342.8	343.6
Biscuits & cakes	12	303.6	307.1	308.8	309.1	309.5	310.0	314.0	314.8	315.0	318.7	320.5	320.4	323.2
Beef	16	305.9	309.7	310.1	310.2	310.8	310.5	310.7	311.5	311.8	312.3	313.6	315.5	313.1
Lamb	6	261.6	266.4	267.7	276.8	280.4	261.6	257.1	248.2	246.4	244.9	246.1	248.9	238.8
of which Home-killed lamb	3	277.8	285.6	290.0	310.0	318.2	280.1	270.5	252.1	248.9	246.6	252.2	258.7	263.0
Pork	6	226.6	226.8	226.8	227.0	226.1	222.2	222.1	221.3	222.3	222.7	223.7	224.6	226.8
Bacon	7	231.9	231.5	231.8	231.9	230.6	231.8	232.1	232.3	233.6	235.7	236.6	239.3	237.2
Poultry & other meat	19	222.1	223.3	224.5	226.0	227.3	228.1	228.8	229.3	229.8	230.0	229.9	230.8	230.6
Fish	7	238.1	237.8	240.6	241.2	242.4	241.0	239.6	241.3	243.0	245.7	249.9	248.9	254.9
of which Fresh/smoked fish	3.08	234.6	233.2	236.0	236.5	239.1	235.8	235.0	236.4	236.8	239.9	242.4	241.5	252.8
Butter	4	411.4	411.1	410.1	409.6	410.7	413.0	415.8	421.4	424.3	423.9	423.3	419.4	418.4
Oils & fats	3	211.8	211.0	212.8	211.2	209.9	210.9	210.3	210.7	209.9	209.6	211.8	212.9	214.2
Cheese	6	345.9	349.7	351.5	351.3	349.5	348.6	351.6	351.8	357.0	357.3	359.7	359.6	359.8
Eggs	5	176.5	179.3	179.4	176.7	172.1	163.7	161.4	154.6	153.1	155.2	156.5	156.5	152.8
Milk, fresh	18	360.4	360.4	360.4	360.4	360.4	360.4	360.4	360.4	360.4	360.4	378.4	378.4	378.4
Milk products	3	355.6	360.0	360.0	356.7	360.7	361.8	361.2	361.9	391.2	392.8	394.7	394.4	395.0
Tea	3	300.0	299.7	299.3	298.9	295.5	295.1	300.3	309.3	315.1	318.7	322.2	323.7	330.7
Coffee & other hot drinks	3	318.2	319.0	320.2	321.0	328.4	331.9	335.4	341.5	343.5	346.6	346.0	343.9	346.6
Soft drinks	4	314.0	318.6	318.8	313.0	311.1	305.8	304.1	308.2	310.5	312.7	313.4	313.6	316.2
Sugar & preserves	4	358.2	359.6	360.0	364.2	366.1	366.0	366.4	374.2	381.6	383.7	384.1	385.8	386.1
Sweets & chocolates	14	383.5	384.7	383.7	387.1	391.4	394.1	397.8	401.5	404.4	405.1	404.9	404.8	408.0
Potatoes	9	425.9	431.5	442.0	434.9	457.2	453.7	352.3	319.2	340.3	358.5	360.0	367.9	374.1
of which Unproc'd potatoes	6.03	410.9	418.9	434.0	421.4	453.4	448.4	302.5	254.8	285.1	310.3	311.2	322.6	331.5
Other vegetables	14	308.8	296.1	314.6	341.0	352.1	335.0	303.4	269.9	270.9	271.0	268.9	270.2	287.4
of which Fresh vegetables	§	336.5	312.4	339.8	383.3	402.8	371.0	314.5	261.0	261.4	260.7	252.1	257.4	278.8
Fruit	11	268.4	272.9	278.7	288.0	303.6	310.5	315.8	287.9	262.9	250.3	249.8	255.7	259.7
of which Fresh fruit	§	289.7	295.4	303.9	318.5	343.2	351.7	356.2	317.6	281.5	264.3	263.2	273.7	276.2
Other foods (excl. petfood)	12	317.2	318.5	320.7	324.4	329.9	331.9	331.8	335.6	336.2	335.8	337.2	337.1	337.2
FOOD (excluding petfood)	201	296.9	297.9	300.4	303.3	306.4	304.7	300.2	296.0	296.5	297.0	299.1	300.5	302.3
Restaurant meals	18	335.8	338.2	341.4	344.4	347.2	349.1	351.1	352.1	353.5	357.0	359.5	361.5	361.8
Canteen meals	8	328.0	331.2	333.8	338.5	338.8	341.2	343.5	345.7	351.1	354.0	355.2	355.5	357.9
Take-away meals & snacks	12	290.1	291.6	292.4	291.8	295.5	295.0	297.5	300.4	302.2	303.7	304.9	305.3	306.2
CATERING	38	329.7	331.9	334.2	336.4	339.1	340.3	342.6	344.5	347.0	349.8	351.6	352.8	353.7
Beer	47	366.0	368.7	380.5	386.3	389.7	388.8	389.6	392.8	399.4	403.8	405.3	403.9	408.1
Wines & spirits	30	262.4	264.8	267.7	275.3	278.7	277.6	282.6	282.4	281.3	283.3	280.9	276.4	281.9
ALCOHOLIC DRINK	77	321.8	324.4	332.1	338.8	342.3	341.3	344.1	345.7	348.8	352.0	351.7	348.8	353.7
Cigarettes	37	393.2	394.9	400.2	403.7	415.3	420.0	420.2	420.7	420.8	425.9	425.3	427.2	426.7
Other tobacco	4	380.0	381.8	387.6	407.7	409.1	409.2	409.9	409.2	410.2	422.4	418.0	417.6	419.1
TOBACCO	41	392.1	393.8	399.1	404.4	414.9	419.2	419.5	419.9	420.0	425.8	424.8	426.5	426.2
Rent	36	312.3	312.3	312.5	340.9	341.0	342.7	343.0	343.7	343.6	347.6	345.7	346.4	346.6
Mortgage interest payments	41	356.1	362.0	365.5	335.6	334.2	337.2	340.0	343.5	312.0	310.6	313.3	268.7	265.8
Rates	33.29	413.0	374.8	374.8	457.5	456.5	456.4	455.0	454.1	451.2	451.2	451.2	451.2	451.2
Water charges	7.71	350.0	350.0	350.0	384.7	384.7	384.7	384.7	384.7	384.7	384.7	384.7	384.7	384.7
Repair/maintenance charges	8	407.9	407.9	407.9	437.8	436.0	437.2	437.2	437.2	437.2	448.9	449.3	450.2	450.2
Do-it-yourself materials	15	314.3	317.1	318.8	319.8	321.4	324.1	326.4	328.3	330.1	331.4	322.8	333.8	333.9
HOUSING #	144	350.0	344.5	345.6	364.9	364.2	365.8	366.8	368.1	359.0	360.4	360.9	348.8	348.1
Coal & solid fuels	9	429.9	430.8	431.8	408.2	404.8	404.8	401.8	432.5	433.3	434.0	454.0	456.2	456.8
Electricity	28	428.7	439.2	447.6	461.6	474.3	486.5	492.4	492.4	492.4	492.4	492.4	492.4	492.4
Gas	20	306.6	306.6	306.6	315.1	326.7	338.0	343.4	343.4	343.4	348.7	361.7	372.1	377.3
Oil & other fuel	5	549.5	549.7	549.7	545.4	545.4	545.4	557.4	558.8	559.2	578.6	593.1	595.7	626.7
FUEL & LIGHT	62	401.9	406.5	410.2	416.2	426.1	436.0	441.2	445.4	445.5	449.0	458.1	462.9	467.0
Furniture	14	239.3	241.1	244.1	244.3	245.1	243.7	241.5	243.5	245.0	245.1	247.3	247.8	244.2
Furnishings	12	256.5	258.3	260.6	262.3	262.1	261.3	258.9	260.7	262.7	262.2	264.6	265.0	261.5
Electrical appliances	17	249.8	252.2	253.5	254.1	254.2	255.0	254.5	256.0	256.7	257.6	259.4	260.8	259.3
Other household equipment	11	310.0	313.3	314.6	316.2	317.8	319.5	323.6	327.8	328.5	330.0	330.5	333.1	335.5
Household consumables	14	356.1	358.2	363.1	364.3	365.5	369.8	370.8	371.8	374.8	376.6	377.4	377.4	378.9
Pet care	5	261.6	266.1	269.5	271.3	270.5	273.8	265.8	268.5	267.9	270.5	279.0	279.1	276.9
HOUSEHOLD GOODS	73	276.2	278.6	281.2	282.2	282.9	283.6	282.7	284.8	286.0	286.9	289.1	289.9	288.6
Postage	2	411.0	446.4	446.4	446.4	446.8	446.8	446.8	446.8	446.8	446.8	446.8	446.8	446.8
Telephone charges etc	16	349.4	348.0	348.0	348.0	339.6	339.6	339.6	339.6	339.6	339.6	339.6	339.6	339.6
Domestic services	5	374.1	378.1	384.2	388.8	390.4	392.5	393.7	397.1	400.5	400.9	402.5	408.5	408.1
Fees & subscriptions	9	359.3	358.4	357.8	361.3	359.5	358.3	368.0	369.8	371.3	373.7	374.3	375.2	380.6
HOUSEHOLD SERVICES	32	368.7	370.4	371.1	372.8	368.1	368.1	371.1	372.2	373.1	373.8	374.3	375.4	377.0
Men's outerwear	12	227.4	229.2	230.5	232.5	231.4	230.0	228.4	227.6	233.9	232.2	233.5	234.0	228.9
Women's outerwear	22	158.9	160.2	160.5	160.2	159.9	159.2	158.4	159.7	160.3	161.0	160.8	161.2	159.3
Children's outerwear	9	216.5	224.7	224.3	226.6	227.2	226.7	225.6	225.4	226.3	226.0	226.5	227.5	226.0
Other clothing	19	245.1	246.6	247.0	247.8	248.5	247.8	249.5	250.6	256.0	255.2	256.9	256.9	254.4
Footwear	15	218.8	219.4	219.4	219.6	220.1	220.0	219.3	220.8	221.1	221.1	221.7	221.7	220.7
CLOTHING & FOOTWEAR	77	207.1	209.3	209.6	210.2	210.2	209.6	209.2	210.0	212.4	212.2	212.8	213.2	210.9
Chemists' goods	13	304.7	307.2	311.0	318.9	319.9	321.9	324.1	325.3	327.5	331.3	335.6	338.2	336.3
Personal services	7	368.0	370.7	373.9	382.3	387.8	390.2	391.5	395.4	400.2	402.6	397.9	398.6	401.2

	Weight *	Jan	Feb	Mar	Apr	May	Jun	Jul	Aug	Sep	Oct	Nov	Dec	Next Jan
						Index: January 1974 = 100								
Purchase of motor vehicles	58	288.5	288.4	288.1	289.5	293.7	293.4	294.3	291.8	288.8	291.0	293.1	296.1	299.4
Maintenance of motor vcles	16	347.6	352.8	355.7	356.1	357.0	354.9	362.6	364.9	368.1	368.1	368.7	372.3	372.3
Petrol & oil	46	392.0	371.0	376.4	391.2	394.3	406.1	408.0	415.2	413.9	417.9	421.4	421.6	410.1
Vehicle tax & insurance	16	288.2	289.2	307.3	307.3	308.2	308.2	308.2	308.2	308.2	313.8	313.8	313.8	313.8
MOTORING EXPENDITURE	136	325.1	319.8	323.9	328.8	331.9	334.9	336.6	337.7	336.2	339.2	341.3	343.2	341.6
Rail fares	6	386.2	386.2	386.2	471.0	471.0	471.0	471.0	473.0	473.0	473.0	473.0	473.0	496.0
Bus & coach fares	10	366.2	370.0	375.2	442.1	442.1	443.8	444.4	444.8	446.2	447.5	448.5	450.3	451.9
Other travel costs	2	268.9	269.9	270.5	268.8	269.8	270.0	266.3	269.3	270.8	271.5	272.2	271.8	269.8
FARES & OTHER TRAVEL COSTS	18	356.2	358.4	361.3	423.2	423.4	424.3	424.1	425.4	426.4	427.2	427.8	428.8	436.4
Audio-visual equipment	10	148.8	148.2	148.6	148.2	148.0	147.2	144.7	144.5	144.8	144.2	144.6	144.8	142.9
Records, toys, photo & sports goods & personal articles	24	248.7	249.8	250.7	252.6	255.2	256.6	256.6	255.5	259.4	261.0	260.7	260.9	260.5
Books & newspapers	17	407.2	410.5	419.3	428.9	429.3	431.7	438.5	438.4	441.8	448.8	454.5	454.6	459.4
Gardening products	4	258.7	258.7	258.7	258.7	261.4	261.4	261.4	261.4	261.4	261.4	265.5	270.3	270.3
TV licences & rentals	13	197.5	199.4	199.4	199.4	199.4	199.4	200.0	200.0	200.0	200.0	200.0	200.0	196.9
Entertainment & recreation	13	367.5	368.0	368.3	378.9	380.2	380.9	381.1	382.8	386.3	384.7	387.5	387.6	397.9
LEISURE SERVICES	26	264.3	265.8	265.9	269.7	270.2	270.5	270.9	271.5	272.8	272.2	273.2	273.2	274.9

* Applied to change since January 1982
§ Variable from month to month
# Includes unpublished components for dwelling insurance & ground rent

	Weight *	Jan	Feb	Mar	Apr	May	Jun	Jul	Aug	Sep	Oct	Nov	Dec	Next Jan
						Index: January 1974 = 100								
Bread	11	302.3	302.4	302.8	303.4	303.3	303.4	302.5	302.4	302.7	302.7	302.0	312.4	314.6
Cereals	5	343.6	348.1	348.7	350.4	351.6	353.6	355.0	356.8	357.7	358.5	357.9	358.0	361.5
Biscuits & cakes	12	323.2	324.5	325.4	326.8	325.3	325.7	328.3	328.8	329.1	329.0	330.4	329.7	334.8
Beef	15	313.1	311.2	309.8	308.3	309.2	316.7	316.6	317.2	317.4	317.4	317.4	319.5	320.4
Lamb	5	238.8	241.7	244.3	255.8	266.0	263.2	244.8	236.2	234.0	235.2	235.8	242.6	243.8
of which Home-killed lamb	2.65	263.0	275.2	279.5	299.2	316.1	306.6	268.1	250.1	246.2	245.2	248.4	257.9	265.5
Pork	5	226.8	221.6	219.5	219.4	219.2	221.5	222.4	222.2	222.7	227.5	230.3	232.7	232.8
Bacon	6	237.2	232.7	230.5	228.9	229.6	230.8	229.8	229.3	230.8	235.4	236.8	237.3	238.9
Poultry & other meat	20	230.6	229.8	228.7	230.1	231.6	233.5	233.3	234.0	236.3	236.6	237.8	238.5	239.3
Fish	6	254.9	255.0	252.2	253.7	255.2	255.2	254.8	257.1	259.2	259.7	261.2	262.5	267.3
of which Fresh/smoked fish	2.58	252.8	252.2	245.9	249.4	249.6	249.8	247.7	249.3	253.1	251.4	253.5	257.4	267.8
Butter	4	418.4	421.4	423.1	421.8	420.1	418.2	416.8	416.2	414.7	414.5	413.2	413.4	413.0
Oils & fats	3	214.2	209.6	210.3	213.0	213.0	215.9	216.6	219.5	219.3	219.5	226.8	229.7	232.0
Cheese	6	359.8	360.5	362.4	361.7	359.1	359.2	360.4	353.0	357.4	357.5	358.4	359.2	362.0
Eggs	4	152.8	146.2	151.0	151.3	149.6	150.3	149.0	154.1	164.7	171.4	173.3	183.5	185.2
Milk, fresh	18	378.4	378.4	378.4	378.4	378.4	378.4	378.4	378.4	378.4	378.4	378.4	378.4	378.4
Milk products	3	395.0	395.2	394.8	402.3	404.2	406.2	403.9	407.4	410.5	410.7	413.1	411.9	411.9
Tea	3	330.7	340.8	344.7	347.0	357.7	365.3	369.0	374.3	373.4	372.5	371.0	371.1	385.3
Coffee & other hot drinks	3	346.6	347.8	349.0	351.5	358.4	362.0	374.5	379.5	380.7	385.3	386.8	384.5	387.9
Soft drinks	5	316.2	324.5	326.6	325.6	325.2	323.7	322.7	328.6	329.6	330.8	331.9	331.3	331.9
Sugar & preserves	4	386.1	386.7	388.0	389.3	391.1	391.8	391.5	396.0	399.1	400.0	400.3	402.9	403.5
Sweets & chocolates	15	408.0	411.5	411.3	412.0	414.1	416.4	413.1	415.6	415.0	413.1	412.2	412.7	413.9
Potatoes	8	374.1	374.9	368.9	362.3	364.7	379.2	362.9	409.9	492.3	522.9	525.2	533.1	525.0
of which Unproc'd potatoes	4.64	331.5	332.7	323.7	313.5	311.3	333.6	308.7	377.4	503.2	535.3	540.8	551.0	553.1
Other vegetables	12	287.4	286.6	286.9	305.1	297.6	313.7	316.3	293.8	306.8	310.0	318.5	329.5	324.6
of which Fresh vegetables	§	278.8	276.9	278.7	308.1	295.7	319.9	324.1	287.8	308.2	313.5	328.0	347.1	340.3
Fruit	10	259.7	267.4	273.9	280.7	287.6	296.0	310.0	310.9	294.4	290.0	292.9	291.2	296.1
of which Fresh fruit	§	276.2	286.0	295.5	305.9	315.7	326.6	344.3	347.7	325.2	320.4	326.6	326.4	325.8
Other foods (excl. petfood)	14	337.2	338.1	337.8	338.5	342.2	343.4	342.6	345.3	345.2	344.5	344.9	345.1	346.8
FOOD (excluding petfood)	197	302.3	302.7	302.9	305.2	306.2	309.6	309.5	310.3	314.0	315.5	317.0	319.5	320.9
Restaurant meals	18	361.8	363.3	364.6	367.8	371.0	373.0	373.6	375.7	377.5	378.3	380.7	383.5	385.6
Canteen meals	8	357.9	358.6	359.1	360.4	361.5	364.0	363.2	365.1	372.6	374.7	377.1	379.4	384.9
Take-away meals & snacks	13	306.2	308.2	309.4	311.3	313.3	315.4	316.5	318.3	319.4	322.3	324.9	326.5	328.4
CATERING	39	353.7	355.3	356.5	358.9	361.4	363.5	364.1	366.1	368.9	370.8	373.4	375.7	378.5
Beer	48	408.1	409.8	411.0	420.0	421.1	423.3	424.9	427.4	428.6	431.8	432.5	434.5	437.2
Wines & spirits	30	281.9	284.9	285.6	290.0	294.5	295.3	296.0	297.3	296.9	296.5	294.3	293.2	296.1
ALCOHOLIC DRINK	78	353.7	356.0	357.0	363.9	366.7	368.2	369.4	371.4	371.8	373.4	372.7	373.2	376.1
Cigarettes	36	426.7	431.3	433.4	440.8	443.9	444.2	444.0	443.7	444.0	444.3	449.1	450.6	451.3
Other tobacco	3	419.1	425.0	425.9	433.2	433.6	434.8	436.2	437.5	437.0	438.4	440.9	441.7	443.1
TOBACCO	39	426.2	430.9	432.9	440.3	443.2	444.0	443.5	443.2	443.5	444.0	448.6	450.0	450.8
Rent	36	346.6	346.9	347.3	362.2	360.2	359.2	359.9	360.0	360.0	363.8	362.5	362.8	363.1
Mortgage interest payments	30	265.8	267.9	270.2	272.5	274.7	277.0	307.3	316.8	319.9	322.6	325.9	328.8	331.7
Rates	35.42	451.2	451.2	451.2	484.6	481.8	481.8	481.8	480.9	480.9	480.9	480.9	480.9	480.9
Water charges	8.58	384.7	384.7	384.7	413.7	413.7	413.7	413.7	413.7	413.7	413.7	413.7	413.7	413.7
Repair/maintenance charges	10	450.2	450.2	450.2	465.2	467.9	467.6	467.6	467.6	467.6	484.4	482.2	481.8	481.8
Do-it-yourself materials	13	333.9	336.4	335.1	335.0	337.2	338.5	339.1	338.5	339.7	340.2	341.3	342.0	342.4
HOUSING #	137	348.1	349.0	349.7	363.5	363.4	364.0	373.0	375.5	376.7	379.6	380.5	381.6	382.6
Coal & solid fuels	8	456.8	456.7	459.9	458.5	433.7	426.4	425.6	452.2	458.1	459.9	477.6	479.1	479.7
Electricity	32	492.4	491.3	491.7	491.8	492.0	492.1	492.1	492.1	492.1	492.1	492.1	492.1	492.1
Gas	24	377.3	373.4	373.8	374.3	374.3	374.3	374.3	374.3	374.3	374.3	374.3	374.3	375.4
Oil & other fuel	5	626.7	626.7	626.0	623.2	623.2	623.2	627.0	630.4	631.3	640.6	641.3	641.3	635.2
FUEL & LIGHT	69	467.0	464.8	465.6	465.5	462.6	461.8	461.9	465.2	466.0	466.7	468.8	469.0	469.3
Furniture	14	244.2	248.1	250.9	252.1	253.6	253.1	250.9	251.3	252.6	253.1	254.7	255.7	258.7
Furnishings	13	261.5	264.1	264.4	264.1	265.7	266.5	264.8	265.7	267.9	269.0	269.2	271.8	267.2
Electrical appliances	16	259.3	260.5	262.3	263.3	263.9	263.9	262.1	263.2	263.5	263.5	262.9	262.7	260.6
Other household equipment	11	335.5	338.1	338.5	339.9	342.0	345.5	349.2	349.7	351.8	352.9	353.0	354.4	356.7
Household consumables	15	378.9	380.4	382.0	390.9	389.8	389.9	393.2	388.6	393.4	395.5	398.4	400.5	401.3
Pet care	6	276.9	273.7	275.7	276.4	276.0	275.3	275.1	272.3	273.1	273.3	278.3	277.0	274.3
HOUSEHOLD GOODS	75	288.6	290.4	292.1	294.1	294.9	295.4	295.1	294.7	296.5	297.4	298.6	299.5	299.1
Postage	2	446.8	446.8	446.8	457.0	457.0	457.0	457.0	456.9	456.9	457.0	457.0	457.0	457.0
Telephone charges etc	16	339.6	336.6	336.2	336.6	336.6	336.6	336.6	336.6	336.6	336.6	346.4	346.4	346.4
Domestic services	5	408.1	410.9	414.1	416.3	418.2	420.9	422.9	424.4	424.5	427.0	427.9	432.4	431.9
Fees & subscriptions	8	380.6	380.6	381.2	390.3	390.3	394.1	395.5	395.8	397.7	399.7	408.9	409.8	409.7
HOUSEHOLD SERVICES	31	377.0	375.7	376.1	379.5	379.8	381.1	381.8	382.1	382.6	383.4	391.3	392.5	392.4
Men's outerwear	11	228.9	233.1	234.3	235.2	234.8	234.9	234.0	234.2	236.1	238.9	237.0	235.0	226.2
Women's outerwear	22	159.3	160.9	160.9	161.0	159.7	158.4	159.1	162.7	162.4	162.5	165.7	165.1	155.0
Children's outerwear	8	226.0	232.9	233.3	234.5	238.3	236.7	236.2	240.6	240.3	240.5	242.3	242.6	240.3
Other clothing	17	254.4	257.0	256.2	257.7	257.0	257.4	257.5	259.6	259.2	261.6	262.2	259.7	255.5
Footwear	16	220.7	222.6	223.2	223.7	223.6	224.3	221.7	221.6	222.2	222.4	222.3	222.6	220.4
CLOTHING & FOOTWEAR	74	210.9	213.6	213.8	214.5	214.2	213.7	213.3	215.5	215.8	216.7	218.0	217.1	210.4
Chemists' goods	13	336.3	338.5	337.9	339.9	342.0	343.8	344.1	345.4	344.9	345.4	346.8	347.5	350.5
Personal services	7	401.2	402.9	405.3	409.3	414.0	415.6	421.4	424.9	425.9	426.3	430.1	431.9	431.8

Index: January 1974 = 100

	Weight *	Jan	Feb	Mar	Apr	May	Jun	Jul	Aug	Sep	Oct	Nov	Dec	Next Jan
Purchase of motor vehicles	55	299.4	302.4	305.6	308.8	312.8	315.1	318.6	319.3	320.2	319.6	318.1	314.7	310.6
Maintenance of motor vcles	16	372.3	376.4	379.0	381.8	381.5	382.0	384.0	385.8	394.1	396.2	393.2	395.5	397.6
Petrol & oil	47	410.1	410.6	406.6	422.7	431.1	431.5	441.0	442.0	442.1	442.2	442.2	442.2	442.3
Vehicle tax & insurance	18	313.8	313.8	313.8	323.7	323.7	321.5	321.5	326.6	326.6	326.6	326.6	329.5	329.5
MOTORING EXPENDITURE	136	341.6	343.5	344.1	351.9	356.2	357.0	361.7	363.2	364.5	364.5	363.5	362.6	360.9
Rail fares	7	496.0	496.0	496.0	496.0	496.0	459.7	459.7	459.7	459.7	459.7	459.7	459.7	479.6
Bus & coach fares	11	451.9	455.0	455.6	457.8	458.4	444.7	445.4	447.3	448.3	447.6	450.2	452.7	453.7
Other travel costs	5	269.8	272.0	272.9	273.0	273.3	273.1	271.0	271.0	273.4	272.8	272.8	273.4	272.5
FARES & OTHER TRAVEL COSTS	23	436.4	438.5	439.2	440.2	440.6	424.4	424.1	424.9	426.2	425.7	426.9	428.3	433.7
Audio-visual equipment	10	142.9	143.6	144.2	143.6	143.7	143.4	142.0	142.3	141.9	141.5	141.5	141.3	139.9
Records, toys, photo & sports goods & personal articles	24	260.5	261.1	261.9	262.6	266.6	266.9	267.4	267.4	267.8	267.4	268.4	269.2	267.1
Books & newspapers	18	459.4	460.7	463.2	465.2	469.5	470.6	473.6	478.5	479.7	484.4	488.2	489.3	490.1
Gardening products	5	270.3	270.3	270.3	270.3	276.2	276.2	276.2	276.2	276.2	276.2	285.3	286.2	286.2
TV licences & rentals	14	196.9	196.9	196.9	196.7	196.7	196.7	196.5	196.5	196.5	196.5	197.1	197.1	195.9
Entertainment & recreation	11	397.9	398.7	399.6	409.9	411.8	411.5	412.2	413.2	414.6	414.7	414.5	415.4	423.2
LEISURE SERVICES	25	274.9	275.1	275.4	278.3	278.9	278.8	278.9	279.2	279.6	279.6	280.0	280.3	281.7

* Applied to change since January 1983
§ Variable from month to month
# Includes unpublished components for dwelling insurance & ground rent

Index: January 1974 = 100

	Weight *	Jan	Feb	Mar	Apr	May	Jun	Jul	Aug	Sep	Oct	Nov	Dec	Next Jan
Bread	11	314.6	315.0	314.9	314.8	315.1	314.7	315.5	314.8	315.3	314.7	314.7	322.7	324.0
Cereals	5	361.5	368.4	369.9	370.1	373.1	374.8	378.8	379.7	378.5	378.9	380.8	382.5	384.0
Biscuits & cakes	10	334.8	332.9	338.6	340.3	342.2	343.8	340.6	341.1	341.2	345.2	345.9	345.0	347.1
Beef	14	320.4	319.4	318.6	319.3	318.7	321.6	320.6	320.2	320.8	319.2	318.9	320.9	321.8
Lamb	5	243.8	252.6	257.7	264.0	279.2	256.1	255.3	251.9	248.9	246.4	256.4	261.0	261.5
of which Home-killed lamb	2.95	265.5	280.8	289.3	298.4	323.7	278.6	276.7	270.5	262.4	262.8	277.0	281.4	279.7
Pork	6	232.8	232.3	237.3	240.2	243.8	246.0	244.6	245.2	245.7	253.2	255.3	257.2	255.6
Bacon	6	238.9	235.7	236.2	238.4	241.1	245.2	243.8	245.3	246.0	248.9	249.9	250.0	250.5
Poultry & other meat	20	239.3	238.9	239.2	239.1	240.7	241.1	241.4	241.5	243.0	243.0	244.4	245.7	243.6
Fish	7	267.3	265.1	263.4	264.3	265.4	266.7	268.4	269.8	271.2	272.9	274.2	276.9	280.4
of which Fresh/smoked fish	3.08	267.8	262.4	257.9	260.4	261.8	264.6	265.8	267.5	269.1	272.0	274.0	279.1	282.6
Butter	3	413.0	411.6	412.0	412.7	418.8	423.2	425.0	430.0	437.1	440.4	442.3	443.0	437.2
Oils & fats	3	232.0	237.6	241.8	243.0	248.7	250.5	251.6	250.4	254.6	256.1	260.0	261.6	263.9
Cheese	5	362.0	361.9	361.7	364.1	359.5	362.1	359.8	362.2	362.4	364.3	367.1	370.2	374.6
Eggs	4	185.2	186.3	188.4	196.9	198.5	194.2	188.2	186.1	184.5	184.6	181.4	188.3	188.6
Milk, fresh	17	378.4	378.4	378.4	378.4	378.4	394.5	395.1	395.1	395.6	395.3	395.6	396.2	396.4
Milk products	3	411.9	397.2	398.6	398.8	402.0	401.1	400.1	401.8	401.8	404.7	407.6	407.9	408.6
Tea	3	385.3	432.8	452.2	481.1	494.0	499.6	499.6	499.3	497.8	512.1	538.5	545.1	545.5
Coffee & other hot drinks	3	387.9	391.7	397.6	415.2	423.1	430.0	432.5	426.4	428.3	430.9	431.8	431.3	440.8
Soft drinks	5	331.9	333.7	334.7	334.3	333.7	333.5	332.0	330.7	329.8	338.7	340.5	338.2	342.9
Sugar & preserves	4	403.5	403.2	404.5	404.4	404.3	402.6	401.6	402.7	402.6	403.1	402.8	402.1	403.3
Sweets & chocolates	13	413.9	417.9	418.7	419.9	425.7	431.7	433.0	436.1	437.2	439.2	439.1	438.4	439.5
Potatoes	11	525.0	526.8	530.2	538.8	489.9	508.4	439.8	426.2	422.7	430.9	420.3	415.4	421.8
of which Unproc'd potatoes	7.37	553.1	563.3	557.1	569.9	492.9	522.0	409.5	380.8	375.3	388.2	371.4	363.8	373.9
Other vegetables	13	324.6	335.3	347.0	364.8	387.0	366.9	360.8	333.7	316.2	321.6	315.3	313.1	339.2
of which Fresh vegetables	§	340.3	356.9	372.6	400.0	438.2	403.6	387.8	343.6	315.5	324.1	314.1	307.2	351.6
Fruit	11	296.1	295.1	299.2	302.1	308.4	315.2	327.0	331.0	310.3	300.8	302.4	300.4	307.9
of which Fresh fruit	§	325.8	322.6	327.8	331.1	339.7	349.1	366.2	373.4	344.4	331.7	336.4	332.0	337.9
Other foods (excl. petfood)	13	346.8	348.3	349.0	353.2	354.3	355.4	359.2	362.1	361.5	361.4	362.4	361.3	364.1
FOOD (excluding petfood)	195	320.9	322.5	324.9	328.4	330.6	331.8	329.8	328.1	326.0	327.2	327.8	328.8	331.9
Restaurant meals	20	385.6	386.6	388.9	390.6	394.9	397.9	396.3	396.8	397.3	401.1	403.6	406.6	406.1
Canteen meals	9	384.9	386.4	387.6	390.3	394.0	396.5	397.4	397.9	403.4	404.1	405.3	405.0	406.5
Take-away meals & snacks	7	328.4	329.4	331.1	334.4	347.5	351.4	352.0	354.3	356.4	358.1	358.7	358.6	359.0
CATERING	36	378.5	379.7	381.6	383.9	390.1	393.2	392.7	393.6	395.7	398.3	400.1	401.6	401.8
Beer	47	437.2	441.0	442.7	452.3	455.1	455.4	455.1	457.6	463.5	470.4	469.5	472.7	473.3
Wines & spirits	28	296.1	298.0	298.7	299.1	300.2	300.4	300.3	300.3	300.7	302.7	298.8	296.2	301.2
ALCOHOLIC DRINK	75	376.1	379.0	380.2	385.6	387.6	387.9	387.7	389.0	392.4	397.1	394.8	395.2	397.9
Cigarettes	33	451.3	455.7	458.2	489.2	499.5	501.1	501.4	500.9	502.8	505.4	508.6	508.1	509.7
Other tobacco	3	443.1	446.7	448.0	473.4	481.1	483.1	483.7	482.9	481.5	486.3	487.4	489.0	488.6
TOBACCO	36	450.8	455.1	457.6	488.0	498.1	499.7	500.1	499.6	501.1	504.0	507.0	506.6	508.1
Rent	35	363.1	363.7	363.3	387.4	382.5	382.3	382.5	382.6	382.8	383.1	383.7	388.5	389.2
Mortgage interest payments	39	331.7	333.7	336.3	313.1	311.5	314.3	317.0	389.0	400.9	406.5	412.1	385.0	386.0
Rates	37.03	480.9	480.9	480.9	515.4	508.5	508.4	509.7	509.7	509.7	509.7	509.7	509.7	509.7
Water charges	8.97	413.7	413.7	413.7	441.2	441.2	441.2	441.2	441.2	441.2	441.2	441.2	441.2	441.2
Repair/maintenance charges	10	481.8	481.8	481.8	512.0	514.2	496.7	496.7	496.7	496.7	509.0	510.4	510.4	510.4
Do-it-yourself materials	14	342.4	348.9	340.1	345.1	348.6	348.7	351.6	351.7	353.4	355.2	356.6	356.2	355.1
HOUSING #	149	382.6	383.8	383.6	393.1	390.6	390.5	392.0	413.9	417.8	420.8	423.1	416.2	416.4
Coal & solid fuels	8	479.7	479.6	479.0	479.0	478.9	481.3	478.7	481.7	483.6	495.2	518.7	529.5	523.0
Electricity	30	492.1	492.1	492.1	493.2	497.5	500.6	502.5	502.5	502.5	502.2	502.2	502.2	502.2
Gas	23	375.4	381.8	386.4	390.1	390.1	390.1	390.1	390.1	390.1	390.1	390.1	390.1	390.1
Oil & other fuel	4	635.2	635.2	634.9	625.4	625.4	626.4	628.8	628.8	628.8	656.3	658.4	658.6	680.3
FUEL & LIGHT	65	469.3	472.1	474.0	475.7	477.6	479.3	479.9	480.3	480.6	483.0	486.0	487.3	487.5
Furniture	14	258.7	263.4	264.5	264.2	264.5	266.9	272.3	272.6	272.2	267.4	269.1	268.4	266.5
Furnishings	13	267.2	270.1	272.6	269.7	271.9	275.8	269.9	277.2	280.4	282.0	282.6	283.7	281.6
Electrical appliances	19	260.6	260.9	263.6	264.0	263.2	264.5	262.0	261.8	262.7	264.3	264.1	264.5	263.6
Other household equipment	11	356.7	363.3	361.4	366.2	366.1	366.7	366.9	369.6	372.0	373.0	373.1	375.7	377.1
Household consumables	15	401.3	404.5	408.4	413.8	416.1	417.3	417.7	420.3	425.2	432.7	434.3	436.1	438.6
Pet care	6	274.3	277.3	280.2	282.1	281.2	282.5	277.9	279.9	281.6	284.3	280.4	279.3	280.6
HOUSEHOLD GOODS	78	299.1	302.1	304.2	305.1	305.7	307.5	306.6	308.9	310.8	312.0	312.2	312.8	312.4
Postage	2	457.0	457.0	457.0	457.0	457.0	457.0	457.0	457.0	478.4	478.4	478.4	478.4	478.4
Telephone charges etc	15	346.4	346.4	346.4	346.4	346.4	346.4	346.4	346.4	346.4	346.4	363.9	366.9	370.0
Domestic services	5	431.9	434.7	438.0	441.3	441.5	442.9	444.7	444.5	446.8	448.1	449.4	450.0	451.7
Fees & subscriptions	11	409.7	407.7	412.8	417.2	417.5	418.9	424.0	425.0	426.7	430.9	433.0	434.3	449.8
HOUSEHOLD SERVICES	33	392.4	392.2	394.2	396.1	396.2	396.8	398.8	399.0	401.0	402.5	412.4	414.4	421.2
Men's outerwear	11	226.2	228.4	231.0	232.8	233.1	231.4	227.4	227.3	227.8	228.6	229.9	231.9	233.1
Women's outerwear	20	155.0	156.6	154.0	155.7	156.1	153.5	156.2	154.9	159.1	156.9	157.2	159.6	158.5
Children's outerwear	8	240.3	240.6	242.2	237.3	244.6	243.8	250.5	260.7	260.7	258.5	258.2	258.8	256.8
Other clothing	16	255.5	259.1	262.4	263.9	264.6	263.7	263.3	264.4	264.5	266.3	267.3	269.3	266.5
Footwear	15	220.4	223.5	224.5	224.4	224.3	225.7	223.5	225.2	224.1	224.5	224.5	225.6	224.9
CLOTHING & FOOTWEAR	70	210.4	212.7	213.0	213.7	214.8	213.5	214.1	215.3	216.7	216.2	216.6	218.5	217.4
Chemists' goods	13	350.5	355.3	356.3	361.2	360.7	361.5	362.2	363.8	366.7	367.2	366.5	368.5	371.8
Personal services	7	431.8	435.4	436.7	438.8	442.8	445.1	448.4	452.7	452.3	454.0	456.9	458.9	462.7

1984 continued]   Index: January 1974 = 100

	Weight *	Jan	Feb	Mar	Apr	May	Jun	Jul	Aug	Sep	Oct	Nov	Dec	Next Jan
Purchase of motor vehicles	58	310.6	308.1	007.6	309.4	313.0	316.0	314.2	312.5	311.0	313.9	313.1	309.3	308.8
Maintenance of motor vcles	16	397.6	398.9	399.9	402.4	408.1	408.4	409.8	413.5	414.9	417.2	420.0	420.6	421.0
Petrol & oil	48	442.3	435.4	434.5	441.1	440.7	442.9	442.4	446.4	445.1	456.0	456.5	456.6	456.2
Vehicle tax & insurance	18	329.5	332.3	332.3	340.9	342.0	342.0	342.6	342.6	342.6	342.6	342.6	344.5	344.5
MOTORING EXPENDITURE	140	360.9	358.4	358.0	362.1	364.5	366.5	365.8	366.4	365.6	370.2	370.3	368.9	368.5
Rail fares	6	479.6	479.6	479.6	479.6	479.6	479.6	479.6	479.6	479.6	479.6	479.6	479.6	510.1
Bus & coach fares	9	453.7	456.2	456.5	461.7	461.8	462.1	462.3	464.6	464.9	464.9	465.3	466.6	474.4
Other travel costs	3	272.5	272.6	272.3	269.8	270.5	271.1	269.5	271.0	272.5	275.2	273.2	279.1	275.4
FARES & OTHER TRAVEL COSTS	18	433.7	435.0	435.1	436.9	437.0	437.4	437.0	438.6	439.1	439.9	440.8	441.7	453.6
Audio-visual equipment	12	139.9	140.0	139.6	140.1	139.5	139.0	137.5	137.0	137.3	136.7	136.6	136.2	134.5
Records, toys, photo & sports goods & personal articles	27	267.1	270.4	271.1	273.8	273.6	274.6	273.6	274.1	274.5	276.4	275.0	275.2	279.1
Books & newspapers	17	490.1	490.6	501.9	508.1	506.5	507.4	508.7	510.9	509.7	516.6	529.1	536.9	541.4
Gardening products	4	286.2	303.1	286.2	286.2	289.0	289.0	289.0	289.0	289.0	289.0	298.4	302.1	302.1
TV licences & rentals	14	195.9	195.9	195.9	196.5	196.5	196.5	196.7	196.7	196.7	196.9	196.9	196.9	196.7
Entertainment & recreation	11	423.2	423.8	423.2	440.0	440.0	439.9	439.9	439.3	442.6	442.9	443.8	444.3	444.8
LEISURE SERVICES	25	281.7	281.9	281.7	287.1	287.1	287.1	287.2	287.1	288.0	288.3	288.6	288.7	288.7

* Applied to change since January 1984
§ Variable from month to month
# Includes unpublished components for dwelling insurance & ground rent

	Weight *	Jan	Feb	Mar	Apr	May	Jun	Jul	Aug	Sep	Oct	Nov	Dec	Next Jan
								Index: January 1974 = 100						
Bread	10	324.0	325.7	325.3	325.9	326.4	326.3	326.4	326.7	326.7	327.9	340.4	342.9	351.5
Cereals	5	384.0	387.2	390.5	392.3	396.0	398.4	396.7	398.2	397.1	399.0	401.0	402.1	406.0
Biscuits & cakes	10	347.1	348.9	349.7	350.0	346.0	346.6	348.6	350.3	351.4	349.7	349.9	349.4	349.6
Beef	13	321.8	321.2	320.1	319.1	318.9	320.3	319.1	319.1	320.1	319.4	319.9	321.3	320.5
Lamb	5	261.5	261.2	263.6	278.4	285.0	253.1	259.2	257.9	253.2	252.6	250.3	253.1	259.6
of which Home-killed lamb	2.95	279.7	277.5	281.8	310.0	321.1	297.6	275.4	272.3	265.6	265.4	266.9	268.8	287.3
Pork	5	255.6	250.8	249.9	248.8	247.2	247.5	247.0	245.5	247.2	248.0	251.0	252.6	252.7
Bacon	6	250.5	251.9	251.4	252.8	252.9	252.0	251.3	251.9	251.9	252.7	253.5	254.8	255.7
Poultry & other meat	19	243.6	244.4	246.1	246.9	247.9	248.6	246.8	247.2	247.4	247.3	247.3	248.0	247.2
Fish	6	280.4	281.7	282.0	288.3	288.7	289.5	293.1	292.7	294.1	297.2	299.4	298.7	304.0
of which Fresh/smoked fish	2.64	282.6	284.5	284.6	289.9	289.7	290.8	290.3	289.7	292.5	294.3	300.7	299.7	306.9
Butter	3	437.2	439.1	439.4	440.2	438.7	438.9	441.1	441.5	439.9	441.1	441.9	442.1	441.8
Oils & fats	3	263.9	263.9	268.9	267.4	268.1	269.1	271.6	272.6	270.0	266.8	268.5	269.6	267.7
Cheese	5	374.6	380.0	381.2	384.4	385.7	386.0	389.4	388.7	389.4	388.9	388.1	387.3	386.6
Eggs	4	188.6	187.9	192.5	193.5	193.1	192.4	191.8	188.8	195.8	197.8	199.0	204.7	206.1
Milk, fresh	16	396.4	395.3	395.6	412.3	413.1	412.7	413.2	418.2	418.2	413.1	413.1	413.3	413.6
Milk products	3	408.6	400.1	401.1	407.3	406.8	407.0	406.2	407.0	409.2	408.5	411.9	411.7	413.0
Tea	4	545.5	541.1	539.9	539.1	538.7	535.2	530.1	522.9	516.2	500.7	486.0	481.5	478.1
Coffee & other hot drinks	4	440.8	442.1	446.9	452.3	459.5	459.9	461.5	465.9	466.2	454.5	454.5	456.9	466.6
Soft drinks	4	342.9	346.2	349.0	348.8	350.9	351.4	347.2	347.6	346.1	349.1	349.7	349.0	350.2
Sugar & preserves	3	403.3	403.2	403.6	404.2	407.2	407.8	410.1	410.1	409.7	409.7	408.2	407.1	406.9
Sweets & chocolates	13	439.5	442.8	445.6	444.8	449.6	452.4	453.9	457.9	461.8	459.1	462.2	462.1	465.7
Potatoes	7	421.8	419.5	420.1	408.1	395.5	429.4	354.1	361.1	394.4	416.9	423.1	433.2	437.9
of which Unproc'd potatoes	4.69	373.9	370.9	371.6	350.7	333.9	379.4	279.2	288.4	332.5	357.1	365.2	378.5	384.8
Other vegetables	12	339.2	351.0	374.5	386.0	386.8	380.8	341.9	334.2	323.8	318.2	326.3	346.2	354.0
of which Fresh vegetables	§	351.6	371.9	409.2	426.8	430.4	417.4	351.5	337.3	319.9	310.3	325.1	356.8	369.6
Fruit	11	307.9	317.2	325.2	333.6	334.4	337.0	335.9	332.6	325.1	323.6	323.1	321.4	321.0
of which Fresh fruit	§	337.9	349.4	360.3	371.9	372.6	375.4	342.0	367.8	352.8	350.7	352.1	351.6	352.3
Other foods (excl. petfood)	13	364.1	365.2	365.3	370.0	370.6	372.0	376.5	376.1	377.3	379.6	380.3	379.5	379.3
FOOD (excluding petfood)	184	331.9	333.7	336.6	340.2	340.7	341.6	336.5	336.7	337.0	336.6	338.3	340.5	342.3
Restaurant meals	21	406.1	407.4	409.1	412.3	414.0	417.0	417.0	420.9	421.7	424.2	426.3	428.5	430.3
Canteen meals	9	406.5	406.1	407.8	412.2	416.3	416.3	418.2	418.2	422.0	423.4	424.9	426.0	431.8
Take-away meals & snacks	15	359.0	360.8	362.5	366.0	369.1	370.7	373.7	375.6	376.5	378.1	379.4	379.9	382.3
CATERING	45	401.8	403.0	404.8	408.4	411.2	413.2	414.6	417.1	418.6	420.7	422.4	423.8	426.7
Beer	44	473.3	474.9	476.3	487.9	489.9	489.0	490.1	494.1	500.2	507.1	507.9	507.1	509.9
Wines & spirits	31	301.2	302.9	303.8	308.6	310.4	311.0	312.6	314.5	316.1	317.6	317.1	311.9	315.5
ALCOHOLIC DRINK	75	397.9	399.7	400.9	409.2	411.2	411.0	412.5	415.5	419.3	423.5	423.7	420.4	423.8
Cigarettes	34	509.7	514.9	516.3	533.2	538.7	540.9	541.6	541.3	541.7	541.9	546.4	547.1	547.7
Other tobacco	3	488.6	491.6	493.8	501.7	509.8	512.1	515.3	513.8	516.3	517.4	519.9	518.4	521.7
TOBACCO	37	508.1	513.1	514.5	530.8	536.4	538.7	539.6	539.2	539.8	540.0	544.4	544.8	545.7
Rent	31	389.2	389.1	389.1	410.7	410.6	410.4	411.2	411.3	411.4	411.9	413.5	417.2	418.0
Mortgage interest payments	46	386.0	420.7	428.2	464.1	469.6	472.9	476.7	479.5	447.4	446.5	450.1	453.6	457.2
Rates	36.22	509.7	509.7	509.7	546.1	549.9	556.8	558.2	558.2	558.2	558.2	558.2	558.2	558.2
Water charges	8.78	441.2	441.2	441.2	491.7	492.5	492.5	492.5	492.5	492.5	492.5	492.5	492.5	492.5
Repair/maintenance charges	9	510.4	510.4	510.4	525.5	525.5	525.5	526.5	526.5	526.5	526.5	538.9	540.4	540.4
Do-it-yourself materials	17	355.1	356.2	361.1	364.3	365.9	368.4	368.6	370.5	371.5	371.6	375.8	376.2	378.8
HOUSING #	153	416.4	427.7	431.2	458.4	461.3	463.8	465.8	467.1	457.0	457.0	459.7	462.0	463.7
Coal & solid fuels	8	523.0	528.6	532.2	531.4	501.1	494.3	493.6	503.7	521.3	523.9	542.1	547.5	543.9
Electricity	29	502.2	502.2	502.2	505.2	511.5	517.7	522.2	522.2	522.2	522.2	522.2	522.2	522.2
Gas	24	390.1	391.4	396.8	403.2	407.2	407.2	408.5	408.5	408.5	408.6	408.6	408.6	408.6
Oil & other fuel	4	680.3	680.4	682.9	717.8	717.8	717.8	685.7	685.7	685.7	680.4	680.4	680.4	678.5
FUEL & LIGHT	65	487.5	488.7	491.7	497.4	498.5	500.4	501.5	502.6	504.7	504.7	506.8	507.4	507.0
Furniture	13	266.5	268.0	271.7	272.6	273.8	273.0	271.2	273.1	275.0	275.3	276.0	275.3	272.4
Furnishings	13	281.6	288.0	288.0	289.6	291.2	293.2	291.9	296.3	297.5	300.0	303.3	303.1	300.6
Electrical appliances	16	263.6	264.5	267.6	268.0	268.7	270.2	267.2	268.0	271.0	272.4	272.2	273.2	266.4
Other household equipment	12	377.1	380.1	384.2	387.9	389.4	392.5	395.3	396.6	396.9	397.5	397.9	398.6	399.7
Household consumables	16	438.6	444.1	448.0	454.8	454.6	456.8	458.1	460.9	460.2	462.6	461.6	464.2	467.4
Pet care	6	280.6	285.4	286.8	284.4	285.1	285.1	286.1	283.2	288.3	290.4	296.3	294.8	291.7
HOUSEHOLD GOODS	76	312.4	315.8	318.6	320.4	321.3	322.8	322.0	323.8	325.6	327.1	328.2	328.6	326.2
Postage	2	478.4	478.4	478.4	478.4	478.4	478.4	478.4	478.4	480.9	480.9	470.5	470.5	470.5
Telephone charges etc	16	370.0	370.0	370.0	370.0	370.0	370.0	370.0	370.0	370.0	370.0	383.1	387.9	391.7
Domestic services	6	451.7	453.5	455.2	458.5	463.3	468.5	468.9	468.8	469.4	470.3	468.1	467.3	469.7
Fees & subscriptions	8	449.8	448.3	452.8	458.2	464.4	464.6	467.6	471.3	473.2	477.1	478.2	479.4	483.2
HOUSEHOLD SERVICES	32	421.2	421.2	422.5	424.4	427.2	427.6	428.4	429.3	430.0	431.0	437.8	440.5	444.1
Men's outerwear	11	233.1	233.0	240.9	241.4	241.6	240.0	239.4	239.2	242.9	245.2	244.2	243.4	239.9
Women's outerwear	24	158.5	155.1	159.1	159.0	160.0	159.8	159.6	161.8	164.7	167.0	168.2	167.9	164.5
Children's outerwear	9	256.8	257.0	261.9	263.5	261.4	261.6	260.4	262.0	262.7	262.1	261.7	260.1	261.9
Other clothing	15	266.5	267.7	274.1	275.8	276.0	272.7	277.2	280.7	281.6	283.0	283.8	283.7	279.3
Footwear	16	224.9	225.8	227.6	227.9	227.3	228.1	227.7	231.0	233.1	235.0	235.5	234.2	232.7
CLOTHING & FOOTWEAR	75	217.4	216.3	221.0	221.6	221.8	221.1	221.4	223.3	226.2	228.1	228.7	227.9	225.2
Chemists' goods	14	371.8	377.4	383.7	390.4	393.4	397.4	398.5	400.3	401.9	403.6	405.6	406.2	410.1
Personal services	7	462.7	466.1	468.1	474.0	477.6	479.6	481.6	482.9	484.1	488.5	490.0	490.0	493.4

	Weight *	Jan	Feb	Mar	Apr	May	Jun	Jul	Aug	Sep	Oct	Nov	Dec	Next Jan
						Index: January 1974 = 100								
Purchase of motor vehicles	55	308.8	311.9	314.6	315.8	319.5	319.8	320.1	320.1	320.7	320.7	318.6	316.5	315.6
Maintenance of motor vcles	15	421.0	425.3	426.0	428.9	402.0	433.7	436.4	440.1	441.8	444.5	447.4	447.8	450.0
Petrol & oil	50	456.2	456.2	476.0	487.3	490.0	488.3	481.6	478.6	475.0	467.5	463.4	462.1	459.4
Vehicle tax & insurance	19	344.5	346.5	346.5	366.3	367.1	367.1	371.5	373.0	373.0	375.7	378.3	381.6	381.6
MOTORING EXPENDITURE	139	368.5	370.7	377.8	384.5	387.8	387.5	386.7	386.3	385.7	384.1	382.7	381.8	380.8
Rail fares	6	510.1	510.1	510.1	510.1	510.1	510.1	510.1	510.1	510.1	510.1	510.1	510.1	544.7
Bus & coach fares	8	474.4	474.9	475.8	479.8	480.5	481.3	481.8	482.7	483.2	484.0	486.1	486.9	497.2
Other travel costs	3	275.4	277.2	277.7	278.7	280.2	280.8	279.0	282.0	283.7	282.9	284.5	282.9	283.6
FARES & OTHER TRAVEL COSTS	17	453.6	454.4	454.9	457.0	457.8	458.3	458.0	459.3	460.0	460.1	461.5	461.4	477.1
Audio-visual equipment	11	134.5	134.2	133.7	133.3	134.1	134.2	132.3	133.0	134.0	133.7	133.4	133.1	132.2
Records, toys, photo & sports goods & personal articles	25	279.1	281.7	284.8	286.6	286.4	286.5	287.4	288.2	290.2	288.8	289.5	290.3	292.8
Books & newspapers	17	541.4	549.8	552.8	556.3	558.7	559.1	561.7	562.5	563.1	570.5	573.6	573.9	577.0
Gardening products	5	302.1	302.1	302.1	302.1	310.0	310.0	310.0	310.0	310.0	310.0	311.3	310.8	310.8
TV licences & rentals	12	196.7	196.7	196.7	215.5	215.5	215.5	212.1	212.1	212.1	212.0	212.0	212.0	211.8
Entertainment & recreation	11	444.8	444.8	444.8	464.0	464.9	464.6	464.7	464.7	467.7	468.2	467.7	468.1	476.9
LEISURE SERVICES	23	288.7	288.7	288.7	309.0	309.3	309.2	306.7	306.7	307.6	307.7	307.5	307.7	310.3

* Applied to change since January 1985
§ Variable from month to month
\# Includes unpublished components for dwelling insurance & ground rent

Index: January 1974 = 100

	Weight *	Jan	Feb	Mar	Apr	May	Jun	Jul	Aug	Sep	Oct	Nov	Dec	Next Jan
Bread	10	351.5	354.4	355.6	356.4	357.0	357.2	357.3	356.1	357.9	358.1	358.7	363.6	365.5
Cereals	5	406.0	407.7	408.2	410.3	413.7	415.2	418.9	419.6	419.6	420.9	421.9	422.8	423.6
Biscuits & cakes	10	349.6	350.8	350.9	352.8	353.4	356.3	358.8	358.7	359.3	361.5	361.4	361.9	363.2
Beef	12	320.5	319.9	320.8	320.3	320.7	323.2	323.4	323.4	322.8	322.4	321.6	322.3	322.7
Lamb	4	259.6	258.0	267.0	284.7	296.5	297.5	279.0	267.1	260.7	249.8	253.1	263.5	269.5
of which Home-killed lamb	2.4	287.3	286.5	299.2	326.8	344.2	342.2	305.3	287.2	276.1	258.2	265.7	283.4	294.7
Pork	5	252.7	251.0	248.6	251.3	250.2	252.0	251.5	252.1	252.6	253.4	252.3	253.9	253.9
Bacon	5	255.7	254.2	255.1	253.1	254.1	254.5	254.4	255.7	257.3	259.9	259.4	260.1	260.0
Poultry & other meat	19	247.2	248.3	247.9	249.1	250.1	250.4	250.6	251.6	251.4	251.8	253.4	255.8	255.5
Fish	5	304.0	306.1	305.6	308.8	310.5	312.2	309.8	311.9	319.1	325.5	328.3	331.2	336.9
of which Fresh/smoked fish	1.9	306.9	307.5	308.5	310.3	312.3	314.6	311.4	312.1	316.2	316.2	322.0	325.2	328.6
Butter	3	441.8	441.2	441.8	442.1	440.5	444.3	450.6	451.7	450.0	447.8	447.2	446.7	447.2
Oils & fats	3	267.7	262.6	260.7	256.7	252.5	250.9	249.9	246.7	243.3	239.5	235.5	233.9	233.8
Cheese	5	386.6	387.3	386.7	388.2	388.8	388.5	387.6	388.3	388.6	388.5	390.8	389.9	395.1
Eggs	4	206.1	205.8	207.6	206.9	204.3	199.6	196.0	196.4	198.4	193.8	195.9	203.1	204.0
Milk, fresh	14	413.6	429.3	430.9	431.5	430.7	431.1	431.1	431.1	431.0	430.9	430.8	430.9	447.4
Milk products	3	413.0	415.1	414.2	413.7	413.2	413.5	413.3	416.8	415.6	415.8	417.3	416.1	416.0
Tea	3	478.1	476.8	472.6	472.3	470.9	471.1	468.7	468.2	468.8	468.8	468.1	467.2	466.5
Coffee & other hot drinks	4	466.6	476.5	488.8	507.2	516.9	520.7	526.9	530.3	529.4	532.1	532.5	531.3	532.0
Soft drinks	6	350.2	352.6	353.3	354.7	354.9	355.2	352.9	350.9	352.1	355.2	354.3	353.9	356.1
Sugar & preserves	3	406.9	407.0	407.0	408.2	407.2	407.4	405.3	406.9	407.1	407.6	409.9	411.1	412.4
Sweets & chocolates	14	465.7	469.1	471.8	474.3	477.4	478.9	480.2	482.7	485.4	484.5	483.8	485.1	487.2
Potatoes	7	437.9	445.8	461.3	467.9	480.9	527.9	480.8	507.8	515.7	513.4	518.7	524.0	538.9
of which Unproc'd potatoes	3.64	384.8	398.0	423.4	429.6	452.7	530.6	449.3	491.8	499.9	494.4	500.7	507.3	529.9
Other vegetables	12	354.0	361.8	369.7	366.5	384.2	375.9	335.1	326.5	323.1	325.2	319.7	332.9	360.9
of which Fresh vegetables	§	369.6	382.5	396.8	390.9	422.2	409.0	341.6	329.9	324.2	328.9	320.2	336.3	380.0
Fruit	10	321.0	323.3	324.5	333.6	337.0	337.3	340.6	351.9	338.0	323.8	316.9	316.9	321.4
of which Fresh fruit	§	352.3	355.9	359.8	377.1	354.7	383.7	389.8	408.9	392.8	373.8	362.7	365.8	364.7
Other foods (excl. petfood)	13	379.3	380.2	379.3	383.9	384.4	385.8	389.2	391.0	392.4	393.4	393.5	394.3	392.3
FOOD (excluding petfood)	179	342.3	344.9	346.5	348.9	351.4	353.1	348.9	350.1	349.8	348.9	348.8	351.3	355.7
Restaurant meals	22	430.3	433.3	434.8	439.6	442.3	446.9	447.4	450.2	452.9	455.7	457.0	462.0	463.1
Canteen meals	8	431.8	432.5	433.3	437.6	437.7	438.0	439.0	440.6	444.2	448.0	450.0	451.4	451.4
Take-away meals & snacks	14	382.3	384.2	384.2	387.9	389.3	391.5	393.3	394.8	396.9	398.2	400.0	402.1	405.6
CATERING	44	426.7	428.9	429.9	434.3	436.2	439.3	440.4	442.6	445.3	447.8	449.5	452.9	454.8
Beer	48	509.9	512.1	513.4	514.9	515.9	516.6	519.0	521.7	525.2	528.6	529.9	531.2	534.2
Wines & spirits	34	315.5	317.4	317.3	318.0	319.2	319.7	320.5	320.7	321.6	322.2	319.9	316.4	324.7
ALCOHOLIC DRINK	82	423.8	425.9	426.5	427.6	428.8	429.4	431.0	432.5	434.6	436.6	436.0	434.6	440.7
Cigarettes	35	547.7	552.0	555.4	585.4	599.8	602.9	602.7	603.0	603.6	605.2	608.0	609.2	608.2
Other tobacco	5	521.7	524.8	528.0	539.2	547.0	548.3	548.4	549.4	551.4	552.8	552.4	550.7	555.4
TOBACCO	40	545.7	549.9	553.2	580.8	594.4	597.3	597.1	597.5	598.3	599.9	602.2	603.1	602.9
Rent	29	418.0	417.8	418.3	438.8	435.9	436.1	436.5	436.8	437.1	437.6	438.2	442.4	442.5
Mortgage interest payments	54	457.2	461.2	464.8	452.0	450.5	417.2	420.7	424.5	428.0	431.6	484.5	491.6	496.3
Rates	33	558.2	558.2	558.2	632.4	634.1	634.0	634.0	634.0	634.0	634.0	634.0	634.0	634.0
Water charges	8	492.5	492.5	492.5	533.3	533.3	533.3	533.3	533.3	533.3	533.3	533.3	533.3	533.3
Repair/maintenance charges	8	540.4	540.4	540.4	559.7	560.2	560.2	560.2	560.2	560.2	547.6	550.1	550.1	550.1
Do-it-yourself materials	16	378.8	381.7	384.6	384.9	383.3	388.0	386.5	392.2	396.1	396.8	392.9	392.9	388.6
HOUSING #	153	463.7	465.7	467.5	483.5	482.7	471.6	472.8	475.2	477.3	478.4	497.4	501.1	502.4
Coal & solid fuels	7	543.9	544.5	544.8	544.7	518.9	513.8	512.4	529.9	539.6	541.5	544.6	545.5	546.6
Electricity	29	522.2	522.2	522.2	526.1	525.3	527.6	528.9	528.8	528.7	527.7	526.1	524.5	523.2
Gas	23	408.6	408.6	408.6	408.6	409.6	410.2	413.6	414.1	414.1	414.1	414.1	414.2	414.2
Oil & other fuel	3	678.5	678.5	678.5	624.3	624.3	618.4	569.4	533.2	533.2	531.2	533.1	527.2	562.0
FUEL & LIGHT	62	507.0	507.0	507.0	506.8	504.2	504.8	505.0	505.8	506.7	506.4	506.1	505.3	506.1
Furniture	13	272.4	275.0	278.3	279.2	281.9	280.6	276.8	276.0	279.1	281.3	284.6	286.1	279.4
Furnishings	13	300.6	306.0	305.6	309.2	312.3	312.9	308.3	308.4	309.3	311.2	313.7	313.0	306.9
Electrical appliances	15	266.4	268.3	270.0	270.2	270.9	270.6	267.2	267.6	270.1	269.1	270.9	271.1	270.5
Other household equipment	11	399.7	400.9	401.1	403.5	408.4	407.3	406.2	399.9	400.5	406.0	411.7	415.2	408.2
Household consumables	17	467.4	469.0	468.1	468.0	467.6	465.1	465.9	467.8	468.7	471.2	471.3	469.1	470.8
Pet care	6	291.7	291.8	293.0	290.9	290.8	290.3	290.3	293.2	293.1	295.1	296.3	294.2	293.1
HOUSEHOLD GOODS	75	326.2	328.6	329.6	330.6	332.5	331.7	329.2	328.9	330.6	332.4	334.7	334.9	331.5
Postage	2	470.5	470.5	470.5	470.5	470.5	470.5	470.5	470.5	470.5	470.5	496.4	486.5	496.4
Telephone charges etc	17	391.7	391.7	391.7	391.7	391.7	391.7	391.7	391.7	391.7	391.7	395.8	397.6	399.8
Domestic services	5	469.7	474.2	480.1	481.1	484.4	488.4	489.2	490.8	493.4	493.8	495.9	498.8	503.3
Fees & subscriptions	2	483.2	485.6	485.4	488.6	492.3	493.6	496.0	498.0	501.4	503.6	506.2	508.6	512.1
HOUSEHOLD SERVICES	26	444.1	445.1	446.1	446.6	447.5	448.2	448.5	449.0	449.7	449.9	455.5	456.8	460.2
Men's outerwear	11	239.9	240.2	241.6	243.8	245.2	245.2	244.6	244.5	247.2	248.2	248.5	249.1	243.4
Women's outerwear	23	164.5	163.4	165.6	164.6	164.4	163.0	162.6	165.7	167.5	169.2	169.9	169.9	165.9
Children's outerwear	9	261.9	263.3	265.1	263.5	261.1	256.7	256.8	265.6	266.2	269.3	272.6	275.7	271.7
Other clothing	16	279.3	280.3	284.6	285.2	284.3	288.2	288.0	288.4	290.3	291.3	292.6	291.5	288.8
Footwear	16	232.7	235.9	236.7	235.0	238.3	238.4	236.9	239.6	240.9	241.9	242.3	242.2	241.9
CLOTHING & FOOTWEAR	75	225.2	225.7	227.9	227.4	227.8	227.5	226.8	229.7	231.5	233.0	234.0	234.2	230.8
Chemists' goods	17	410.1	410.6	413.4	419.3	416.8	419.5	420.9	421.6	423.8	424.3	425.4	427.6	426.3
Personal services	8	493.4	497.2	498.6	504.0	506.8	509.5	512.1	513.5	515.6	520.6	521.7	521.0	527.3

	Weight *	Jan	Feb	Mar	Apr	May	Jun	Jul	Aug	Sep	Oct	Nov	Dec	Next Jan
						Index: January 1974 = 100								
Purchase of motor vehicles	59	315.6	316.3	317.6	322.0	326.3	327.5	328.2	330.5	331.0	331.1	332.2	332.8	335.2
Maintenance of motor vcles	15	450.0	456.2	456.4	457.0	458.8	461.2	461.7	465.6	470.9	469.7	470.7	471.7	471.0
Petrol & oil	47	459.4	447.5	427.4	412.8	392.0	399.6	392.7	385.6	407.0	407.8	407.4	406.4	412.1
Vehicle tax & insurance	19	381.6	386.1	386.1	386.1	389.5	401.0	401.0	405.7	405.7	405.7	417.9	424.3	424.8
MOTORING EXPENDITURE	140	380.8	379.0	374.1	372.4	369.3	373.9	372.3	372.5	379.2	379.3	381.5	382.5	385.3
Rail fares	6	544.7	544.7	544.7	544.7	544.7	544.7	544.7	544.7	544.7	544.7	544.7	544.7	569.3
Bus & coach fares	8	497.2	493.7	493.7	526.8	526.8	530.7	530.9	530.9	531.5	531.5	531.5	531.5	533.7
Other travel costs	3	283.6	282.1	282.5	275.5	278.1	277.5	285.1	287.8	289.2	287.3	289.2	291.4	293.6
FARES & OTHER TRAVEL COSTS	17	477.1	475.0	475.2	488.1	488.8	490.4	492.7	493.5	494.2	493.6	494.2	494.8	504.1
Audio-visual equipment	11	132.2	133.7	133.8	127.0	126.5	125.9	123.9	122.6	116.9	116.2	117.6	117.3	120.7
Records, toys, photo & sports goods & personal articles	25	292.8	296.8	294.5	296.6	296.6	297.6	294.5	298.0	299.7	299.0	300.7	302.2	298.7
Books & newspapers	17	577.0	579.1	579.9	583.2	587.0	588.1	589.6	590.9	591.4	592.0	593.4	595.0	597.9
Gardening products	5	310.8	321.1	321.8	327.1	325.0	326.3	321.2	316.6	318.4	325.2	316.3	317.8	318.2
TV licences & rentals	13	211.8	211.8	211.8	211.5	211.5	211.5	211.0	211.0	211.0	211.0	211.0	211.0	211.1
Entertainment & recreation	11	476.9	478.4	478.4	502.9	507.4	507.8	508.4	509.8	513.8	515.4	514.4	515.2	515.3
LEISURE SERVICES	24	310.3	310.8	310.7	317.8	319.1	319.2	319.0	319.4	320.6	321.1	320.8	321.1	321.1

* Applied to change since January 1986
§ Variable from month to month
\# Includes unpublished components for dwelling insurance & ground rent

Index: January 1974 = 100

	Weight *	Jan	Feb	Mar	Apr	May	Jun	Jul	Aug	Sep	Oct	Nov	Dec	Next Jan
Bread	9	100.0	99.9	99.8	100.1	100.3	100.4	100.7	100.8	100.8	101.1	104.2	105.4	105.8
Cereals	4	100.0	101.0	101.4	102.0	102.5	102.9	101.8	101.5	102.3	102.1	102.6	103.0	103.8
Biscuits & cakes	10	100.0	99.9	100.1	100.7	100.9	101.4	101.9	102.1	102.1	102.5	102.7	102.5	103.0
Beef	10	100.0	99.5	99.0	100.0	100.7	101.2	100.9	100.5	101.6	102.0	102.2	103.8	104.8
Lamb	4	100.0	99.3	98.8	109.9	113.8	108.9	101.8	102.8	94.5	94.4	97.7	100.3	99.3
of which Home-killed lamb	3	100.0	98.3	98.2	112.9	118.1	111.7	102.1	103.6	93.2	92.6	97.0	100.4	99.3
Pork	4	100.0	97.7	98.8	98.7	99.8	100.6	101.1	100.0	100.4	100.9	101.5	102.0	101.1
Bacon	4	100.0	99.1	98.6	99.4	100.1	99.2	99.9	99.7	99.8	100.8	101.7	101.8	102.2
Poultry	7	100.0	102.1	100.9	102.6	100.4	102.2	103.9	103.3	104.5	104.5	103.3	102.6	101.5
Other meat	11	100.0	100.4	100.7	100.9	101.3	101.0	100.9	100.8	100.3	100.5	100.5	100.9	100.7
Fish	6	100.0	100.2	100.5	101.5	102.6	102.5	102.4	102.8	102.7	103.3	102.8	103.6	105.1
of which Fresh fish	2	100.0	98.4	99.7	99.6	100.9	100.4	100.5	101.6	101.6	102.1	100.7	103.4	108.1
Butter	2	100.0	99.5	100.2	99.9	99.4	99.2	98.9	98.8	100.0	100.2	100.8	101.1	101.5
Oils & fats	3	100.0	100.5	98.9	98.4	97.3	97.7	97.1	97.2	97.5	98.1	98.6	100.0	99.5
Cheese	5	100.0	99.9	100.1	99.4	100.2	100.4	101.0	101.0	100.8	101.5	102.5	102.4	104.2
Eggs	3	100.0	100.1	101.4	107.2	105.1	104.2	103.0	101.5	105.1	103.2	107.7	109.2	110.7
Milk, fresh	14	100.0	100.3	100.4	100.4	100.4	100.4	100.1	100.4	100.4	103.9	104.1	104.2	104.2
Milk products	2	100.0	100.4	100.8	101.9	99.8	102.0	101.9	102.2	102.6	103.7	105.0	105.3	105.7
Tea	3	100.0	100.3	100.4	100.3	100.3	100.2	100.3	100.1	100.3	100.3	100.6	100.3	100.6
Coffee & other hot drinks	4	100.0	99.5	98.9	95.4	94.9	94.5	93.8	94.0	93.1	92.3	92.4	91.9	91.9
Soft drinks	7	100.0	100.9	102.1	102.0	102.6	103.0	102.9	103.6	104.0	104.7	106.0	106.2	107.7
Sugar & preserves	3	100.0	100.4	100.7	101.3	102.3	102.7	103.0	104.1	105.4	105.9	106.3	107.0	107.6
Sweets & chocolates	13	100.0	100.1	99.9	99.9	99.9	100.4	100.4	100.4	100.6	100.6	100.2	100.3	100.7
Potatoes	7	100.0	103.3	101.5	101.5	103.5	105.6	92.0	92.8	94.0	94.3	96.9	98.7	99.8
of which Unproc'd potatoes	4	100.0	105.8	102.8	102.1	105.4	108.8	85.0	86.1	87.9	87.5	93.3	96.1	97.9
Other vegetables	11	100.0	105.5	105.3	110.4	113.5	102.2	96.3	98.2	97.1	98.1	99.2	103.7	105.0
of which Fresh vegetables	7	100.0	107.7	107.5	115.1	119.9	102.0	94.1	96.7	95.0	96.3	98.7	105.8	107.2
Fruit	9	100.0	101.8	102.4	102.7	105.5	104.9	101.8	103.6	98.0	100.6	99.3	100.7	101.3
of which Fresh fruit	7	100.0	101.9	102.3	102.8	106.1	105.3	101.0	103.6	96.4	100.1	98.6	100.4	101.2
Other foods	12	100.0	100.2	100.7	100.8	101.2	100.9	101.9	101.2	102.1	102.3	102.0	102.0	102.8
FOOD	167	100.0	100.7	100.7	101.6	102.2	101.6	100.4	100.7	100.4	101.1	101.6	102.4	102.9
Restaurant meals	23	100.0	100.5	101.0	101.5	102.0	102.7	103.3	104.2	104.8	105.3	105.5	106.0	106.5
Canteen meals	7	100.0	100.6	100.6	101.2	101.6	101.9	102.2	102.5	103.9	104.0	105.0	105.6	106.5
Take-away meals & snacks	16	100.0	100.4	100.6	101.2	101.5	101.9	102.8	103.1	103.8	104.2	105.1	105.6	106.3
CATERING	46	100.0	100.4	100.8	101.4	101.8	102.3	102.9	103.6	104.3	104.7	105.3	105.8	106.4
Beer	45	100.0	100.3	100.6	100.8	101.0	101.2	101.4	101.8	102.8	103.7	104.0	104.0	104.3
Wines & spirits	31	100.0	100.4	100.6	100.8	101.5	101.8	102.2	102.5	102.7	103.2	102.3	101.7	102.8
ALCOHOLIC DRINK	76	100.0	100.3	100.6	100.8	101.2	101.4	101.7	102.1	102.8	103.5	103.3	103.1	103.7
Cigarettes	33	100.0	99.9	100.0	99.9	99.9	99.9	99.8	99.7	99.9	100.7	101.4	101.5	101.7
Other tobacco	5	100.0	100.1	99.7	99.4	99.3	99.3	99.1	98.5	98.5	99.2	99.4	99.3	99.7
TOBACCO	38	100.0	99.9	99.9	99.8	99.8	99.8	99.7	99.5	99.7	100.5	101.1	101.2	101.4
Rent	34	100.0	100.2	100.2	103.8	104.3	104.7	104.7	104.6	104.6	105.1	105.6	105.6	105.7
Mortgage interest payments	44	100.0	100.9	101.6	105.6	99.7	98.2	99.2	100.2	101.0	102.1	103.1	96.6	96.3
Rates	42	100.0	100.0	100.0	107.7	107.7	107.7	107.7	107.7	107.7	107.7	107.7	107.7	107.7
Water charges	7	100.0	100.0	100.0	105.6	105.6	105.6	105.6	105.6	105.6	105.6	107.6	107.6	107.6
Repair/maintenance charges	8	100.0	100.0	100.3	101.1	101.1	101.5	101.8	101.6	101.6	102.2	103.0	103.3	104.1
Do-it-yourself materials	16	100.0	100.2	101.2	101.4	102.1	102.5	102.7	102.6	102.7	103.2	104.2	104.7	104.7
HOUSING	157	100.0	100.3	100.7	105.0	103.6	103.4	103.8	104.1	104.4	104.9	105.6	103.9	103.9
Coal & solid fuels	6	100.0	100.1	100.2	100.3	96.6	95.5	95.3	98.3	99.2	99.8	100.2	100.3	101.8
Electricity	28	100.0	100.0	100.0	100.0	100.0	100.0	100.0	100.0	100.0	100.0	100.0	100.0	100.0
Gas	24	100.0	100.0	100.0	100.0	100.0	100.0	99.3	97.9	96.5	95.5	95.5	95.5	95.5
Oil & other fuel	3	100.0	99.6	96.0	96.4	94.9	96.9	95.9	99.0	98.0	96.6	101.2	98.2	97.3
FUEL & LIGHT	61	100.0	100.0	99.8	99.9	99.4	99.4	99.1	99.0	98.5	98.0	98.3	98.2	98.3
Furniture	13	100.0	100.7	101.3	101.7	102.3	102.2	100.9	101.5	102.7	103.4	104.5	104.5	102.7
Furnishings	11	100.0	100.8	101.2	102.1	102.3	102.2	101.5	102.1	102.3	104.1	105.1	105.2	103.3
Electrical appliances	15	100.0	100.4	101.3	101.8	102.3	102.4	101.8	102.1	102.8	103.3	104.4	104.3	102.8
Other household equipment	12	100.0	100.8	101.0	101.6	102.3	102.6	101.9	102.2	102.9	103.0	103.8	104.3	103.6
Household consumables	14	100.0	100.0	100.2	101.1	101.9	101.5	102.6	103.1	103.3	103.9	105.2	105.5	105.6
Pet care	8	100.0	99.9	100.7	100.4	100.4	99.9	99.8	99.8	100.7	101.0	100.8	100.5	100.5
HOUSEHOLD GOODS	73	100.0	100.4	101.0	101.5	102.0	101.9	101.6	101.9	102.7	103.3	104.2	104.3	103.3
Postage	2	100.0	100.0	100.1	100.1	100.1	100.1	100.1	100.1	100.6	100.6	100.6	100.3	100.6
Telephone charges etc	16	100.0	100.2	100.2	100.2	100.2	100.2	100.2	100.2	100.2	100.2	100.9	101.0	101.2
Domestic services	7	100.0	100.1	100.6	101.1	101.2	101.7	102.0	102.5	102.7	103.3	104.3	104.5	105.8
Fees & subscriptions	19	100.0	100.1	100.3	101.4	102.6	103.0	103.7	104.5	105.5	105.9	106.4	106.6	108.4
HOUSEHOLD SERVICES	44	100.0	100.1	100.3	100.9	101.4	101.6	102.0	102.4	102.9	103.2	103.8	104.0	105.0
Men's outerwear	15	100.0	100.7	101.2	101.8	101.6	101.5	100.0	100.3	102.5	102.9	103.8	104.1	101.6
Women's outerwear	22	100.0	99.8	100.9	100.5	100.4		97.2	97.9	101.2	101.7	102.2	103.0	99.2
Children's outerwear	9	100.0	100.1	100.4	100.2	100.6	100.4	98.2	99.0	102.1	103.3	103.8	104.3	101.0
Other clothing	12	100.0	100.5	101.0	101.3	101.6	101.8	101.2	102.0	102.1	102.6	103.2	103.6	103.0
Footwear	16	100.0	100.5	100.5	101.2	101.1	101.3	100.1	100.7	101.6	101.5	102.1	102.6	101.8
CLOTHING & FOOTWEAR	74	100.0	100.3	100.8	101.0	101.0	100.8	99.2	99.8	101.8	102.3	102.9	103.4	101.1

Index: January 1974 = 100

	Weight *	Jan	Feb	Mar	Apr	May	Jun	Jul	Aug	Sep	Oct	Nov	Dec	Next Jan
Personal articles	11	100.0	100.0	100.1	100.1	99.3	99.2	99.3	99.3	99.5	99.8	100.9	100.9	100.6
Chemists' goods	16	100.0	100.6	101.1	101.8	102.6	103.2	103.3	103.7	102.1	102.9	104.6	104.7	105.1
Personal services	11	100.0	100.2	100.8	101.6	101.9	102.8	102.7	103.4	104.0	104.8	105.9	106.4	106.9
PERSONAL GOODS & SERVICES	38	100.0	100.3	100.7	101.3	101.4	101.9	101.9	102.4	101.9	102.6	103.9	104.1	104.3
Purchase of motor vehicles	52	100.0	100.6	101.4	102.5	104.1	105.2	106.6	107.2	108.0	108.3	108.2	107.6	106.9
Maintenance of motor vcles	20	100.0	101.4	101.2	101.6	102.7	102.9	103.1	103.9	103.9	104.2	104.9	105.3	105.8
Petrol & oil	37	100.0	102.0	101.8	101.3	101.1	100.7	101.1	101.1	101.0	100.4	100.2	99.7	98.9
Vehicle tax & insurance	18	100.0	100.0	100.0	103.1	103.1	103.1	106.2	106.2	106.2	108.3	108.3	108.3	112.2
MOTORING EXPENDITURE	127	100.0	101.0	101.3	102.1	102.8	103.2	104.4	104.8	105.1	105.4	105.4	105.0	105.1
Rail fares	7	100.0	100.0	100.1	100.1	100.1	100.1	101.1	101.1	101.1	101.1	101.1	101.1	107.1
Bus & coach fares	7	100.0	100.0	100.0	100.9	103.1	103.5	104.9	104.9	104.9	105.3	106.7	106.7	106.7
Other travel costs	8	100.0	99.5	99.6	99.7	100.8	100.9	100.8	101.1	101.0	101.5	101.8	102.0	102.0
FARES & OTHER TRAVEL COSTS	22	100.0	99.8	99.9	100.2	101.3	101.5	102.2	102.3	102.3	102.6	103.1	103.2	105.1
Audio-visual equipment	12	100.0	99.4	99.6	99.2	99.1	98.4	96.9	96.9	96.7	96.5	96.9	96.9	95.3
Records & tapes	3	100.0	100.1	99.9	100.1	100.1	99.9	99.7	99.6	100.0	103.3	103.9	104.0	100.0
Toys, photo & sports goods	11	100.0	100.0	100.7	100.1	100.8	101.4	101.5	101.8	101.9	101.8	102.3	102.3	102.2
Books & newspapers	16	100.0	100.8	101.1	103.5	104.5	105.6	106.0	106.1	106.5	107.8	108.4	108.4	109.0
Gardening products	5	100.0	100.5	98.2	98.9	100.8	101.5	100.5	100.2	101.0	102.0	102.1	103.4	104.3
LEISURE GOODS	47	100.0	100.2	100.3	100.9	101.6	102.0	101.6	101.7	101.9	102.6	103.1	103.2	102.8
TV licences & rentals	13	100.0	100.5	100.6	101.0	100.2	100.2	100.0	100.0	100.0	99.9	99.9	100.0	99.4
Entertainment & recreation	17	100.0	99.9	99.7	102.0	101.8	102.1	102.4	102.4	103.4	105.8	106.6	106.4	106.9
LEISURE SERVICES	30	100.0	100.1	100.1	101.5	101.1	101.3	101.4	101.4	101.9	103.3	103.7	103.6	103.6

* Applied to change since January 1987

Index: January 1974 = 100

	Weight *	Jan	Feb	Mar	Apr	May	Jun	Jul	Aug	Sep	Oct	Nov	Dec	Next Jan
Bread	9	105.8	106.2	106.2	106.5	107.4	108.0	108.3	108.7	108.8	109.0	109.0	110.8	111.6
Cereals	4	103.8	105.5	106.2	107.1	107.8	107.8	108.3	108.6	109.9	110.5	110.8	111.0	112.2
Biscuits & cakes	9	103.0	103.1	102.9	103.1	104.2	104.5	105.3	104.6	105.4	106.0	106.4	107.2	108.3
Beef	10	104.8	104.9	105.7	106.2	107.8	109.0	109.6	111.3	112.1	112.3	113.8	115.1	115.4
Lamb	3	99.3	97.5	98.0	102.6	106.9	108.9	102.4	103.8	100.9	96.5	98.8	99.6	99.0
of which Home-killed lamb	2	99.3	92.7	95.7	106.2	110.3	113.2	103.0	104.9	100.6	93.9	97.7	98.5	96.9
Pork	4	101.1	100.1	100.9	99.9	99.6	101.8	100.9	100.5	101.3	101.6	104.3	104.7	105.0
Bacon	4	102.2	102.2	102.3	101.9	102.4	103.0	103.1	103.5	104.1	104.7	105.2	105.4	105.8
Poultry	7	101.5	100.2	101.9	100.7	101.4	101.5	101.8	101.6	102.1	101.2	102.7	102.0	102.2
Other meat	10	100.7	100.5	100.0	99.8	99.9	99.9	99.7	99.6	100.1	99.9	100.6	101.0	101.2
Fish	5	105.1	106.1	105.1	104.9	103.8	104.3	103.7	103.3	104.2	103.0	103.1	104.1	105.9
of which Fresh fish	2	108.1	107.9	106.0	105.7	103.5	105.0	105.9	106.2	107.7	104.6	103.5	105.2	107.8
Butter	2	101.5	101.7	102.5	103.1	103.2	103.4	104.5	105.4	107.6	108.5	110.0	110.3	110.8
Oils & fats	3	99.5	100.8	101.0	101.3	101.5	101.0	101.5	102.8	104.3	105.2	106.5	107.2	107.2
Cheese	5	104.2	104.7	106.0	106.6	106.8	106.9	107.2	107.0	108.4	109.2	109.8	109.1	110.3
Eggs	3	110.7	110.6	108.7	110.5	108.0	104.2	102.4	101.7	101.5	102.8	104.9	106.4	103.7
Milk, fresh	13	104.2	104.1	104.1	104.4	104.5	104.6	104.6	107.8	107.9	108.0	108.4	108.5	111.7
Milk products	3	105.7	105.7	106.1	107.5	107.5	107.7	108.3	110.1	109.5	110.8	111.4	112.9	112.5
Tea	3	100.6	100.8	100.6	101.0	100.7	103.9	107.1	106.7	107.8	108.3	108.3	108.5	108.9
Coffee & other hot drinks	3	91.9	92.3	92.4	92.5	92.4	93.0	93.0	93.5	93.1	93.0	92.9	92.7	92.9
Soft drinks	8	107.7	109.3	110.3	112.2	114.8	115.4	115.8	117.2	118.2	118.5	119.2	119.9	120.7
Sugar & preserves	3	107.6	107.6	109.3	109.8	110.1	110.1	110.7	110.5	110.7	111.5	112.0	112.1	114.2
Sweets & chocolates	13	100.7	100.6	100.8	101.1	101.1	101.0	101.0	101.2	101.5	101.4	101.4	101.5	101.8
Potatoes	7	99.8	100.9	99.6	99.6	100.1	95.8	90.2	94.4	95.5	95.4	97.6	99.5	99.7
of which Unproc'd potatoes	4	97.9	100.3	97.7	98.2	98.0	89.5	79.6	86.0	87.9	87.6	91.3	94.3	94.6
Other vegetables	12	105.0	110.2	112.9	114.2	110.5	107.5	97.2	96.5	97.5	99.9	102.6	105.8	108.3
of which Fresh vegetables	8	107.2	114.2	117.0	117.6	111.5	106.8	90.7	89.5	90.8	94.4	97.7	102.2	105.5
Fruit	8	101.3	104.1	104.0	105.3	106.1	110.5	111.5	107.5	105.1	103.2	101.5	102.8	106.1
of which Fresh fruit	6	101.2	104.3	104.4	106.2	107.8	113.1	114.3	109.2	106.1	103.9	102.1	103.9	107.6
Other foods	12	102.8	103.0	103.2	104.0	105.1	105.2	105.4	106.0	105.8	106.4	106.8	107.0	107.3
FOOD	163	102.9	103.6	103.9	104.4	104.7	104.8	104.0	104.4	104.8	104.9	105.7	106.5	107.4
Restaurant meals	25	106.5	107.5	107.8	108.6	109.1	109.8	110.0	111.1	111.9	112.6	113.2	113.3	113.9
Canteen meals	8	106.5	107.1	107.5	109.0	109.2	109.5	109.6	109.6	110.8	110.9	110.8	111.3	112.2
Take-away meals & snacks	17	106.3	106.6	107.1	108.1	108.6	109.1	109.3	109.8	110.1	110.7	111.2	111.6	112.3
CATERING	50	106.4	107.1	107.5	108.5	108.9	109.5	109.7	110.4	111.1	111.7	112.1	112.4	113.1
Beer	46	104.3	104.8	105.1	106.8	107.4	107.6	108.0	108.8	109.8	110.6	111.0	111.2	111.8
Wines & spirits	32	102.8	103.4	103.9	105.1	105.5	105.7	105.8	106.2	106.5	106.8	106.3	105.7	107.2
ALCOHOLIC DRINK	78	103.7	104.2	104.6	106.1	106.6	106.8	107.1	107.7	108.4	109.1	109.1	108.9	109.9
Cigarettes	32	101.7	101.9	101.9	103.5	104.0	103.9	103.8	104.0	104.1	104.5	105.4	105.6	105.9
Other tobacco	4	99.7	99.7	99.5	100.7	101.3	100.8	100.8	100.9	101.3	102.3	103.0	102.9	103.9
TOBACCO	36	101.4	101.6	101.6	103.2	103.7	103.6	103.4	103.6	103.7	104.2	105.1	105.2	105.6
Rent	33	105.7	105.8	105.9	111.9	112.0	112.5	112.9	112.8	113.0	114.0	114.4	114.0	114.4
Mortgage interest payments	42	96.3	96.8	97.8	101.6	98.9	99.3	99.9	118.8	121.0	134.8	137.6	139.2	144.4
Rates	43	107.7	107.7	107.7	116.8	116.8	116.8	116.8	116.8	116.8	116.8	116.8	116.8	116.8
Water charges	7	107.6	107.6	107.6	115.5	115.6	115.6	115.6	115.6	115.6	115.6	115.6	115.6	116.2
Repair/maintenance charges	9	104.1	104.3	104.4	105.5	106.3	106.6	106.9	107.3	107.8	108.5	109.1	109.3	110.7
Do-it-yourself materials	19	104.7	105.4	105.8	106.0	106.4	107.1	107.9	108.4	108.3	108.5	109.1	109.3	109.3
HOUSING	160	103.9	104.3	104.7	109.9	109.4	109.8	110.2	115.8	116.5	120.7	122.1	122.5	124.6
Coal & solid fuels	5	101.8	102.0	101.9	101.9	97.2	96.6	96.2	95.8	100.3	101.1	102.0	102.3	103.1
Electricity	26	100.0	100.0	100.0	101.7	104.4	107.1	108.6	108.6	108.6	108.6	108.6	108.6	108.6
Gas	21	95.5	95.5	95.5	96.6	98.4	100.1	101.2	101.2	101.2	101.2	101.2	101.2	101.2
Oil & other fuel	3	97.3	92.9	89.4	89.5	90.1	88.7	89.9	86.5	83.6	84.5	85.6	89.2	89.3
FUEL & LIGHT	55	98.3	98.0	97.8	99.1	100.7	102.4	103.6	103.4	103.6	103.7	103.9	104.1	104.2
Furniture	14	102.7	103.9	105.0	105.5	106.3	105.8	105.7	106.5	107.5	107.9	108.7	108.7	107.3
Furnishings	12	103.3	104.7	105.7	105.9	106.5	106.5	106.2	106.9	107.8	108.1	108.5	108.8	108.7
Electrical appliances	16	102.8	103.0	103.6	104.1	104.8	104.7	103.9	104.3	105.1	105.3	105.8	105.6	104.6
Other household equipment	10	103.6	104.1	104.4	105.3	105.8	105.9	106.3	107.3	107.7	108.0	108.3	108.5	108.5
Household consumables	14	105.6	105.9	106.2	106.7	106.9	107.6	109.9	110.6	111.3	111.7	111.6	111.8	112.2
Pet care	8	100.5	100.7	100.8	100.6	101.1	101.2	101.9	102.4	102.3	102.7	102.7	102.2	102.4
HOUSEHOLD GOODS	74	103.3	103.9	104.5	105.0	105.5	105.6	105.9	106.5	107.2	107.6	107.9	107.9	107.5
Postage	2	100.6	100.6	100.6	100.6	100.6	100.6	100.6	100.6	106.5	106.5	106.5	106.5	106.5
Telephone charges etc	16	101.2	101.2	101.2	101.2	101.2	101.2	101.2	101.2	101.2	101.2	101.2	101.2	101.2
Domestic services	7	105.8	106.1	106.7	107.3	107.6	108.3	108.7	109.3	109.8	110.6	111.1	111.5	113.2
Fees & subscriptions	16	108.4	108.9	109.1	109.7	110.2	110.5	112.5	113.0	113.3	113.8	114.9	115.1	118.3
HOUSEHOLD SERVICES	41	105.0	105.3	105.4	105.7	106.0	106.2	107.1	107.4	107.8	108.2	108.7	108.8	110.3
Men's outerwear	14	101.6	102.9	104.4	104.4	105.9	106.6	103.9	104.0	105.3	107.2	108.1	108.3	106.2
Women's outerwear	22	99.2	99.8	100.7	100.9	100.3	104.3	101.1	100.7	103.5	105.0	105.9	106.2	102.5
Children's outerwear	9	101.0	102.1	102.6	102.3	107.2	107.3	104.5	104.1	104.4	107.8	108.8	109.0	106.8
Other clothing	12	103.0	103.5	104.3	104.6	104.8	105.1	104.8	104.9	105.9	108.0	108.5	109.0	109.0
Footwear	15	101.8	102.4	103.8	104.1	104.4	104.3	103.8	104.7	105.5	108.0	108.3	108.5	107.6
CLOTHING & FOOTWEAR	72	101.1	101.9	102.9	103.1	104.8	105.3	103.3	103.3	104.8	106.9	107.6	107.9	105.9

	Weight *	Jan	Feb	Mar	Apr	May	Jun	Jul	Aug	Sep	Oct	Nov	Dec	Next Jan
							Index: January 1974 = 100								
Personal articles	11	100.6	100.9	100.9	101.0	101.2	101.3	101.5	101.8	102.1	102.5	103.0	103.2	102.9
Chemists' goods	15	105.1	105.4	105.9	106.9	107.3	107.8	108.0	108.4	108.6	108.9	109.9	110.1	111.1
Personal services	11	106.9	107.7	108.1	109.8	110.1	110.4	111.5	112.0	112.5	112.7	113.3	110.5	117.1
PERSONAL GOODS & SERVICES	37	104.3	104.7	105.1	106.0	106.3	106.6.	107.1	107.5	107.8	108.1	108.8	109.1	110.4
Purchase of motor vehicles	58	106.9	106.5	107.8	109.5	110.1	111.3	112.3	113.3	113.8	114.3	114.2	113.6	113.5
Maintenance of motor vcles	18	105.8	107.5	108.0	108.6	108.8	109.6	110.1	109.9	110.4	110.6	111.1	111.0	113.1
Petrol & oil	36	98.9	98.0	98.0	99.9	99.7	100.7	100.9	100.8	100.5	100.3	100.0	99.8	99.7
Vehicle tax & insurance	20	112.2	112.2	112.2	112.9	113.1	113.1	115.9	115.9	115.9	117.6	117.6	117.6	121.9
MOTORING EXPENDITURE	132	105.1	105.0	105.6	107.0	107.3	108.2	109.2	109.5	109.7	110.2	110.1	109.8	110.6
Rail fares	7	107.1	107.1	107.1	107.1	107.8	107.8	107.8	107.8	107.8	107.8	107.8	107.8	117.4
Bus & coach fares	7	106.7	108.2	108.2	108.3	109.5	109.7	111.3	112.4	112.5	113.4	113.7	113.7	115.3
Other travel costs	9	102.0	102.3	102.2	102.6	103.4	103.6	104.9	105.9	106.3	106.7	107.0	107.5	107.3
FARES & OTHER TRAVEL COSTS	23	105.1	105.7	105.6	105.8	106.7	106.9	107.9	108.6	108.8	109.2	109.5	109.6	112.9
Audio-visual equipment	13	95.3	95.1	94.6	95.1	95.1	94.2	93.3	93.4	92.1	92.0	91.9	91.7	90.9
Records & tapes	5	100.0	99.3	99.5	99.6	99.5	99.6	99.6	99.7	99.5	99.7	97.8	97.8	97.8
Toys, photo & sports goods	11	102.2	102.8	103.1	104.3	104.4	104.5	105.8	106.3	106.5	106.4	106.8	106.9	106.8
Books & newspapers	16	109.0	110.2	110.3	110.9	111.9	111.9	112.6	113.1	113.3	114.5	114.7	114.7	115.4
Gardening products	5	104.3	105.0	105.9	105.3	107.2	107.7	107.0	107.2	108.1	109.5	109.5	110.8	112.2
LEISURE GOODS	50	102.8	103.3	103.3	103.9	104.3	104.2	104.4	104.7	104.5	105.0	104.9	105.0	105.1
TV licences & rentals	11	99.4	99.4	99.5	103.6	103.6	103.6	103.3	103.3	103.3	103.4	103.4	103.5	103.7
Entertainment & recreation	18	106.9	107.0	107.1	111.8	112.0	112.0	112.1	112.4	115.9	115.8	117.5	117.6	118.1
LEISURE SERVICES	29	103.6	103.7	103.8	108.3	108.4	108.4	108.3	108.5	110.6	110.5	111.6	111.7	112.1

* Applied to change since January 1988

Index: January 1974 = 100

	Weight	Jan	Feb	Mar	Apr	May	Jun	Jul	Aug	Sep	Oct	Nov	Dec	Next Jan
Bread	9	111.6	112.6	113.0	113.9	113.1	114.4	115.0	113.8	114.6	115.1	115.0	117.6	118.6
Cereals	4	112.2	113.5	114.8	115.6	115.6	115.8	116.2	115.6	115.9	115.9	117.1	117.4	118.8
Biscuits & cakes	9	108.3	109.0	109.9	110.8	111.2	111.3	111.2	112.2	112.7	113.3	114.0	114.4	115.0
Beef	10	115.4	115.4	115.4	119.1	120.3	121.0	121.7	121.8	122.6	122.3	122.0	123.1	124.2
Lamb	3	99.0	95.5	98.5	108.3	116.2	113.9	106.5	101.7	101.6	101.0	105.4	109.0	110.9
of which Home-killed lamb	2	96.9	92.4	96.3	110.2	120.6	117.0	105.7	97.9	96.6	96.1	102.3	106.5	109.8
Pork	3	105.0	104.1	105.3	108.0	109.7	109.6	113.9	113.1	116.7	122.1	124.2	121.3	121.3
Bacon	4	105.8	105.6	105.6	105.8	106.7	108.8	112.8	115.4	118.7	122.7	124.4	123.3	123.3
Poultry	6	102.2	100.9	101.6	101.8	101.5	103.4	104.6	105.1	107.3	107.9	108.3	108.4	111.6
Other meat	9	101.2	101.0	101.5	102.3	103.8	104.2	106.4	107.4	109.7	110.9	112.0	113.0	112.7
Fish	5	105.9	106.6	106.1	106.4	106.1	106.5	106.8	106.6	107.1	108.2	107.9	107.1	111.1
of which Fresh fish	2	107.8	108.7	108.2	108.1	107.2	108.1	108.3	108.7	108.7	111.3	112.2	111.1	118.4
Butter	2	110.8	113.1	114.6	114.9	115.6	116.5	120.6	121.5	122.5	121.8	123.9	125.3	124.8
Oils & fats	3	107.2	107.1	106.3	107.0	106.9	107.6	108.3	108.6	108.4	108.6	109.9	110.7	111.0
Cheese	4	110.3	110.6	110.6	111.3	110.9	111.5	112.2	113.0	115.4	117.1	117.9	117.7	118.5
Eggs	2	103.7	102.0	101.0	101.0	105.0	107.3	106.3	107.1	111.4	111.0	116.2	115.0	118.7
Milk, fresh	12	111.7	112.3	112.5	112.6	112.6	112.6	112.7	112.0	112.6	119.5	119.7	119.8	120.1
Milk products	3	112.5	113.4	114.3	114.6	116.3	116.6	115.2	117.4	119.3	121.1	121.2	121.7	122.0
Tea	2	108.9	108.9	109.0	109.0	109.3	109.3	109.5	112.4	113.4	114.3	115.0	118.8	122.0
Coffee & other hot drinks	3	92.9	.92.8	92.7	95.5	96.6	97.0	98.0	98.0	97.8	97.8	97.9	97.8	97.9
Soft drinks	9	120.7	121.5	122.5	122.6	122.7	122.8	122.9	123.5	124.0	124.2	123.8	123.6	124.0
Sugar & preserves	2	114.2	114.8	115.0	116.1	116.1	116.3	117.6	118.0	118.8	119.8	120.9	121.3	121.7
Sweets & chocolates	12	101.8	102.1	102.5	103.4	104.0	104.4	105.2	105.6	105.3	105.4	105.6	105.4	105.7
Potatoes	6	99.7	101.1	102.0	105.3	110.2	111.3	100.5	111.6	113.3	110.1	113.3	115.0	118.6
of which Unproc'd potatoes	3	94.6	97.3	99.1	104.9	114.0	115.8	93.6	113.0	115.2	108.9	114.0	117.1	123.1
Other vegetables	11	108.3	110.7	112.6	114.2	110.4	107.5	100.6	100.7	102.3	106.7	111.0	117.5	119.9
of which Fresh vegetables	7	105.5	108.6	111.1	113.3	107.3	102.5	91.4	91.1	93.7	99.8	106.3	116.2	119.5
Fruit	9	106.1	104.8	104.9	106.5	109.9	111.5	109.0	104.0	100.2	99.3	101.5	105.1	111.1
of which Fresh fruit	7	107.6	105.5	105.9	107.5	111.7	113.7	110.1	103.4	98.5	97.8	100.9	105.5	112.8
Fresh fruit	7	107.6	105.5	105.9	107.5	111.7	113.7	110.1	103.4	98.5	97.8	100.9	105.5	112.8
Other foods	12	107.3	107.5	108.0	109.3	109.7	110.9	111.5	112.5	112.8	112.6	113.0	112.5	114.7
FOOD	154	107.4	107.7	108.3	109.6	110.3	110.7	110.1	110.6	111.3	112.4	113.5	114.5	116.0
Restaurant meals	26	113.9	114.3	115.1	115.9	116.6	117.2	117.8	118.3	119.1	120.1	120.8	121.3	122.2
Canteen meals	7	112.2	112.7	113.3	114.2	114.5	115.0	115.8	116.2	117.0	118.1	118.3	118.8	120.6
Take-away meals & snacks	16	112.3	112.7	113.0	113.9	114.6	115.1	115.8	116.5	116.9	117.4	118.1	118.9	120.0
CATERING	49	113.1	113.5	114.1	115.0	115.6	116.2	116.8	117.4	118.0	118.9	119.5	120.1	121.2
Beer	50	111.8	112.3	112.8	113.1	113.5	113.8	114.6	116.1	116.9	117.9	118.0	118.4	119.0
Wines & spirits	33	107.2	107.9	108.3	109.1	109.7	110.0	110.4	110.9	111.5	112.0	111.7	111.3	112.5
ALCOHOLIC DRINK	83	109.9	110.5	110.9	111.5	111.9	112.2	112.9	114.0	114.7	115.5	115.4	115.5	116.3
Cigarettes	32	105.9	106.0	106.0	106.1	106.1	106.2	106.1	106.0	106.7	107.9	108.3	108.3	108.4
Other tobacco	4	103.9	104.2	104.2	104.0	103.8	103.8	103.8	103.9	104.6	106.9	107.2	107.2	107.8
TOBACCO	36	105.6	105.7	105.8	105.8	105.8	105.9	105.8	105.8	106.4	107.7	108.1	108.2	108.3
Rent	32	114.4	114.5	114.6	122.5	122.7	123.2	123.3	123.4	123.7	124.8	124.9	125.2	125.9
Mortgage interest payments	60	144.4	152.0	154.2	156.7	159.0	161.1	163.4	165.9	168.2	171.7	185.7	188.4	190.6
Rates & community charge	42	116.8	116.8	116.8	128.0	128.0	128.0	128.0	128.0	128.0	128.0	128.0	128.0	128.0
Water charges	7	116.2	116.2	116.2	133.6	131.4	131.4	131.4	130.1	130.3	130.3	130.3	130.3	131.5
Repair/maintenance charges	9	110.7	110.9	111.2	113.1	113.7	114.0	114.7	115.1	115.5	116.3	116.7	117.4	120.1
Do-it-yourself materials	17	109.3	109.8	110.4	111.5	111.8	112.5	113.4	113.8	114.3	115.0	115.4	115.7	116.2
HOUSING	175	124.6	127.0	127.7	134.0	134.7	135.5	136.6	137.4	138.2	139.6	143.9	144.8	145.8
Coal & solid fuels	4	103.1	103.1	103.4.	102.5	97.9	96.8	96.4	101.0	101.6	102.4	104.2	104.8	105.4
Electricity	26	108.6	108.6	108.6	110.0	112.3	114.4	115.7	115.7	115.7	115.7	115.7	115.7	115.7
Gas	22	101.2	101.2	101.2	101.8	102.9	103.9	104.6	104.6	104.6	104.6	104.6	104.6	104.6
Oil & other fuel	2	89.3	88.7	91.5	96.3	93.7	90.1	90.9	90.0	95.1	101.9	108.0	113.4	124.5
FUEL & LIGHT	54	104.2	104.2	104.3	105.4	106.4	107.6	108.4	108.7	109.0	109.4	109.7	110.0	110.6
Furniture	13	107.3	108.1	109.5	109.9	110.4	110.5	110.0	110.7	111.1	111.9	112.2	112.9	112.7
Furnishings	12	108.7	109.8	110.7	111.6	111.7	112.0.	110.9	112.0	112.4	113.3	113.7	114.1	112.6
Electrical appliances	14	104.6.	104.6	104.7	105.0	105.0	104.6	104.3	104.6	105.1	105.2	105.6	105.3	104.3
Other household equipment	10	108.5	109.0	109.6	110.2	111.0	111.8	112.3	112.5	113.1	114.1	114.2	114.9	114.9
Household consumables	14	112.2	113.3	113.9	114.8	115.8	116.1	116.7	117.0	117.2	118.0	118.8	119.2	119.9
Pet care	8	102.4	103.8	103.7	104.1	104.1	104.3	105.1	105.4	105.5	105.5	105.1	105.6	106.9
HOUSEHOLD GOODS	71	107.5	108.3	108.9	109.5	109.9	110.1	110.0	110.5	110.9	111.5	111.8	112.2	112.0
Postage	2	106.5	106.5	106.5	106.5	106.5	106.5	106.5	106.5	106.5	112.6	112.6	112.6	112.6
Telephone charges etc	15	101.2	101.2	101.2	101.2	101.2	101.2	101.2	101.2	103.5	104.4	105.4	105.5	105.7
Domestic services	8	113.2	113.7	114.6	115.3	116.1	116.9	118.0	118.1	118.6	119.2	120.0	120.3	122.3
Fees & subscriptions	16	118.3	119.4	119.4	121.0	120.9	120.4	121.2	121.0	120.9	121.4	122.5	122.4	124.4
HOUSEHOLD SERVICES	41	110.3	110.8	110.9	111.7	111.8	111.8	112.2	112.2	113.2	114.2	115.1	115.2	116.3
Men's outerwear	14	106.2	107.5	108.5	109.9	110.6	110.1	109.2	109.5	110.4	111.5	113.0	113.2	110.7
Women's outerwear	22	102.5	103.8	104.4	107.5	108.0	108.3	104.6	104.3	109.2	110.1	110.6	110.7	106.7
Children's outerwear	9	106.8	108.5	109.1	114.0	115.6	116.1	112.7	112.6	112.6	114.5	114.9	114.6	111.7
Other clothing	13	109.0	110.1	110.6	111.4	111.6	111.7	110.8	111.4	113.0	114.9	115.4	115.8	115.0
Footwear	15	107.6	108.7	108.8	109.3	109.8	110.2	109.8	109.9	110.1	111.4	113.0	113.5	113.0
CLOTHING & FOOTWEAR	73	105.9	107.2	107.7	109.8	110.5	110.6	108.6	108.7	111.0	112.3	113.0	113.2	110.8

	Weight *	Jan	Feb	Mar	Apr	May	Jun	Jul	Aug	Sep	Oct	Nov	Dec	Next Jan
						Index: January 1974 = 100								
Personal articles	11	102.9	103.4	103.3	103.8	104.3	104.5	104.4	104.7	105.0	105.4	105.7	105.9	105.9
Chemists' goods	15	111.1	111.6	112.2	114.1	114.7	115.0	115.8	116.2	116.5	117.4	117.9	119.0	120.2
Personal services	11	117.1	117.4	117.8	121.6	122.0	122.5	124.8	125.2	125.5	126.3	126.7	127.0	130.0
PERSONAL GOODS & SERVICES	37	110.4	110.9	111.1	113.1	113.7	114.0	114.9	115.3	115.6	116.3	116.7	117.3	118.6
Purchase of motor vehicles	55	113.5	113.1	114.2	115.1	115.3	115.9	116.1	116.0	116.4	116.3	115.6	113.8	113.1
Maintenance of motor vcles	19	113.1	113.3	113.8	114.4	115.1	115.4	117.0	117.5	118.0	118.3	118.3	118.4	121.9
Petrol & oil	34	99.7	101.6	102.6	108.7	111.2	111.5	110.0	106.9	107.6	108.3	107.9	107.0	109.0
Vehicle tax & insurance	20	121.9	121.9	121.9	122.9	122.9	122.9	122.9	123.5	123.5	124.5	124.5	124.5	125.9
MOTORING EXPENDITURE	128	110.6	111.0	111.8	114.2	115.2	115.5	115.4	114.6	115.1	115.4	115.0	114.0	115.0
Rail fares	7	117.4	117.4	117.4	117.4	117.4	117.4	117.4	117.4	117.4	117.4	117.4	117.4	117.4
Bus & coach fares	7	115.3	115.9	116.0	116.2	119.6	120.3	120.6	120.8	120.8	121.4	122.4	122.4	123.2
Other travel costs	9	107.3	107.5	107.7	107.9	108.4	110.1	110.7	111.0	111.5	111.9	112.0	112.3	112.7
FARES & OTHER TRAVEL COSTS	23	112.9	113.2	113.3	113.4	114.6	115.6	115.9	116.1	116.3	116.6	117.0	117.1	117.5
Audio-visual equipment	11	90.9	90.9	90.8	90.7	90.5	90.4	90.3	90.2	90.3	90.3	90.8	90.4	89.5
Records & tapes	5	97.8	98.0	97.9	98.2	98.2	98.3	98.3	98.5	98.6	98.7	98.7	98.7	98.9
Toys, photo & sports goods	10	106.8	107.0	107.6	107.8	107.9	108.2	108.5	108.0	108.3	109.4	110.6	111.0	111.2
Books & newspapers	16	115.4	116.1	116.4	117.0	120.7	121.1	121.6	121.6	122.0	124.1	125.9	126.3	126.7
Gardening products	5	112.2	112.9	113.8	114.7	114.9	115.3	115.8	116.0	116.2	116.9	118.5	119.4	120.4
LEISURE GOODS	47	105.1	105.5	105.7	106.0	107.2	107.4	107.6	107.6	107.8	108.7	109.9	110.0	110.1
TV licences & rentals	10	103.7	103.7	103.7	104.1	104.2	104.2	105.4	105.5	105.5	105.3	105.4	105.3	105.9
Entertainment & recreation	19	118.1	118.3	118.4	120.2	121.3	121.6	122.1	122.7	125.3	125.7	127.3	127.3	128.8
LEISURE SERVICES	29	112.1	112.2	112.3	113.5	114.3	114.5	115.2	115.6	117.2	117.4	118.4	118.4	119.6

* Applied to change since January 1989

	Weight *	Jan	Feb	Mar	Apr	May	Jun	Jul	Aug	Sep	Oct	Nov	Dec	Next Jan
						Index: January 1974 = 100								
Bread	8	118.6	119.3	119.3	120.1	119.8	120.7	120.7	121.1	121.1	122.6	124.1	124.6	130.1
Cereals	4	118.8	120.6	121.9	122.9	123.6	123.8	124.2	125.0	125.3	125.3	125.8	126.8	127.7
Biscuits & cakes	9	115.0	115.9	116.4	117.7	119.9	119.7	120.1	121.3	122.3	123.2	124.7	125.7	125.7
Beef	9	124.2	124.1	124.4	125.1	125.6	124.0	124.3	123.3	123.9	123.3	123.6	124.1	124.7
Lamb	3	110.9	111.2	113.9	118.6	119.4	118.3	112.7	108.6	106.8	105.7	108.9	110.2	111.5
of which Home-killed lamb	2	109.8	110.4	113.3	121.6	122.7	119.5	111.7	106.0	104.0	102.3	106.3	107.5	110.7
Pork	4	121.3	121.5	120.8	121.8	125.4	129.5	127.9	126.0	126.0	123.0	123.1	121.8	118.3
Bacon	4	123.3	122.7	122.0	123.8	127.0	128.3	129.6	128.9	130.0	129.1	128.7	127.8	127.5
Poultry	7	111.6	112.2	112.6	112.9	114.8	116.7	117.7	118.8	119.6	119.2	118.5	116.7	117.1
Other meat	10	112.7	114.3	114.8	114.9	116.4	118.0	120.1	120.9	120.9	121.2	121.3	122.1	122.5
Fish	5	111.1	113.3	113.4	115.0	116.3	117.7	119.9	120.1	120.7	123.2	123.5	123.2	124.5
of which Fresh fish	2	118.4	122.7	124.2	126.7	126.1	126.9	131.4	132.0	131.7	138.0	137.5	138.7	139.9
Butter	2	124.8	123.1	121.8	120.3	119.4	121.7	122.5	122.8	120.7	121.2	120.7	120.2	120.0
Oils & fats	2	111.0	112.1	113.6	114.9	116.0	116.6	117.0	118.7	119.2	118.3	120.0	120.4	121.3
Cheese	5	118.5	118.6	118.3	116.4	120.0	120.2	120.4	120.7	120.9	118.6	119.4	119.1	120.1
Eggs	2	118.7	118.8	116.3	117.6	117.7	116.9	116.1	117.5	110.9	114.0	110.6	114.6	112.8
Milk, fresh	11	120.1	120.1	120.2	121.0	121.4	121.6	121.6	123.3	125.1	127.5	128.3	128.8	129.9
Milk products	3	122.0	122.8	123.5	123.7	124.3	125.8	125.3	128.1	128.5	130.0	130.0	132.6	133.9
Tea	2	122.0	123.5	124.6	125.5	130.1	132.2	134.0	134.9	134.8	136.7	139.9	140.5	141.7
Coffee & other hot drinks	3	97.9	91.8	90.9	90.5	90.7	90.5	90.1	90.3	90.3	89.5	89.9	89.8	89.8
Soft drinks	11	124.0	127.4	131.1	133.6	136.6	137.6	137.8	138.6	138.7	138.4	137.7	136.9	134.6
Sugar & preserves	2	121.7	121.9	122.5	123.2	123.6	124.5	128.4	130.1	131.2	131.8	132.3	132.7	134.5
Sweets & chocolates	13	105.7	106.4	106.8	106.9	108.3	108.8	109.2	109.2	109.4	109.5	109.7	109.8	110.7
Potatoes	6	118.6	119.8	119.6	121.7	126.5	117.9	104.2	113.1	114.0	112.1	114.2	117.2	118.2
of which Unproc'd potatoes	3	123.1	125.3	124.1	127.6	135.9	116.4	84.5	101.1	103.6	99.8	103.4	110.1	112.8
Other vegetables	12	119.9	122.2	123.9	127.0	122.3	111.4	104.5	110.2	112.1	114.0	118.5	123.1	124.4
of which Fresh vegetables	8	119.5	122.8	124.6	129.1	121.5	105.2	95.2	103.2	105.9	108.6	114.5	121.3	123.1
Fruit	9	111.1	113.6	114.5	116.9	121.6	128.4	121.7	121.4	118.6	116.1	116.9	120.0	122.7
of which Fresh fruit	7	112.8	114.9	115.6	118.6	124.2	132.6	123.3	122.8	119.1	116.8	117.7	121.6	124.6
Other foods	12	114.7	115.6	116.9	117.7	119.0	119.9	119.5	121.2	121.8	122.1	122.9	123.2	124.0
FOOD	158	116.0	117.0	117.7	118.8	120.1	120.0	118.8	120.0	120.3	120.4	121.3	122.1	122.9
Restaurant meals	24	122.2	122.8	123.2	124.8	125.9	126.9	127.9	128.5	129.7	130.4	131.2	131.8	132.3
Canteen meals	7	120.6	121.3	122.1	123.5	124.7	125.4	126.0	126.5	128.8	130.3	130.9	131.6	132.9
Take-away meals & snacks	16	120.0	120.6	121.4	122.8	123.7	124.8	126.4	127.2	128.5	129.4	130.2	130.7	131.8
CATERING	47	121.2	121.8	122.4	123.9	125.0	125.9	127.1	127.7	129.1	130.0	130.8	131.4	132.2
Beer	47	119.0	119.6	120.2	123.8	125.9	126.2	127.8	129.4	130.2	131.1	131.5	132.2	133.0
Wines & spirits	30	112.5	113.4	114.3	118.2	120.8	121.6	123.0	122.9	123.4	123.9	123.6	123.4	124.9
ALCOHOLIC DRINK	77	116.3	117.1	117.8	121.5	123.8	124.3	125.8	126.7	127.4	128.2	128.3	128.6	129.7
Cigarettes	30	108.4	108.5	108.5	112.5	115.1	115.3	115.3	115.4	115.5	116.7	117.2	117.9	118.4
Other tobacco	4	107.8	108.2	108.4	111.4	112.9	112.8	113.1	113.1	113.3	115.2	115.4	116.1	116.9
TOBACCO	34	108.3	108.4	108.4	112.4	114.8	115.0	115.0	115.1	115.2	116.5	116.9	117.6	118.2
Rent	32	125.9	126.0	126.2	136.7	136.9	137.4	139.6	140.0	140.2	141.1	141.3	141.9	142.3
Mortgage interest payments	75	190.6	192.9	205.9	208.3	211.5	213.7	215.9	218.5	220.7	223.0	215.4	214.2	216.2
Rates & community charge	40	128.0	128.0	128.0	171.6	171.7	171.6	171.8	171.8	171.8	171.8	171.8	171.8	171.8
Water charges	7	131.5	131.5	131.5	148.4	148.4	148.4	148.4	148.4	148.4	148.4	148.3	148.3	148.3
Repair/maintenance charges	8	120.1	120.3	120.8	121.8	122.7	123.3	123.7	124.4	124.9	126.3	126.7	127.7	129.5
Do-it-yourself materials	15	116.2	117.5	118.5	119.3	120.9	121.7	122.7	124.2	125.3	125.9	126.3	126.7	128.9
HOUSING	185	145.8	146.7	151.0	165.4	166.7	167.6	169.0	170.1	171.0	172.0	169.7	169.6	170.6
Coal & solid fuels	4	105.4	105.5	105.5	105.5	100.2	99.9	99.6	103.7	106.2	107.4	110.9	111.6	112.5
Electricity	24	115.7	115.7	115.7	116.9	121.1	124.3	126.2	126.2	126.2	126.2	126.2	126.2	126.2
Gas	19	104.6	104.6	106.1	108.5	111.5	112.4	112.4	112.4	112.4	112.4	112.9	114.0	115.3
Oil & other fuel	3	124.5	111.7	104.7	105.6	104.3	100.7	98.0	128.7	140.3	184.0	154.6	140.5	148.8
FUEL & LIGHT	50	110.6	109.9	110.1	111.7	114.3	116.0	116.7	118.6	119.5	121.9	120.8	120.5	121.6
Furniture	14	112.7	113.4	115.5	115.6	116.3	116.7	115.3	117.3	118.7	119.2	120.0	120.5	117.3
Furnishings	11	112.6	113.9	115.2	115.5	116.6	117.1	115.2	116.4	118.3	117.9	119.1	119.7	115.9
Electrical appliances	13	104.3	104.6	105.1	105.7	106.2	106.1	105.0	105.2	106.2	107.1	107.4	107.9	104.7
Other household equipment	9	114.9	116.1	116.9	118.3	119.0	119.1	119.7	120.4	120.6	121.3	121.7	122.7	120.7
Household consumables	16	119.9	120.8	121.9	122.7	123.3	124.4	124.4	124.6	125.7	126.6	127.8	128.2	129.4
Pet care	8	106.9	107.9	108.1	108.9	108.8	108.6	108.9	110.2	110.4	110.5	111.0	111.3	111.6
HOUSEHOLD GOODS	71	112.0	112.8	113.9	114.5	115.1	115.5	114.7	115.7	116.7	117.2	118.0	118.5	116.7
Postage	2	112.6	112.6	112.6	112.6	112.6	112.6	112.6	112.6	112.6	125.2	125.2	125.2	125.2
Telephone charges etc	15	105.7	105.8	105.8	105.8	106.1	106.2	106.2	106.2	111.5	112.6	113.7	113.9	114.0
Domestic services	8	122.3	123.1	124.1	125.5	127.0	127.6	128.8	130.0	131.1	132.3	133.8	134.4	136.3
Fees & subscriptions	15	124.4	124.7	124.7	124.5	125.7	126.7	128.7	128.4	128.0	128.4	128.5	128.1	131.2
HOUSEHOLD SERVICES	40	116.3	116.7	116.8	117.1	117.9	118.4	119.3	119.5	121.7	123.2	124.0	124.0	125.5
Men's outerwear	14	110.7	112.7	114.3	115.0	116.7	116.3	113.0	113.8	115.9	117.6	118.4	118.0	114.6
Women's outerwear	22	106.7	108.4	108.6	111.7	111.4	110.9	106.5	107.9	112.6	113.6	114.3	114.2	106.7
Children's outerwear	8	111.7	113.0	114.3	116.6	117.6	117.0	114.5	116.3	118.0	118.7	119.7	119.5	114.7
Other clothing	11	115.0	116.3	117.7	118.3	118.8	119.0	117.9	118.7	120.2	121.2	123.3	123.5	121.6
Footwear	14	113.0	114.3	114.9	115.7	116.5	116.9	115.8	117.4	118.4	119.8	120.7	121.1	119.5
CLOTHING & FOOTWEAR	69	110.8	112.4	113.3	115.0	115.6	115.3	112.5	113.8	116.4	117.6	118.6	118.6	114.2

	Weight *	Jan	Feb	Mar	Apr	May	Jun	Jul	Aug	Sep	Oct	Nov	Dec	Next Jan
							Index: January 1974 = 100							
Personal articles	12	105.9	106.4	106.6	106.9	107.2	107.5	107.0	108.3	109.0	109.4	109.3	109.0	108.5
Chemists' goods	17	120.2	121.4	122.8	124.1	124.7	124.9	125.6	126.5	128.0	128.9	129.9	130.3	130.6
Personal services	10	130.0	130.5	130.8	131.6	132.8	133.2	136.5	137.4	138.0	138.5	130.9	100.3	143.0
PERSONAL GOODS & SERVICES	39	118.6	119.4	120.2	121.1	121.7	122.0	122.8	123.9	124.9	125.6	126.1	126.2	127.2
Purchase of motor vehicles	58	113.1	113.7	114.8	115.9	116.8	117.9	119.0	119.9	119.9	119.9	119.3	118.0	116.7
Maintenance of motor vcles	20	121.9	123.0	123.7	125.1	126.8	127.8	129.1	130.0	130.8	131.2	132.4	132.7	135.0
Petrol & oil	33	109.0	108.8	108.7	116.5	116.3	115.7	114.8	123.5	133.7	136.4	128.8	121.8	120.1
Vehicle tax & insurance	20	125.9	125.9	125.9	126.3	126.3	126.3	128.9	128.9	128.9	131.6	131.6	131.6	135.8
MOTORING EXPENDITURE	131	115.0	115.4	116.0	118.8	119.4	119.9	120.7	123.5	126.3	127.5	125.4	123.0	122.8
Rail fares	6	117.4	128.3	128.3	128.3	128.2	128.2	128.2	128.2	128.2	129.7	129.7	129.7	140.3
Bus & coach fares	7	123.2	124.5	124.6	124.6	125.8	125.9	126.3	126.3	126.5	127.8	127.6	127.9	132.6
Other travel costs	8	112.7	113.5	113.9	114.7	115.3	118.8	119.3	120.9	121.2	121.6	122.0	122.0	122.1
FARES & OTHER TRAVEL COSTS	21	117.5	121.4	121.5	121.8	122.4	123.8	124.2	124.8	125.0	126.0	126.1	126.2	130.8
Audio-visual equipment	11	89.5	89.7	90.0	90.0	89.9	89.5	88.8	89.0	89.2	89.6	89.6	89.3	86.9
Records & tapes	6	98.9	99.2	99.4	99.6	100.0	100.1	100.4	100.5	101.0	101.6	102.4	103.1	104.1
Toys, photo & sports goods	10	111.2	112.0	112.5	113.2	113.8	114.1	113.8	114.5	115.0	115.2	115.3	115.5	114.9
Books & newspapers	15	126.7	126.9	127.4	128.4	130.3	130.4	130.6	131.0	131.7	135.6	137.4	137.5	138.4
Gardening products	6	120.4	121.4	122.6	123.0	123.2	123.8	123.9	124.3	124.1	124.7	125.4	126.1	127.8
LEISURE GOODS	48	110.1	110.5	111.0	111.5	112.2	112.3	112.1	112.5	112.9	114.2	114.9	115.1	114.9
TV licences & rentals	9	105.9	105.9	105.9	110.1	110.1	110.2	109.9	109.9	110.0	110.5	110.5	110.7	111.3
Entertainment & recreation	21	128.8	129.2	129.4	131.5	132.5	133.6	134.1	134.7	139.1	140.1	141.2	141.7	143.2
LEISURE SERVICES	30	119.6	119.9	120.0	122.8	123.4	124.1	124.4	124.8	127.7	128.4	129.2	129.6	130.7

* Applied to change since January 1990

78 PENSIONER PRICE INDICES *

(excluding housing costs)

	1-person households					2-person households			
	Q1	Q2	Q3	Q4		Q1	Q2	Q3	Q4
Indices: January 1962 = 100									
1962	100.2	102.1	101.2	101.9		100.2	102.1	101.2	101.7
1963	104.4	104.1	102.7	104.5		104.0	103.8	102.6	104.3
1964	105.4	106.6	107.2	108.7		105.3	106.8	107.6	109.0
1965	110.4	110.7	111.6	113.4		110.5	111.4	112.3	113.8
1966	114.3	116.4	116.4	117.9		114.6	116.6	116.7	118.0
1967	118.8	119.2	117.6	120.5		118.9	119.4	118.0	120.3
1968	122.9	124.0	124.3	126.8		122.7	124.3	124.6	126.7
1969	129.4	130.8	130.6	133.6		129.6	131.3	131.4	133.8
1970	136.9	139.3	140.3	144.1		137.0	139.4	140.6	144.0
1971	148.5	153.4	156.5	159.3		148.4	153.4	156.2	158.6
1972	162.5	164.4	167.0	171.0		161.8	163.7	166.7	170.3
1973	175.3	180.8	182.5	190.3		175.2	181.1	183.0	190.6
1974	199.4					199.5			
Indices: January 1974 = 100									
1974	101.1	105.2	108.6	114.2		101.1	105.8	108.7	114.1
1975	121.3	134.3	139.2	145.0		121.0	134.0	139.1	144.4
1976	152.3	158.3	161.4	171.3		151.5	157.3	160.5	170.2
1977	179.0	186.9	191.1	194.2		178.9	186.3	189.4	192.3
1978	197.5	202.5	205.1	207.1		195.8	200.9	203.6	205.9
1979	214.9	220.6	231.9	239.8		213.4	219.3	231.1	238.5
1980	250.7	262.1	268.9	275.0		248.9	260.5	266.4	271.8
1981	283.2	292.1	297.2	304.5		280.3	290.3	295.6	303.0
1982	314.2	322.4	323.0	327.4		311.8	319.4	319.8	324.1
1983	331.1	334.3	337.0	342.3		327.5	331.5	334.4	339.7
1984	346.7	353.6	353.8	357.5		343.8	351.4	351.3	355.1
1985	363.2	371.4	371.3	374.5		360.7	369.0	368.7	371.8
1986	378.4	382.8	382.6	384.3		375.4	379.6	379.9	382.0
1987 Jan	386.5					384.2			
Indices: January 1987 = 100									
1987	100.3	101.2	100.9	102.0		100.3	101.3	101.1	102.3
1988	102.8	104.6	105.3	106.6		103.1	104.8	105.5	106.8
1989	108.0	110.0	111.0	113.2		108.2	110.4	111.3	113.4
1990	115.3	118.1	119.9	122.4		115.4	118.3	120.2	122.6

* For the purposes of these indices pensioner households are defined as those where the head of household is aged 65+ if male
or 60+ if female and at least three-quarters of the total income of the household is derived from national insurance pensions and related benefits.

79 COMPONENTS OF THE INDEX OF MORTGAGE INTEREST PAYMENTS

	Jan	Feb	Mar	Apr	May	Jun	Jul	Aug	Sep	Oct	Nov	Dec
Indices of average outstanding mortgage debt: January 1975 = 100												
1975	100.0	101.1	102.1	103.2	104.2	105.3	106.4	107.4	108.6	109.7	110.7	111.8
1976	112.9	114.0	115.0	121.5	117.2	118.3	119.4	120.7	121.7	122.9	124.1	125.4
1977	126.5	127.0	128.8	120.9	131.0	132.1	133.3	134.5	135.8	136.9	137.9	139.1
1978	140.5	141.9	143.1	144.1	145.5	146.7	148.4	149.8	151.4	153.0	154.6	156.2
1979	157.8	159.5	161.5	163.3	165.1	166.9	168.9	171.3	173.6	175.8	178.1	180.4
1980	182.8	185.2	187.4	190.1	192.6	195.1	197.9	200.5	203.1	205.9	208.7	211.2
1981	213.7	216.3	219.0	221.6	224.1	226.7	229.1	231.7	234.4	236.9	239.3	241.8
1982	244.3	246.7	249.1	251.2	253.0	255.3	257.4	260.1	262.3	264.6	266.9	269.3
1983	271.7	273.8	276.2	278.5	280.8	283.1	285.6	287.7	290.5	292.9	295.9	298.6
1984	301.2	303.0	305.4	308.2	310.4	313.2	315.9	318.5	321.2	324.3	326.9	305.4
1985	306.2	334.5	338.6	341.3	343.9	346.3	349.1	352.3	354.9	357.8	360.7	363.5
1986	366.3	369.5	372.4	375.6	378.8	382.2	385.4	388.9	392.1	395.4	399.4	402.9
1987	406.8											
Indices of average outstanding mortgage debt: January 1987 = 100												
1987	100.0	100.9	101.6	102.8	103.5	104.4	105.5	106.5	107.4	108.6	109.6	110.5
1988	111.8	113.0	114.1	115.5	116.7	118.1	119.3	120.7	122.0	123.4	125.7	127.1
1989	129.2	130.9	132.5	134.4	136.1	137.6	139.4	141.2	143.0	144.7	146.4	148.2
1990	149.8	151.5	153.1	154.6	156.2	157.7	159.2	160.9	162.3	163.8	165.2	166.5
1991	168.0											
Interest rates net of tax relief at standard rate on whole of debt (% pa)												
1975	7.4	7.4	7.4	7.2	7.2	7.2	7.2	7.2	7.2	7.2	7.2	7.2
1976	7.2	7.2	7.2	6.8	6.8	6.8	6.8	6.8	6.8	6.8	6.8	8.0
1977	8.0	8.0	8.0	8.0	7.5	7.3	7.0	7.0	7.0	6.4	6.3	6.3
1978	6.3	5.8	5.7	5.7	5.7	5.7	5.9	6.5	6.5	6.5	6.5	7.1
1979	7.8	7.8	7.9	7.9	7.9	8.3	8.3	8.3	8.3	8.3	8.3	8.3
1980	10.2	10.6	10.6	10.5	10.5	10.5	10.5	10.5	10.5	10.5	10.5	10.5
1981	10.1	9.8	9.8	9.3	9.1	9.1	9.1	9.1	9.1	9.1	10.0	10.4
1982	10.4	10.5	10.5	9.6	9.5	9.5	9.5	9.5	8.5	8.4	8.4	7.1
1983	7.0	7.0	7.0	7.0	7.0	7.0	7.7	7.9	7.9	7.9	7.9	7.9
1984	7.9	7.9	7.9	7.3	7.2	7.2	7.2	8.7	8.9	9.0	9.0	9.0
1985	9.0	9.0	9.1	9.7	9.8	9.8	9.8	9.7	9.0	8.9	8.9	8.9
1986	8.9	8.9	8.9	8.6	8.5	7.8	7.8	7.8	7.8	7.8	8.7	8.7
1987	8.7	8.7	8.7	9.0	8.4	8.2	8.2	8.2	8.2	8.2	8.2	7.6
1988	7.5	7.5	7.5	7.7	7.4	7.3	7.3	8.6	8.7	9.5	9.6	9.6
1989	9.8											
Interest rates net of tax relief at standard rate on appropriate part of debt												
1989	9.9	10.3	10.3	10.4	10.4	10.4	10.4	10.4	10.4	10.5	11.3	11.3
1990	11.3	11.3	12.0	12.0	12.1	12.1	12.1	12.1	12.1	12.1	11.6	11.4
1991	11.5											

Note: The index of mortgage interest payments is the product of (a) an index based on the interest rates shown above and (b) the index of average outstanding mortgage debt.

RPI section	Categories of expenditure represented
Bread	Loaves & rolls
Cereals	Flour, proprietary breakfast foods, rice & other dry cereals
Biscuits & cakes	Chocolate-coated & other biscuits & wafers; cakes, buns, fruit pies, scones etc
Beef	Beef & veal, including minced beef & burgers but excluding sausages
Lamb	Mutton & lamb
Pork	Pork, excluding sausages
Bacon	Bacon, gammon & uncooked ham
Poultry	Cooked & uncooked, fresh & frozen poultry & game
Other meat	Liver & other offal, uncooked sausages & sausage meat, cooked & canned meat & meat products
Fish	Fresh, smoked, canned & frozen fish; shellfish
Butter	Butter
Oils & fats	Margarine, lard, lower-fat spreads, cooking fats & oils
Cheese	Cheese, including processed varieties
Eggs	Eggs, including dried eggs
Milk	Fresh, sterilised & UHT milk, including skimmed milk
Milk products	Cream; dried & canned milk; yoghurt
Tea	Packeted tea & tea bags
Coffee & other hot drinks	Coffee, cocoa & proprietary food drinks
Soft drinks	Fruit juices & squashes; carbonated drinks; cordials
Sugar & preserves	Sugar, syrup, honey, marmalade & jam
Sweets & chocolates	Sweets, chocolates & other confectionery
Potatoes	Unprocessed & canned potatoes, instant potato powder, frozen chips, crisps etc
Vegetables	Fresh, canned, dried & frozen vegetables (including tomatoes)
Fruit	Fresh, canned, dried & frozen fruit, excluding fruit juices but including nuts
Other foods	Ice cream, canned & packeted food (e.g. "ready meals", soups, jelly); sauces, flavourings & additives
Restaurant meals	All meals eaten on the caterer's premises, apart from canteens
Canteen meals	State school & workplace meals
Take-away meals & snacks	All meals eaten off the caterer's premises
Beer	Beer, stout, ale, shandy, cider etc
Wines & spirits	Spirits & liqueurs; fortified & non-fortified wines
Cigarettes	Cigarettes
Other tobacco	Pipe tobacco, cigars & snuff
Rent	Rent, excluding rates & other charges paid together with rent
Mortgage interest payments	Interest payments on a representative mortgage
House insurance & ground rent	Insurance premia on structure of houses & flats; ground rent & other housing charges
Rates	Local authority rates
Water & other charges	Charges for water supply, sewerage & related services
Repair & maintenance charges	Payments to contractors, including those for house painting & decorating
Do-it-yourself materials	Purchase of materials and tools (other than electrical tools); tool hire
Coal & solid fuels	Coal, coke & proprietary smokeless fuels

RPI section	Categories of expenditure represented
Electricity	Account & slot meter payments for electricity
Gas	Account & slot meter payments for gas
Oil & other fuel	Fuel oil for central heating, bottled gas, paraffin, firewood, candles etc
Furniture	New & second-hand furniture, including built-in units
Furnishings	Floor coverings, household textiles, mattresses, pillows, cushions etc
Electrical appliances	New & second-hand appliances, repairs & spare parts, including electrical tools but excluding audio-visual equipment & structural space heating appliances
Other household equipment	Gas cookers, china, glass, cutlery, hardware, ironmongery etc, including garden tools
Household consumables	Electrical consumables, soap & detergents, other cleaning materials, matches, toilet paper & other paper products
Pet care	Food & other expenditure on animals & pets, including veterinary services
Postal charges	Postage & poundage
Telephone charges	Telephone account & call box charges; telemessages
Domestic services	Domestic help & chimney sweeping; footwear & other repairs; laundry, launderette & dry cleaning charges
Fees & subscriptions	Subscriptions to trade unions, social clubs etc; bank charges (to be excluded from 1991); licences (except for motoring & television); house contents insurance; miscellaneous expenditure on services, other than that on second homes
Men's outerwear	Men's outerwear, including shirts & sportswear
Women's outerwear	Women's outerwear, including sportswear
Children's outerwear	Boys' & girls' outer clothing (including shirts) & infants' clothing
Other clothing	Underwear, hosiery, nightwear, headgear, gloves, scarves, handkerchiefs, ties, clothing materials & other clothing charges
Footwear	Shoes, boots, wellingtons, leggings, slippers etc
Personal articles	Handbags, wallets & other leather goods; walking sticks, umbrellas & other travel goods; jewellery & watches; lighters & other smokers' requisites; decorative fancy goods; spectacles
Chemists' goods	Medicines & surgical goods, toilet requisites & cosmetics
Personal services	Hairdressing, manicure & beauty treatment; medical, dental, optical & nursing fees
Purchase of motor vehicles	Net purchases of new & second-hamd cars, vans, motor cycles, scooters etc
Maintenance of motor vehicles	Repair & servicing of motor vehicles; spares & accessories; motoring association subscriptions
Petrol & oil	Petrol, diesel oil & other motor oils
Vehicle tax & insurance	Taxation payments (less refunds) & motor vehicle insurance
Rail fares	Rail & tube fares, including combined rail/tube/bus & other season tickets
Bus & coach fares	Fares on regular bus & coach services
Other travel costs	Taxi fares, car hire charges, contributions to cost of travel in friends' vehicles, water transport, household removals etc
Audio-visual equipment	Television sets, radios, audio & video cassette recorders, musical instruments; repairs
Records & tapes	Discs (including CDs) & cassettes
Toys, photo & sports goods	Toys, indoor games, playing cards, fireworks; expenditure on hobbies (e.g. stamp collecting); cameras & other photographic equipment; sports goods (excluding clothes)
Books & newspapers	Books & book tokens (but not library subscriptions), programmes, maps, diaries, timetables, catalogues & sheet music
Gardening products	Seeds, plants, flowers, fertilizers & other horticultural supplies (but not garden tools)
TV licences & rentals	Television licence fee; TV rentals & slot meter payments (less refunds); video recorder rentals
Entertainment & recreation	Admission to cinemas, dances, theatres, concerts, circuses, spectator sports, stately homes, exhibitions, shows, whist drives, fun fares etc; subscriptions for participant sports; educational & training expenses

81 AVERAGE WEEKLY EXPENDITURES UNDERLYING THE WEIGHTS FOR THE GENERAL RPI IN 1987, 1988 AND 1989 (AT PRICES RULING IN JANUARY OF EACH YEAR)

	Used in weights for				Notes
	1987	1988	1989	1990	
Bread	1.68	1.74	1.77	1.86	
Cereals	.77	.83	.90	1.00	
Biscuits & cakes	1.70	1.80	1.93	2.06	
Beef	1.83	1.97	2.13	2.11	
Home-killed lamb	.45	.32	.30	.48	
Imported lamb	.27	.33	.30	.23	
Pork	.71	.69	.68	.81	
Bacon	.79	.77	.78	.92	
Poultry	1.18	1.25	1.29	1.54	
Other meat	1.87	2.01	1.96	2.26	
Fresh fish	.33	.36	.38	.45	[1]
Processed fish	.72	.67	.59	.68	[2]
Butter	.43	.37	.32	.38	
Oils & fats	.47	.50	.53	.57	
Cheese	.83	.87	.93	1.04	
Eggs	.53	.56	.48	.47	
Fresh milk	2.46	2.44	2.50	2.63	[3]
Milk products	.45	.55	.57	.70	[4]
Tea	.49	.48	.49	.53	
Coffee & other hot drinks	.69	.63	.64	.68	
Soft drinks	1.28	1.53	1.89	2.55	[5]
Sugar & preserves	.48	.50	.49	.50	
Sweets & chocolates	2.36	2.47	2.59	3.10	[6]
Unprocessed potatoes	.68	.67	.62	.75	
Potato products	.64	.62	.65	.77	
Fresh vegetables	1.34	1.48	1.47	1.84	
Processed vegetables	.72	.76	.76	.85	
Fresh fruit	1.15	1.23	1.36	1.51	
Processed fruit	.33	.35	.36	.37	[7]
Other foods	2.08	2.30	2.48	2.78	
FOOD	**29.72**	**31.05**	**32.13**	**36.42**	
Restaurant meals	4.13	4.93	5.30	5.47	
Canteen meals	1.29	1.48	1.48	1.70	
Takeaway meals & snacks	2.82	3.21	3.43	3.61	
CATERING	**8.24**	**9.62**	**10.21**	**10.78**	
Beer "on" sales	7.11	7.91	9.20	9.48	[6][8]
Beer "off" sales	.94	.99	1.23	1.38	[8]
Wines & spirits "on" sales	2.37	2.70	2.95	3.11	[8]
Wines & spirits "off" sales	3.12	3.34	4.00	3.94	[8]
ALCOHOLIC DRINK	**13.54**	**14.94**	**17.37**	**17.91**	
Cigarettes	5.85	5.98	6.62	6.99	[6]
Other tobacco	.82	.84	.85	.89	[6]
TOBACCO	**6.68**	**6.82**	**7.47**	**7.88**	
Rent	5.92	6.24	6.55	7.40	[9]
Mortgage interest payments	7.81	8.13	12.47	17.32	[10]
Rates / community charge	7.41	8.24	8.61	9.23	[11]
Water charges	1.29	1.36	1.48	1.73	
House insurance & ground rent	1.13	1.27	1.67	1.79	
Repair & maintenance charges	1.38	1.67	1.91	1.95	[12]
Do-it-yourself materials	2.82	3.70	3.45	3.57	
HOUSING	**27.76**	**30.61**	**36.14**	**42.99**	
Coal & solid fuels	1.08	.92	.90	.82	
Electricity	4.97	4.97	5.34	5.56	
Gas	4.25	4.16	4.51	4.29	
Oil & other fuels	.51	.51	.42	.71	
FUEL & LIGHT	**10.81**	**10.56**	**11.17**	**11.38**	
Furniture	2.27	2.59	2.75	3.15	[12]
Furnishings	1.89	2.33	2.39	2.57	[12]
Electrical appliances	2.60	3.01	2.82	3.02	
Other household equipment	2.21	1.94	2.01	2.15	
Household consumables	2.45	2.73	3.03	3.75	
Pet care	1.40	1.53	1.69	1.73	
HOUSEHOLD GOODS	**12.82**	**14.13**	**14.68**	**16.37**	

	Used in weights for				Notes
	1987	1988	1989	1990	
Postal charges	.36	.38	.41	.42	
Telephone charges	2.76	3.00	3.12	3.49	
Domestic services	1.31	1.36	1.61	1.79	
Fees & subscriptions	3.27	3.09	3.30	3.38	
HOUSEHOLD SERVICES	**7.70**	**7.83**	**8.43**	**9.08**	
Men's outerwear	2.66	2.65	3.05	3.34	
Women's outerwear	3.84	4.26	4.58	5.01	
Children's outerwear	1.55	1.82	1.78	1.77	
Other clothing	2.07	2.26	2.66	2.58	
Footwear	2.74	2.83	3.06	3.12	
CLOTHING & FOOTWEAR	**12.86**	**13.82**	**15.12**	**15.82**	
Personal articles	1.93	2.01	2.40	2.85	
Chemists' goods	2.74	2.94	3.21	3.86	
Personal services	1.91	2.06	2.23	2.25	
PERSONAL GOODS & SERVICES	**6.58**	**7.01**	**7.84**	**8.96**	
Purchase of motor vehicles	9.21	11.02	11.33	13.30	
Maintenance of motor vehicles	3.56	3.46	3.93	4.54	
Petrol & oil	6.54	6.85	6.99	7.69	
Vehicle tax & insurance	3.25	3.74	4.13	4.63	
MOTORING EXPENDITURE	**22.57**	**25.07**	**26.38**	**30.16**	
Rail fares	1.24	1.32	1.45	1.44	
Bus & coach fares	1.22	1.29	1.40	1.51	
Other travel costs	1.44	1.73	1.85	1.90	
FARES & OTHER TRAVEL COSTS	**3.90**	**4.34**	**4.70**	**4.85**	
Audio-visual equipment	2.04	2.41	2.34	2.45	
Records & tapes	.50	.96	1.03	1.27	
Toys, photo & optical goods	1.88	2.09	2.10	2.45	
Books & newspapers	2.83	3.12	3.25	3.50	
Gardening products	.85	.93	1.11	1.40	
LEISURE GOODS	**8.10**	**9.51**	**9.73**	**11.07**	
TV licences & rentals	2.31	2.06	2.08	2.08	
Entertainment & recreation	2.99	3.39	3.92	4.91	
LEISURE SERVICES	**5.30**	**5.45**	**6.01**	**6.99**	
ALL ITEMS IN THE RPI	**176.58**	**190.76**	**207.37**	**230.66**	

Notes

[1] Excludes smoked fish
[2] Includes smoked fish
[3] Includes skimmed milk
[4] Excludes skimmed milk
[5] Includes fruit juices; adjusted for under-recording in the Family Expenditure Survey
[6] Adjusted for under-recording in the FES
[7] Excludes fruit juices
[8] Undefined drink allocated according to relative amounts of defined expenditure in the FES; all amounts adjusted for under-recording
[9] 20 per cent of FES expenditure recorded as rent has been reallocated to rates (where applicable) in respect of composite payments to landlords
[10] Imputed expenditure, not based on payments recorded in the FES
[11] Includes expenditure transferred from rent to rates
[12] Three-year average of FES figures

82 AVERAGE WEEKLY EXPENDITURE FOR CALENDAR YEARS BY TYPE OF HOUSEHOLD (£ per household per week) CLASSIFIED AS IN THE RETAIL PRICES INDEX

(derived from the Family Expenditure Survey and consistent with published FES reports)

	General index					1-person pensioner					2-person pensioner				
	1985	1986	1987	1988	1989	1985	1986	1987	1988	1989	1985	1986	1987	1988	1989
Bread	1.51	1.63	1.60	1.72	1.78	.75	.84	.82	.86	.93	1.35	1.49	1.38	1.56	1.55
Cereals	.72	.77	.82	.88	.99	.29	.31	.32	.33	.38	.54	.61	.55	.61	.74
Biscuits & cakes	1.65	1.70	1.78	1.92	2.04	.74	.85	.82	.86	.87	1.29	1.24	1.35	1.65	1.63
Beef	1.87	1.83	1.83	1.91	2.00	.64	.62	.64	.65	.69	1.71	1.59	1.52	1.62	1.73
Lamb	.72	.66	.61	.64	.68	.38	.38	.31	.35	.42	.84	.73	.68	.84	.83
Pork	.73	.67	.65	.67	.71	.24	.25	.25	.30	.26	.55	.64	.55	.66	.64
Bacon	.78	.74	.73	.76	.81	.36	.37	.35	.38	.42	.87	.83	.77	.75	.93
Poultry	1.08	1.20	1.26	1.43	1.44	.35	.49	.45	.50	.42	.78	.87	.87	.96	.87
Other meat	1.99	1.96	1.97	1.96	2.14	.86	.99	.89	.96	1.04	1.71	1.80	1.69	1.68	1.90
Fish	.90	.95	.93	.99	1.18	.49	.54	.53	.59	.66	.98	1.06	1.21	1.20	1.31
Butter	.44	.40	.33	.35	.35	.30	.29	.23	.25	.26	.47	.50	.40	.37	.39
Oils & fats	.55	.53	.49	.51	.56	.24	.25	.22	.24	.26	.55	.52	.45	.51	.53
Cheese	.83	.82	.83	.95	.97	.30	.31	.30	.31	.35	.52	.56	.56	.61	.71
Eggs	.52	.51	.48	.48	.43	.29	.31	.28	.28	.28	.52	.59	.49	.46	.42
Milk & milk products	2.70	2.78	2.81	2.91	3.23	1.23	1.30	1.36	1.38	1.56	2.15	2.30	2.17	2.43	2.53
Tea	.56	.48	.46	.46	.48	.46	.39	.39	.40	.38	.68	.73	.63	.66	.63
Coffee & hot drinks	.60	.66	.65	.64	.67	.23	.26	.29	.28	.32	.37	.43	.40	.42	.42
Sugar & preserves	.49	.47	.45	.46	.47	.34	.35	.36	.35	.40	.64	.61	.63	.59	.63
Sweets & chocolates	.91	.93	.99	1.08	1.22	.30	.34	.36	.31	.33	.56	.64	.68	.67	.75
Potatoes	1.04	1.16	1.26	1.27	1.40	.31	.36	.40	.39	.44	.62	.70	.78	.76	.83
Other vegetables	1.94	2.04	2.11	2.22	2.56	.76	.79	.79	.81	.95	1.35	1.44	1.54	1.48	1.87
Fruit & soft drinks	2.38	2.59	2.68	3.01	3.49	.91	.99	1.04	1.05	1.16	1.53	1.77	1.79	1.85	2.22
Other foods	2.00	2.00	2.33	2.75	3.13	.62	.73	.76	.85	.96	1.15	1.26	1.37	1.52	1.79
FOOD	**26.90**	**27.48**	**28.04**	**29.93**	**32.72**	**11.38**	**12.30**	**12.14**	**12.68**	**13.73**	**21.72**	**22.90**	**22.45**	**23.85**	**25.85**
Restaurant meals	3.60	4.23	4.78	5.05	5.41	.67	.77	.58	.71	.77	.68	.81	.90	1.23	1.94
Canteen meals	1.25	1.38	1.34	1.46	1.70	.01	.02	.02	.01	.01	.00	.02	.03	.05	.01
Take-aways & snacks	2.42	2.95	3.13	3.01	3.35	.50	.52	.50	.40	.44	.78	.77	.60	.58	.67
CATERING	**7.27**	**8.56**	**9.24**	**9.52**	**10.46**	**1.17**	**1.30**	**1.10**	**1.12**	**1.22**	**1.45**	**1.59**	**1.53**	**1.86**	**2.62**
Beer, wines & spirits:															
"On" sales	6.17	6.32	6.65	6.78	6.95	.48	.68	.39	.61	.60	1.41	1.49	1.69	1.51	1.55
"Off" sales	2.23	2.32	2.48	2.86	3.12	.54	.57	.67	.52	.49	1.09	1.44	1.07	1.13	1.77
ALCOHOLIC DRINK	**8.39**	**8.64**	**9.13**	**9.65**	**10.08**	**1.00**	**1.25**	**1.06**	**1.13**	**1.09**	**2.49**	**2.93**	**2.76**	**2.64**	**3.32**
Cigarettes	4.51	4.65	4.79	4.59	4.85	1.11	.96	1.32	1.13	1.29	2.38	2.55	2.46	1.85	2.44
Other tobacco	.36	.34	.34	.30	.31	.09	.08	.06	.13	.11	.30	.41	.27	.32	.35
TOBACCO	**4.86**	**4.99**	**5.12**	**4.89**	**5.16**	**1.20**	**1.04**	**1.38**	**1.26**	**1.41**	**2.68**	**2.96**	**2.74**	**2.17**	**2.79**
Gross rent, rates, water charges, etc, of households paying rent	7.44	8.30	8.68	8.49	9.74	13.36	14.71	14.84	16.94	18.16	10.92	12.28	12.22	13.42	15.37
Gross rates, water charges, ground rent, nsurance of structure, etc, of owner- occupiers and rent-free	6.18	7.16	7.79	8.90	9.70	1.87	2.88	2.45	1.86	2.60	3.04	4.24	4.85	3.77	4.33
Maintenance charges	1.48	2.28	1.67	1.33	1.58	.15	.36	.29	.16	.23	.35	1.05	.57	1.50	.31
DIY materials	3.22	3.30	3.02	3.34	3.03	.31	.20	.22	.20	.22	1.45	.96	.85	1.71	.94
HOUSING	**18.33**	**21.05**	**21.16**	**22.05**	**24.05**	**15.69**	**18.15**	**17.79**	**19.17**	**21.21**	**15.76**	**18.53**	**18.50**	**20.40**	**20.95**
Coal & solid fuels	1.02	.95	.88	.81	.70	1.00	1.08	.97	.76	.99	2.24	1.84	1.04	1.52	1.15
Electricity	4.60	4.83	4.99	5.01	5.43	3.00	3.27	3.25	3.35	3.39	3.70	4.17	4.20	4.29	4.04
Gas	3.81	4.20	4.39	4.24	4.18	2.29	2.42	2.44	2.43	2.34	2.91	3.05	3.13	2.93	3.05
Oil & other fuels	.60	.58	.48	.51	.47	.61	.55	.56	.57	.61	.78	.64	.69	.60	.41
FUEL & LIGHT	**10.01**	**10.55**	**10.74**	**10.58**	**10.78**	**6.86**	**7.32**	**7.22**	**7.12**	**7.33**	**9.63**	**9.70**	**9.06**	**9.33**	**8.64**
Furniture	1.93	3.15	2.58	3.15	5.30	.05	.16	.43	.12	.64	.09	1.09	.61	.80	1.76
Furnishings	1.81	1.98	2.45	2.46	3.62	.38	.67	.53	1.78	.97	1.11	1.31	.49	1.04	1.15
Electrical appliances	2.61	2.81	2.86	2.92	3.07	.56	.65	.52	.66	.99	1.36	.78	1.24	1.53	1.31
Other household equipment	2.13	2.00	1.93	1.97	2.15	.27	.34	.26	.24	.25	.64	.78	.74	1.61	1.61
Household consumables	2.37	2.52	2.69	3.41	3.80	1.01	1.04	1.05	1.34	1.34	1.52	1.70	1.69	2.17	2.26
Pet care	1.31	1.40	1.66	1.71	1.75	.26	.31	.33	.47	.47	.38	.59	.46	.61	.70
HOUSEHOLD GOODS	**12.16**	**13.85**	**14.17**	**15.63**	**19.69**	**2.53**	**3.17**	**3.11**	**4.62**	**4.67**	**5.10**	**6.25**	**5.23**	**7.75**	**8.79**
Postal charges	.34	.36	.38	.37	.45	.19	.25	.22	.19	.22	.30	.37	.33	.31	.41
Telephone charges	2.55	2.84	3.07	3.30	3.38	1.44	1.67	1.72	1.81	2.00	1.78	2.10	2.33	2.26	2.44
Domestic services	1.05	1.36	1.39	1.60	1.79	.58	.66	.74	.62	.91	.49	.57	.80	.66	.77
Fees & subscriptions	2.55	3.23	2.85	3.32	3.55	.31	.86	.43	.46	.51	.55	.62	.40	.57	.88
HOUSEHOLD SERVICES	**6.49**	**7.81**	**7.69**	**8.58**	**9.16**	**2.52**	**3.44**	**3.11**	**3.08**	**3.64**	**3.12**	**3.66**	**3.86**	**3.80**	**4.50**
Men's outerwear	2.50	2.80	2.84	2.99	3.46	.22	.50	.21	.27	.31	1.08	.96	.84	1.00	.98
Women's outerwear	3.77	4.14	4.34	4.91	5.04	.85	1.03	.75	.87	.84	1.34	1.33	.89	1.39	1.11
Children's outerwear	1.59	1.70	1.68	1.66	1.80	.05	.12	.07	.03	.13	.11	.14	.19	.06	.11
Other clothing	1.96	2.24	2.17	2.38	3.62	.68	.77	.59	.68	.82	1.17	1.48	1.39	1.45	1.27
Footwear	2.64	2.79	2.81	2.92	3.02	.66	.80	.56	.56	.68	1.28	1.34	1.42	.91	1.17
CLOTHING & FOOTWEAR	**12.46**	**13.66**	**13.83**	**14.86**	**15.70**	**2.45**	**3.22**	**2.17**	**2.41**	**2.70**	**4.98**	**5.25**	**4.73**	**4.81**	**4.54**

(derived from the Family Expenditure Survey and consistent with published FES reports)

	General index					1-person pensioner					2-person pensioner				
	1985	1986	1987	1988	1989	1985	1986	1987	1988	1989	1985	1986	1987	1988	1989
Personal articles	1.74	2.06	2.19	2.71	2.70	.20	.34	.14	.20	.35	.43	.57	1.08	.49	.93
Chemists' goods	2.48	2.77	2.92	3.34	3.74	.61	.69	.74	.88	.84	1.08	1.48	1.20	1.54	1.59
Personal services	1.70	1.84	1.99	1.99	2.25	.91	.77	1.02	.99	.77	1.08	1.15	1.76	1.39	1.44
PERSONAL GOODS & SERVICES	**5.92**	**6.67**	**7.11**	**8.04**	**8.68**	**1.72**	**1.79**	**1.90**	**2.07**	**1.96**	**2.59**	**3.19**	**4.04**	**3.42**	**3.96**
Purchase of motor vehicles	8.44	8.85	11.21	11.59	15.46	.02	.14	.23	.00	.26	1.45	1.26	2.54	.84	.16
Maintenance of vehicles	3.32	3.45	3.74	4.28	4.50	.19	.30	.16	.27	.09	.83	1.24	.97	.93	.75
Petrol & oil	7.59	6.81	6.90	7.11	7.75	.27	.34	.39	.39	.34	2.06	2.44	2.57	2.30	2.31
Vehicle tax & insurance	2.83	3.06	3.45	4.20	4.58	.15	.23	.15	.28	.31	1.03	1.37	1.48	1.82	1.49
MOTORING EXPENDITURE	**22.18**	**22.16**	**25.30**	**27.18**	**32.30**	**.63**	**1.01**	**.93**	**.94**	**1.01**	**5.37**	**6.30**	**7.56**	**5.89**	**4.72**
Rail fares	1.15	1.17	1.20	1.36	1.21	.08	.07	.07	.14	.05	.06	.11	.04	.06	.25
Bus & coach fares	1.12	1.15	1.27	1.30	1.46	.33	.39	.32	.48	.37	.56	.59	.47	.83	.95
Other travel costs	1.28	1.47	1.76	1.68	1.98	.20	.36	.23	.34	.36	.36	.25	.41	.20	.49
FARES & OTHER TRAVEL COSTS	**3.55**	**3.79**	**4.23**	**4.34**	**4.64**	**.61**	**.82**	**.62**	**.96**	**.78**	**.98**	**.95**	**.92**	**1.08**	**1.69**
Audio-visual equipment	2.19	2.46	2.46	2.40	2.81	.15	.07	.21	.38	.22	.18	.19	.48	.34	.18
Records & tapes	.74	.87	1.03	1.18	1.43	.17	.02	.02	.02	.04	.05	.11	.05	.09	.19
Toys, photo & sports goods	1.81	2.02	2.09	2.18	2.73	.10	.12	.09	.07	.34	.13	.14	.32	.20	.31
Books & newspapers	2.66	2.78	2.96	3.09	3.36	1.16	1.18	1.31	1.29	1.41	1.88	1.94	2.12	2.25	2.40
Gardening products	.81	.88	.94	1.10	1.22	.24	.20	.16	.21	.27	.52	.56	.33	.87	.86
LEISURE GOODS	**8.21**	**9.02**	**9.49**	**9.94**	**11.55**	**1.82**	**1.59**	**1.78**	**1.97**	**2.28**	**2.76**	**2.92**	**3.31**	**3.74**	**3.93**
TV licences & rentals	1.98	2.04	2.06	2.01	2.06	1.34	1.36	1.42	1.51	1.44	1.51	1.72	1.60	1.76	1.87
Entertainment & recreation	2.78	3.00	3.19	4.29	4.64	.10	.11	.10	.13	.14	.23	.19	.22	.32	.40
LEISURE SERVICES	**4.76**	**5.04**	**5.25**	**6.30**	**6.69**	**1.44**	**1.47**	**1.52**	**1.64**	**1.57**	**1.74**	**1.91**	**1.83**	**2.07**	**2.27**
TOTAL COVERED BY THE RPI	**151.48**	**163.37**	**170.50**	**181.46**	**201.66**	**51.01**	**57.87**	**55.82**	**60.15**	**64.60**	**80.32**	**89.04**	**88.51**	**92.80**	**98.57**
Expenditure not in RPI:															
Imputed rent	11.67	12.82	13.21	16.03	16.97	3.67	4.50	4.80	5.41	6.36	5.49	7.02	7.22	8.76	9.35
Gifts, donations etc	1.73	2.26	3.78	2.89	3.80	.51	.80	.68	.74	.74	.84	1.24	1.01	1.07	.81
Holiday expenditure	5.54	6.18	7.95	8.45	8.66	.44	.53	.59	.50	.81	3.03	.79	2.27	1.03	.68
Credit card interest	.30	.77	.29	.40	.43	.03	.01	.00	.00	.01	.04	.03	.00	.06	.01
Miscellaneous	.62	.77	.95	.82	.96	.06	.10	.04	.16	.04	.12	.06	.03	.03	.05
Gross expenditure	171.34	186.16	196.68	210.05	232.48	55.72	63.80	61.93	66.96	72.56	89.84	98.19	99.05	103.75	109.47
Housing benefit	2.64	2.84	3.10	2.48	2.77	11.33	11.99	11.79	11.37	12.79	6.75	7.69	7.34	6.10	7.91
Net expenditure	168.70	183.32	193.58	207.57	229.71	44.39	51.81	50.14	55.59	59.77	83.09	90.50	91.71	97.65	101.56
NUMBER OF HOUSEHOLDS	**5,773**	**5,855**	**6,134**	**5,999**	**6,163**	**630**	**655**	**650**	**613**	**618**	**345**	**338**	**307**	**318**	**311**
Percentage of households:															
Tenants paying rent	34	34	33	32	30	71	70	67	71	67	60	58	55	57	53
Owner-occupiers & rent-free	66	66	67	68	70	29	30	33	29	33	40	42	45	43	47
People per household:															
Retired people *	.30	.26	.28	.28	.28	1.00	1.00	1.00	.99	.96	2.00	2.00	2.00	1.90	1.89
All	2.72	2.71	2.69	2.65	2.64	1.00	1.00	1.00	1.00	1.00	2.00	2.00	2.00	2.00	2.00

Note: The expenditure figures given above differ in two respects from those used in constructing the weights for the general RPI and pensioner price indices. In the first place they relate to calendar years whereas the weighting information is (usually) for periods ending in mid-year (four quarters in the case of the general index and twelve quarters for the pensioner indices). Secondly the weighting information is "revalued" to the prices ruling in the January at the beginning of the year in which the weights are to be used, by scaling each component of recorded expenditure up or down according to the change in the corresponding price index between the date of recording and the January in question. The above figures are not revalued in this way. Nevertheless they give a broad indication of the way the expenditure patterns for the various types of household differ from one another.

*   Men aged 65 and over, women aged 60 and over, in receipt of national insurance retirement pension

(derived from the Family Expenditure Survey and consistent with published FES reports)

	High income households					All households				
	1985	1986	1987	1988	1989	1985	1986	1987	1988	1989
Bread	1.88	1.90	1.70	1.93	2.09	1.45	1.56	1.53	1.65	1.71
Cereals	1.12	1.07	1.05	1.44	1.39	.69	.73	.78	.84	.95
Biscuits & cakes	2.32	2.41	2.44	2.66	2.50	1.57	1.63	1.70	1.85	1.94
Beef	3.05	2.99	2.54	3.57	3.13	1.79	1.76	1.74	1.86	1.93
Lamb	1.25	.97	.91	1.07	1.13	.71	.65	.60	.64	.68
Pork	1.07	1.03	.82	1.02	.96	.69	.65	.62	.66	.68
Bacon	1.21	1.11	1.03	1.04	1.05	.76	.73	.71	.74	.79
Poultry	1.86	2.13	2.19	2.73	2.47	1.03	1.16	1.21	1.39	1.37
Other meat	2.63	2.45	2.53	2.37	2.58	1.90	1.88	1.88	1.89	2.06
Fish	1.35	1.54	1.72	2.19	2.10	.88	.95	.94	1.02	1.18
Butter	.66	.59	.53	.61	.59	.44	.40	.33	.35	.35
Oils & fats	.61	.54	.50	.58	.65	.53	.50	.46	.50	.54
Cheese	1.47	1.45	1.52	1.68	1.77	.79	.79	.80	.91	.94
Eggs	.69	.61	.54	.50	.54	.51	.50	.47	.44	.42
Milk & milk products	3.82	3.60	3.66	4.16	4.08	2.59	2.66	2.69	2.82	3.09
Tea	.58	.46	.45	.44	.47	.56	.48	.46	.46	.48
Coffee & hot drinks	.92	1.06	1.11	.94	1.15	.57	.63	.63	.61	.65
Sugar & preserves	.60	.54	.50	.55	.51	.49	.47	.45	.46	.48
Sweets & chocolates	1.26	1.42	1.41	1.95	1.87	.85	.88	.94	1.03	1.15
Potatoes	1.19	1.27	1.45	1.49	1.54	.96	1.07	1.17	1.18	1.30
Other vegetables	3.27	3.35	3.72	3.74	4.12	1.85	1.95	2.03	2.14	2.46
Fruit & soft drinks	4.87	4.59	4.95	5.89	6.78	2.29	2.50	2.59	2.93	3.38
Other foods	3.09	3.45	3.65	5.04	4.57	1.88	2.01	2.20	2.63	2.95
FOOD	**40.76**	**40.54**	**40.91**	**47.56**	**48.01**	**25.77**	**26.56**	**26.93**	**28.99**	**31.47**
Restaurant meals	13.22	18.08	16.21	18.87	20.53	3.55	4.37	4.70	5.13	5.51
Canteen meals	2.85	3.20	2.41	2.69	2.75	1.13	1.27	1.21	1.34	1.54
Take-aways & snacks	5.41	6.14	7.31	5.88	6.94	2.27	2.77	2.96	2.82	3.15
CATERING	**21.47**	**27.41**	**25.93**	**27.44**	**30.22**	**6.94**	**8.41**	**8.86**	**9.29**	**10.20**
Beer, wines & spirits:										
"On" sales	15.48	14.32	15.85	12.34	14.03	5.75	5.93	6.25	6.29	6.50
"Off" sales	7.05	6.05	7.01	10.10	7.70	2.19	2.28	2.45	2.90	3.03
ALCOHOLIC DRINK	**22.52**	**20.36**	**22.86**	**22.44**	**21.73**	**7.95**	**8.21**	**8.70**	**9.19**	**9.53**
Cigarettes	4.40	4.88	3.79	4.22	5.09	4.10	4.23	4.35	4.16	4.46
Other tobacco	.41	.66	.72	.33	.65	.33	.33	.32	.28	.31
TOBACCO	**4.81**	**5.55**	**4.52**	**4.55**	**5.74**	**4.42**	**4.55**	**4.67**	**4.45**	**4.77**
Gross rent, rates, water charges, etc, of households paying rent	2.91	2.90	5.17	4.19	3.58	8.00	8.83	9.24	9.25	10.44
Gross rates, water charges, ground rent, insurance of structure, etc, of owner-occupiers and rent-free	13.28	16.32	17.48	20.82	19.94	5.89	7.04	7.58	8.62	9.30
Maintenance charges	3.39	5.61	4.51	22.06	39.17	1.37	2.20	1.61	2.17	2.98
DIY materials	9.12	6.74	10.27	9.01	7.26	3.09	3.06	2.97	3.25	2.89
HOUSING	**28.70**	**31.57**	**37.43**	**56.07**	**69.94**	**18.35**	**21.13**	**21.39**	**23.27**	**25.61**
Coal & solid fuels	1.58	.24	.13	.23	.14	1.10	.97	.87	.82	.72
Electricity	6.51	6.78	6.60	6.96	7.13	4.48	4.74	4.87	4.93	5.27
Gas	6.04	6.94	7.69	6.89	6.86	3.68	4.11	4.30	4.15	4.09
Oil & other fuels	2.82	1.37	.85	1.81	.99	.69	.62	.51	.58	.50
FUEL & LIGHT	**16.95**	**15.33**	**15.26**	**15.88**	**15.11**	**9.95**	**10.43**	**10.55**	**10.48**	**10.58**
Furniture	7.03	9.10	4.09	4.45	12.68	1.87	3.05	2.37	2.85	5.06
Furnishings	5.44	12.84	6.63	7.43	12.53	1.78	2.31	2.36	2.56	3.66
Electrical appliances	5.34	5.33	4.67	4.74	6.14	2.46	2.63	2.66	2.75	2.94
Other household equipment	6.81	5.25	5.61	4.94	6.06	2.07	1.94	1.87	1.95	2.14
Household consumables	4.27	4.28	5.06	6.46	7.16	2.27	2.42	2.59	3.26	3.67
Pet care	2.61	2.94	4.80	3.67	3.90	1.22	1.33	1.62	1.64	1.69
HOUSEHOLD GOODS	**31.50**	**39.74**	**30.86**	**31.69**	**48.49**	**11.67**	**13.67**	**13.48**	**15.01**	**19.17**
Postal charges	.65	.92	.82	.75	.89	.34	.38	.38	.37	.44
Telephone charges	4.72	4.81	4.77	6.82	5.67	2.49	2.79	2.99	3.28	3.32
Domestic services	5.07	5.04	9.80	9.62	8.97	1.13	1.43	1.64	1.83	1.96
Fees & subscriptions	6.66	9.19	7.82	13.18	10.44	2.39	3.16	.73	3.39	3.47
HOUSEHOLD SERVICES	**17.10**	**19.97**	**23.21**	**30.36**	**25.97**	**6.35**	**7.75**	**5.74**	**8.88**	**9.21**
Men's outerwear	8.26	8.60	9.86	9.33	10.70	2.43	2.76	2.80	2.95	3.40
Women's outerwear	12.01	16.13	13.30	15.23	14.93	3.70	4.26	4.23	4.88	4.93
Children's outerwear	2.02	2.72	2.61	3.81	3.79	1.39	1.52	1.51	1.54	1.68
Other clothing	3.93	5.45	5.44	6.22	8.84	1.88	2.21	2.12	2.37	3.50
Footwear	6.28	6.32	5.56	5.97	6.75	2.53	2.70	2.66	2.77	2.90
CLOTHING & FOOTWEAR	**32.48**	**39.22**	**36.77**	**40.57**	**42.44**	**11.92**	**13.45**	**13.32**	**14.52**	**15.25**

AVERAGE WEEKLY EXPENDITURE FOR CALENDAR YEARS BY TYPE OF HOUSEHOLD (£ per household per week) CLASSIFIED AS IN THE RETAIL PRICES INDEX (cont.)

(derived from the Family Expenditure Survey and consistent with published FES reports)

	High income households					All households				
	1985	1986	1987	1988	1989	1985	1986	1987	1988	1989
Personal articles	6.16	6.94	8.45	10.97	7.92	1.70	2.05	2.22	2.77	2.64
Chemists' goods	5.09	5.02	5.54	7.51	7.43	2.34	2.62	2.76	3.25	3.56
Personal services	4.19	4.19	5.64	7.28	6.84	1.69	1.82	2.04	2.11	2.29
PERSONAL GOODS & SERVICES	**15.44**	**16.15**	**19.63**	**25.76**	**22.19**	**5.73**	**6.48**	**7.02**	**8.13**	**8.48**
Purchase of motor vehicles	24.16	32.03	28.03	28.07	44.91	7.90	8.72	10.54	10.86	14.76
Maintenance of vehicles	9.12	7.79	11.57	6.55	9.88	3.12	3.25	3.62	3.90	4.19
Petrol & oil	18.40	14.66	13.67	13.46	14.39	7.05	6.36	6.41	6.61	7.17
Vehicle tax & insurance	7.11	6.90	7.47	8.16	9.16	2.65	2.89	3.23	3.93	4.29
MOTORING EXPENDITURE	**58.79**	**61.38**	**60.74**	**56.24**	**78.34**	**20.72**	**21.22**	**23.80**	**25.31**	**30.42**
Rail fares	4.07	4.92	5.18	6.14	5.57	1.11	1.19	1.21	1.42	1.25
Bus & coach fares	1.13	1.17	.82	1.06	1.10	1.02	1.06	1.14	1.19	1.33
Other travel costs	3.44	6.22	2.92	3.81	10.17	1.22	1.52	1.61	1.59	2.12
FARES & OTHER TRAVEL COSTS	**8.64**	**12.31**	**8.92**	**11.01**	**16.83**	**3.35**	**3.76**	**3.96**	**4.21**	**4.70**
Audio-visual equipment	6.15	5.59	4.27	5.68	4.15	2.05	2.28	2.25	2.28	2.54
Records & tapes	2.01	2.06	2.08	2.48	3.15	.70	.81	.94	1.09	1.33
Toys, photo & sports goods	4.36	4.08	5.05	6.48	6.19	1.66	1.85	1.96	2.10	2.57
Books & newspapers	5.41	5.66	6.66	6.68	6.94	2.59	2.73	2.93	3.06	3.31
Gardening products	2.68	2.63	3.54	3.42	3.64	.81	.88	.95	1.12	1.22
LEISURE GOODS	**20.61**	**20.02**	**21.60**	**24.74**	**24.08**	**7.81**	**8.55**	**9.03**	**9.65**	**10.97**
TV licences & rentals	2.27	2.50	2.34	2.60	2.49	1.91	1.98	1.99	1.98	2.02
Entertainment & recreation	14.77	15.07	15.94	27.83	26.63	2.86	3.14	3.30	4.82	5.00
LEISURE SERVICES	**17.04**	**17.57**	**18.28**	**30.43**	**29.12**	**4.77**	**5.12**	**5.30**	**6.79**	**7.01**
TOTAL COVERED BY THE RPI	**336.78**	**367.11**	**366.91**	**424.75**	**478.21**	**145.68**	**159.31**	**164.77**	**178.17**	**197.36**
Expenditure not in RPI:										
Imputed rent	27.27	30.45	31.88	38.82	36.30	11.20	12.58	12.95	15.83	16.56
Gifts, donations etc	6.20	9.14	53.93	30.20	14.16	1.74	2.39	5.38	3.85	3.84
Holiday expenditure	30.16	23.07	36.90	36.54	39.62	5.85	6.16	8.31	8.71	8.95
Credit card interest	.51	1.71	.65	.76	1.12	.27	.71	.26	.37	.41
Miscellaneous	4.38	2.24	1.84	1.92	3.21	.68	.74	.88	.78	.93
Gross expenditure	405.30	433.72	492.11	532.99	572.62	165.42	181.88	192.55	207.70	228.05
Housing benefit	.00	.11	.23	.18	.07	3.55	3.78	3.93	3.29	3.73
Net expenditure	405.30	433.62	491.88	532.81	572.55	161.87	178.10	188.62	204.41	224.32
NUMBER OF HOUSEHOLDS	**256**	**322**	**294**	**326**	**309**	**7,012**	**7,178**	**7,396**	**7,265**	**7,410**
Percentage of households:										
Tenants paying rent	7	7	8	6	6	37	37	36	35	33
Owner-occupiers & rent-free	93	93	92	94	94	63	63	64	65	67
People per household:										
Retired people *	.10	.08	.12	.12	.12	.40	.40	.40	.40	.40
All	3.29	3.37	3.30	3.46	3.32	2.60	2.55	2.53	2.52	2.51

Note: The expenditure figures given above differ in two respects from those used in constructing the weights for the general RPI and pensioner price indices. In the first place they relate to calendar years whereas the weighting information is (usually) for periods ending in mid-year (four quarters in the case of the general index and twelve quarters for the pensioner indices). Secondly the weighting information is "revalued" to the prices ruling in the January at the beginning of the year in which the weights are to be used, by scaling each component of recorded expenditure up or down according to the change in the corresponding price index between the date of recording and the January in question. The above figures are not revalued in this way. Nevertheless they give a broad indication of the way the expenditure patterns for the various types of household differ from one another.

Men aged 65 and over, women aged 60 and over, in receipt of national insurance retirement pension

83 RELATIONSHIP BETWEEN PRESENT RPI STRUCTURE AND THAT USED UP TO JANUARY 1987

Present sub-categories	Pre-1987 equivalents
Sub-groups	
Food	Food
	- Food for animals
Catering	Meals bought & consumed outside the home
Alcoholic drink	Alcoholic drink
Tobacco	Tobacco
Housing	Housing
Fuel & light	Fuel & light
Household goods	Food for animals
	+ Furniture, floor coverings & soft furnishings
	+ **Part of** Radio, television & other household appliances
	+ Pottery, glassware & hardware
	+ Soap, detergents, polishes, matches etc
	+ **Part of** Stationery, travel & sports goods, toys, photographic & optical goods, plants etc
Household services	Postage & telephone charges
	+ Other services
	- Hairdressing
Clothing & footwear	Clothing & footwear
Personal goods & services	Medicines, surgical etc goods & toiletries
	+ **Part of** Stationery, travel & sports goods, toys, photographic & optical goods, plants etc
	+ Hairdressing
Motoring expenditure	Purchase of motor vehicles
	+ Maintenance of motor vehicles
	+ Petrol & oil
	+ Motor licences
	+ Motor insurance
Fares & other travel costs	Fares
	+ Motoring & cycling
	- Purchase of motor vehicles
	- Maintenance of motor vehicles
	- Petrol & oil
	- Motor licences
	- Motor insurance
Leisure goods	**Part of** Radio, television & other household appliances
	+ Books, newspapers & periodicals
	+ **Part of** Stationery, travel & sports goods, toys, photographic & optical goods, plants etc
Leisure services	Entertainment
Sections	
Bread	Bread
Cereals	Flour
	+ Other cereals
Biscuits & cakes	Bread, flour, cereals, biscuits & cakes
	- Bread
	- Flour
	- Other cereals
Beef	Beef
Lamb	Lamb
Pork	Pork
Bacon	Bacon
Poultry	**Part of** Other meat & meat products
Other meat	**Part of** Other meat & meat products
	+ Ham (cooked)
Fish	Fish
Butter	Butter
Oils & fats	Margarine
	+ Lard & other cooking fats

Present sub-categories	Pre-1987 equivalents
Sections (cont.)	
Cheese	Cheese
Eggs	Eggs
Milk, fresh	Milk, fresh
Milk products	Milk, canned, dried etc
Tea	Tea
Coffee & other hot drinks	Coffee, cocoa, proprietary drinks
Soft drinks	Soft drinks
Sugar & preserves	Sugar + Jam, marmalade & syrup
Sweets & chocolates	Sweets & chocolates
Potatoes	Potatoes
Other vegetables	Other vegetables
Fruit	Fruit, fresh, dried & canned
Other foods	Other foods − Food for animals
Restaurant meals	**Part of** Meals bought & consumed outside the home
Canteen meals	**Part of** Meals bought & consumed outside the home
Take-away meals & snacks	**Part of** Meals bought & consumed outside the home
Beer	Beer
Wines & spirits	Spirits, wines etc
Cigarettes	Cigarettes
Other tobacco	Tobacco
Rent	Rent
Mortgage interest payments	Mortgage interest payments
Rates	**Part of** Rates & water charges
Water charges	**Part of** Rates & water charges
Repair & maintenance charges	**Part of** Materials & charges for repairs & maintenance
Do-it-yourself materials	**Part of** Materials & charges for repairs & maintenance
Coal & solid fuels	Coal & smokeless fuels
Electricity	Electricity
Gas	Gas
Oil & other fuel	Oil & other fuel & light
Furniture	**Part of** Furniture, floor coverings & soft furnishings
Furnishings	Part of Furniture, floor coverings & soft furnishings
Electrical appliances	**Part of** Radio, television & other household appliances
Other household equipment	Pottery, glassware & hardware
Household consumables	Soap, detergents, polishes, matches etc + **Part of** Stationery, travel & sports goods, toys, photographic & optical goods, plants etc
Pet care	Food for animals
Postage	Postage
Telephone charges etc	Telephones & telemessages
Domestic services	Domestic help + Boot & shoe repairing + Laundering

Present sub-categories	Pre-1987 equivalents
Sections (cont.)	
Fees & subscriptions	Other services
	- Domestic help
	- Boot & shoe repairing
	- Laundering
	- Hairdressing
Men's outerwear	Men's outer clothing
Women's outerwear	Women's outer clothing
Children's outerwear	**Part of** Children's clothing
Other clothing	Men's underclothing
	+ Women's underclothing
	+ **Part of** Children's clothing
	+ Other clothing, including hose, haberdashery, hats & materials
Footwear	Footwear
Personal articles	**Part of** Stationery, travel & sports goods, toys, photographic & optical goods, plants etc
Chemists' goods	Medicines, surgical etc goods & toiletries
Personal services	Hairdressing
Purchase of motor vehicles	Purchase of motor vehicles
Maintenance of motor vehicles	Maintenance of motor vehicles
Petrol & oil	Petrol & oil
Vehicle tax & insurance	Motor licences
	+ Motor insurance
Present sub-categories	Pre-1987 equivalents
Rail fares	Rail transport
Bus & coach fares	Road transport
Other travel costs	Motoring & cycling
	- Purchase of motor vehicles
	- Maintenance of motor vehicles
	- Petrol & oil
	- Motor licences
	- Motor insurance
Audio-visual equipment	**Part of** Radio, television & other household appliances
Records & tapes	**Part of** Stationery, travel & sports goods, toys, photographic & optical goods, plants etc
Toys, photo & sports goods	**Part of** Stationery, travel & sports goods, toys, photographic & optical goods, plants etc
Books & newspapers	Books, newspapers & periodicals
Gardening products	**Part of** Stationery, travel & sports goods, toys, photographic & optical goods, plants etc
TV licences & rentals	Entertainment
	- Entertainment other than TV
Entertainment & recreation	Entertainment other than TV

84 "ALL ITEMS" COST OF LIVING INDEX

	Jan	Feb	Mar	Apr	May	Jun	Jul	Aug	Sep	Oct	Nov	Dec
Indices: July 1914 = 100												
1914							100	100-	110-*	110-	110-*	110
1915	110+	115	115+	115+	120	125	125	125	125	130*	130+	135
1916	135	135	135+	135+*	140+	145	145+*	145ı	150	150+	160	165
1917	165	165+	170	170+	175	175+	180	180	180+	175+	185	185
1918	185+	190	190	190+	195+	200	200+	210	210	215+	220+	220
1919	220	220	215	210	205	205	205+	215	215	220	225	225
1920	225	230	230	232	241	250	252	255*	261	264	276	269
1921	265	251	241	233	228*	219	219	222	220	210	203	199
1922	192*	188	186	182	181	180	184	181	179	178*	180	180
1923	178	177	176	174*	170	169	169*	171	173	175	175	177
1924	177	179	178	173	171	169*	170	171	172	176	180	181
1925	180	179*	179*	175	173	172	173	173	174	176	176*	177
1926	175	173	172	168	167	168	170	170*	172	174	179	179
1927	175	172	171	165	164*	163	166	164	165	167	169	169
1928	168*	166	164	164*	164	165	165*	165	165	166	167	168
1929	167	165	166	162	161	160	161	163	164*	165	167	167*
1930	166	164	161	157	155	154*	155	157	157	156	157	155
1931	153	152*	150*	147	147	145	147	145	145	145	146*	148
1932	147	147	146	144	143*	142	143	141	141	143	143	143
1933	142*	141	139	137	136	136	138	139	141	141*	143	143
1934	142	141	140	139*	137	138	141*	142	143	143	144	144
1935	143	142	141	139	139	140	143	143	143*	145	147	147*
1936	147	147	146*	144	144	144	146	146	147	148	151*	151
1937	151	151	151	151	152	152	155	155*	155	158	160	160
1938	159	157	156	154	156*	155	159	156	156	155	156	156
1939	155*	155	153	153	153	153	156	155	155	165*	169	173
1940	174	177	179	178	180	181	187	185	187*	189	192	195*
1941	196	197	197	198	200	200*	199	199	199	199	200	201
1942	200	200*	200*	199	200	199	200	201	200	200	200*	200
1943	199	199	199	198	199	198	200	199*	198	199	199	199
1944	199	200	200	200	200	200	201	202	202	201*	201	201
1945	202	202	202	202	203	204	207*	205	203	203	203	203
1946	203	203	203	203	204	203	205	205	203*	203	203	204*
1947	204	203	204	203	203	203*	203§					

- Less than the figure shown
+ More than the figure shown (by up to 5 index points)
* Figure for end of previous month
§ Figure for 17 June 1947

85 COST OF LIVING INDEX FOR FOOD

	Jan	Feb	Mar	Apr	May	Jun	Jul	Aug	Sep	Oct	Nov	Dec
Indices: July 1914 = 100												
1914							100	115	110*	112	113*	116
1915	118	122	124	124	126	132	132	134	135	140*	141	144
1916	145	147	148	149*	155	159	161*	160	165	168	178	184
1917	187	189	192	194	198	202	204	202	206	197	206	205
1918	206	208	207	206	207	208	210	218	216	229	233	229
1919	230	230	220	213	207	204	209	217	216	222	231	234
1920	236	235	233	235	246	255	258	262*	267	270	291	282
1921	278	263	249	238	232*	218	220	226	225	210	200	195
1922	185*	179	177	173	172	170	180	175	172	172*	176	178
1923	175	173	171	168*	162	160	162*	165	168	172	173	176
1924	175	177	176	167	163	160*	162	164	166	172	179	180
1925	178	176*	176*	170	167	166	167	168	170	172	172*	174
1926	171	168	165	159	158	158	161	161*	162	163	169	169
1927	167	164	162	155	154*	154	159	156	157	161	163	163
1928	162*	159	155	155*	154	156	157*	156	156	157	159	160
1929	159	156	157	150	149	147	149	153	154*	156	159	159*
1930	157	154	150	143	140	138*	141	144	144	143	144	141
1931	138	136*	134*	129	129	127	130	128	128	128	130*	132
1932	131	131	129	126	125*	123	125	123	123	125	125	125
1933	123*	122	119	115	114	114	118	119	122	123*	126	126
1934	124	122	120	118*	116	117	122*	123	126	125	127	127
1935	125	124	122	119	118	120	126	126	125*	128	131	131*
1936	131	130	129*	126	125	126	129	129	131	132	136*	136
1937	136	135	135	135	136	136	140	140*	140	143	146	146
1938	145	142	140	137	139*	138	146	141	140	139	140	139
1939	138*	138	135	135	134	134	139	137	138	150*	154	157
1940	157	161	161	158	159	158	168	164	166*	169	172	173*
1941	172	171	169	170	171	170*	167	167	166	165	165	165
1942	163	163*	162*	160	160	159	160	160	160	162	163*	164
1943	164	164	165	165	165	165	168	167*	166	168	168	168
1944	168	168	168	168	168	168	169	170	169	168*	168	168
1945	168	168	168	168	168	170	176*	172	169	169	169	169
1946	169	169	169	169	169	169	171	171	168*	168	168	168*
1947	168	168	169	168	162	161*	161§					

* Figure for end of previous month
§ Figure for 17 June 1947

	Jan	Fob	Mar	Apr	May	Jun	Jul	Aug	Sep	Oct	Nov	Dec
Indices: July 1914 = 100												
1914							100	100	100*	100	100*	100
1915	100	100	100	100	100	100	100	100	101	102*	102	102
1916	100	100	100	100*	100	100	100*	100	100	100	100	100
1917	100	100	100	100	100	100	100	100	100	100	100	100
1918	100	100	100	100	101	102	102	102	102	102	102	102
1919	102	102	102	102	103	105	106	107	107	108	108	108
1920	108	108	108	108	115	115+	115+	115+*	135	139	142	142
1921	142	143	144	144	144*	145	145	153	153	153	155	155
1922	155*	155	155	155	154	154	153	153	153	152*	150	150
1923	150	150	150	150*	148	148	147*	147	147	148	147	147
1924	147	147	147	147	147	147*	147	147	147	147	147	147
1925	147	147*	147*	147	147	147	147	147	147	148	148*	148
1926	148	148	148	148	149	149	150	150*	150	150	150	150
1927	151	151	151	151	151*	151	151	151	151	151	151	151
1928	151*	151	151	151*	151	151	151*	151	151	151	150	152
1929	152	152	152	152	153	153	153	153	153*	153	152	152*
1930	152	152	152	152	153	153*	153	153	153	153	153	154
1931	154	154*	154*	154	154	154	154	154	154	154	154*	154
1932	154	154	154	154	154*	154	154	154	154	154	155	155
1933	155*	155	155	155	156	156	156	156	156	156*	156	156
1934	156	156	156	156*	156	156	156*	156	156	156	156	156
1935	156	156	156	156	158	158	158	158	158*	158	158	158*
1936	158	158	158*	158	159	159	159	159	159	159	159*	159
1937	159	159	159	159	159	159	159	159*	159	159	159	159
1938	159	159	159	159	160*	160	160	160	160	160	161	161
1939	161*	161	161	161	162	162	162	162	162	162*	162	162
1940	162	162	162	162	164	164	164	164	164*	164	164	164*
1941	164	164	164	164	164	164*	164	164	164	164	164	164
1942	164	164*	164*	164	164	164	164	164	164	164	164*	164
1943	164	164	164	164	164	164	164	164*	164	164	164	164
1944	164	164	164	164	164	164	164	164	164	164*	164	164
1945	164	164	164	164	165	166	166*	166	166	166	166	166
1946	166	166	166	166	168	168	168	168	168*	168	168	168*
1947	168	168	168	168	174	175*	175§					

+ More than the figure shown (by up to 5 index points)
* Figure for end of previous month
§ Figure for 17 June 1947

	Jan	Feb	Mar	Apr	May	Jun	Jul	Aug	Sep	Oct	Nov	Dec
Indices: July 1914 = 100												
1914							100	..	..	..	..	..
1915	105	110+	120	125	125	125	125	125	125	125*	125+	125+
1916	125+	125+	130	130*	135	135	135*	135	135+	135+	135+	140
1917	140	140	140+	140+	140+	140+	140+	140+	145	145+	155	155+
1918	160	160	160	160	165+	165+	175+	180+	185	185+	185+	190
1919	185+	185+	185+	185+	185+	185+	185+	205	205	205+	205+	180+
1920	175	180	180+	180+	185	225	230	230*	235	240	240	240
1921	240	240+	240	245	245+*	250+	260	250	240	235	230	225+
1922	220+*	220	220	215	210	205	190	190	190	185+*	185+	185+
1923	185+	185+	185+	185*	185+	185	180+*	180	180	180	180	180
1924	185	185+	185+	190	190	185*	185	180+	185	185	185	185
1925	185	185*	185*	185	185	180	180	180	180	180	180*	180
1926	185	185	185	185	185	190	195	200*	215	230	255	250
1927	215	210	200+	190	185*	175	170	170	170	170	170	170
1928	170*	170	170	165+*	170	165+	165*	165	165+	170	170	170
1929	170	170+	170+	170+	170	170	165+	165+	170*	170+	175	175*
1930	175	175	175	175	170	170*	170	170	170	170+	170+	175
1931	175	175*	175*	175	175	170	170	170	170+	175	175*	175
1932	175	175	175	175	170+*	170	165+	165+	170	170+	170+	170+
1933	170+*	170+	170+	170+	165+	165+	165+	165+	170	170*	170	170
1934	170+	170+	170+	170+*	170	165+	165+*	165+	170	170	170	170
1935	170+	170+	170+	170+	170	170	165+	165+	165+*	170	170	170*
1936	175	175	175*	175+	175	170+	170+	170+	170+	175	175*	175
1937	175+	175+	175+	175+	175+	175	175	175*	175+	180	180	180+
1938	180+	180+	180+	180+	180+*	175+	175+	175+	180	180	180+	180+
1939	180+*	185	185	185	180+	175+	180	180	180+	185*	185+	195
1940	200	202	205	205	208	212	212	212	212*	214	215	219*
1941	223	225	225	225	226	226*	228	228	228	229	229	230
1942	230	230*	230*	232	232	232	232	240	240	241	241*	241
1943	244	244	244	244	244	244	244	244*	244	244	244	244
1944	244	252	251	252	252	253	253	263	263	263*	264	264
1945	265	267	266	266	275	275	275*	276	276	276	276	275
1946	275	275	275	275	276	276	276	278	278*	278	278	279*
1947	279	279	280	283	282	283*	283§					

+ More than the figure shown (by up to 5 index points)
* Figure for end of previous month
§ Figure for 17 June 1947

	Jan	Feb	Mar	Apr	May	Jun	Jul	Aug	Sep	Oct	Nov	Dec
Indices: July 1914 = 100												
1914							100	..	..	..	..	..
1915	110	110	110+	115	120	120	125	125	130	130*	135	135
1916	140	140	145	150*	150	155	160*	100	165	170	175	180
1917	185	185	190	195	195	200	205	210	220	225	230	240
1918	250	260	270	285	300	310	320	330	340	350	360	360
1919	360	360	360	360	360	360	360	360	360	360	360	370
1920	380	400	410	415	425	425	425	430*	430	430	420	405
1921	390	355	340	325	310*	300	290	280	270	265	260	255
1922	250*	250	245	240	240	240	240	235	235	230*	230	225
1923	225	225	225	225*	225	225	220*	220	220	220	220	220
1924	220+	220+	225	225	225	225*	225	225+	225+	225+	225+	225+
1925	225+	230*	230*	230	230	230	230	225+	225+	225+	225+*	225
1926	225	225	225	220+	220+	220+	220	220*	220	220	215+	215+
1927	215+	215	215	215	215*	210+	210+	210+	210+	215	215	215
1928	215*	215	215+	215+*	220	220	220*	220	220	220	220	220
1929	220	220	220	220	215+	215+	215+	215+	215+*	215	215	215*
1930	215	215	215	210+	210+	210+*	210+	210	210	205+	205+	205
1931	205	200+*	200*	200	195+	195	195	195	190+	190	190*	190
1932	190	190	190	190	190*	190	185+	185+	185+	185+	185+	185+
1933	185*	185	185	185	185	185	180+	180+	180+	185*	185	185
1934	185	185	185	185*	185	185+	185+*	185+	185+	185+	185+	185+
1935	185+	185+	185+	185+	185+	185+	185+	185+	185*	185	185	185*
1936	185	185+	185+*	185+	190	190	190	190	190	190	190*	190
1937	190+	195	195	195+	200	200+	205	205*	205	205+	210	210
1938	210	210	210	210	210*	210	210	210	210	205+	205+	205+
1939	205+*	205+	205+	205+	205+	205+	205+	205+	205+	220+*	235	245
1940	250	260	265+	270+	280	285	290	290	295*	300	305+	320*
1941	330	340+	350	355+	365	370*	375	380	380+	385+	395	395+
1942	400	400+*	405*	405	405	405	405	405	395+	390	385*	375+
1943	370	365	360	355	350+	350	345+	345*	345	340+	340+	340+
1944	340+	340+	340+	340+	345	345	345	345	345	345*	345+	345+
1945	345+	345+	345+	345+	345+	345+	345+*	345+	345	345	345	345
1946	345	345	345	345	345	345	345+	345+	345+*	345+	345+	345+*
1947	345+	340+	340	340+	340+	345*	345§					

+ More than the figure shown (by up to 5 index points)
* Figure for end of previous month
§ Figure for 17 June 1947

COST OF LIVING INDEX FOR ALL ITEMS EXCEPT FOOD,
RENT AND RATES, CLOTHING, FUEL AND LIGHT

	Jan	Feb	Mar	Apr	May	Jun	Jul	Aug	Sep	Oct	Nov	Dec
Indices: July 1914 = 100												
1914							100	100	100*	100	100*	100
1915	100	100	100	105	105	105	105	105	105	110*	110	110
1916	110	110	110	115*	115	120	120*	120	120	120	120	120
1917	120	120	125	130	130	140	140	140	140	140	140	150
1918	150	155	155	165	175	180	180	185	185	185	190	190
1919	190	190	190	185	185	190	195	195	200	200	200	200
1920	200	210	220	220	220	220	220	220*	230	230	230	230
1921	230	220	210	210	210*	210	210	210	210	210	210	200
1922	200*	195	195	195	195	195	195	195	195	195*	190	190
1923	185	185	185	185*	185	185	185*	185	185	185	180	180
1924	180	180	180	180	180	180*	180	180	180	180	180	180
1925	180	180*	180*	180	180	180	180	180	180	180	180*	180
1926	180	180	180	180	180	180	180	180*	180	180	180	180
1927	180	180	180	180	180*	180	180	180	180	180	180	180
1928	180*	180	180	180*	180	180	180*	180	180	180	180	180
1929	180	180	180	180	180	180	180	180	180*	180	180	180*
1930	180	180	180	180	180	180*	175	175	175	175	175	175
1931	175	175*	175*	175	175	175	175	175	175	175	175*	175
1932	175	175	175	175	175*	170+	170+	170+	170	170	170	170
1933	170+*	170+	170+	170+	170+	170+	170+	170+	170+	170+*	170+	170+
1934	170+	170+	170+	170+*	170+	170+	170+*	170+	170+	170+	170+	170+
1935	170+	170	170	170	170	170	170	170	170*	170	170	170*
1936	170	170	170*	170	170	170	170	170	170	170	170*	170
1937	170	170+	170+	170+	170+	175	175	175*	175	175	175	175
1938	175	175	175	175	175*	175	175	175	175	175	175	175
1939	175*	170+	170+	170+	175+	175+	180	180	180	185*	185+	189
1940	190	190	193	193	210	210	210	219	219*	219	220	221*
1941	222	223	224	226	226	227*	227	229	230	231	231	232
1942	233	234*	234*	235	263	263	264	264	265	266	267*	268
1943	268	268	268	268	286	286	286	286*	291	291	291	291
1944	291	291	291	291	291	291	291	291	291	291*	291	291
1945	291	291	291	291	291	291	291*	291	292	292	292	292
1946	293	293	293	293	291	290	294	296	296*	297	297	297*
1947	297	297	299	302	356	356*	356§					

+ More than the figure shown (by up to 5 index points)
* Figure for end of previous month
§ Figure for 17 June 1947

COMBINATION OF COMPONENT PRICE INDICES

The detailed indices given on pages 31 to 80 can be combined to suit users' particular requirements where the standard aggregates are not appropriate, by making use of the "weights" which are given in the tables. Up to January 1962 aggregate indices should be calculated as conventional weighted averages of the component indices. Since then, however, the weights have related only to the current year: not to the whole period since the "reference date" (i.e. the date taken as 100). The aggregate indices therefore need to be calculated in several stages, as follows:

a)   For each component, calculate an index for the current month based on the previous January. This is done by dividing the current month's index by the January index and multiplying by 100.

b)   Calculate a weighted average of these January-based indices, using the current year's weights. (Each year's weights come into use in February and remain current up to and including the following January.)

c)   Convert this January-based aggregate index back to the standard reference base. This is done by multiplying it by the aggregate index for the January in question and dividing by 100.

If a January index for the aggregate (on the standard reference base) is not available for the current year (say year T) then it can be calculated sequentially from the component indices, as follows:

a)   Use the above method with January of year T as the "current" month, to calculate the aggregate index for January of year T with January of year T-1 as 100.

b)   Then calculate an index for January of year T-1 with January of year T-2 as 100.

c)   Similarly for as many years (say N) as are necessary to get back to the reference base (January 1987 at present).

d)   Multiply the N January-on-January indices together and divide by 100 to the power N-1.

For example, suppose the objective is to calculate an aggregate index for *Catering* in respect of December 1989, with January 1987 taken as 100, from its three components - *Restaurants, Canteen meals and Take-away meals/snacks*. The data required are as follows:

	Indices (reference base = 100			Weights		
	Restaurants	Canteens	Takeaways	Restaurants	Canteens	Takeaways
Dec 1990	131.8	131.6	130.7	24	7	16
Jan 1990	122.2	120.6	120.0	26	7	16
Jan 1989	113.9	112.2	112.3	25	8	17
Jan 1988	106.5	106.5	106.3	23	7	16
Jan 1987	100.0	100.0	100.0			

The aggregate index for December 1990 (January 1990 = 100) is:

$$\frac{24 \times 131.8 / 122.2 \; + \; 7 \times 131.6 / 120.6 \; + \; 16 \times 130.7 / 120.0 \quad \times 100}{24 + 7 + 16} = 108.41$$

The aggregate index for January 1990 (January 1989 = 100) is:

$$\frac{26 \times 122.2 / 113.9 + 7 \times 120.6 / 112.2 + 16 \times 120.0 / 112.3 \quad \times 100}{26 + 7 + 16} = 107.18$$

The aggregate index for January 1989 (January 1988 = 100) is:

$$\frac{25 \times 113.9 / 106.5 + 8 \times 112.2 / 106.5 + 17 \times 112.3 / 106.3 \quad \times 100}{25 + 8 + 17} = 106.25$$

The aggregate index for January 1988 (January 1987 = 100) is:

$$\frac{23 \times 106.5 / 100.0 + 7 \times 106.5 / 100 + 16 \times 106.3 / 100.0 \quad \times 100}{23 + 7 + 16} = 106.43$$

The linked aggregate index for December 1990 (January 1987 = 100) is therefore:

$$\frac{108.41 \times 107.18 \times 106.25 \times 106.43}{100 \times 100 \times 100} = 131.4$$

This simple example can be generalised to deal with any number of components and any number of linking years. For example, the index for Food is made up from twenty four separate components and calculating special aggregate indices for 1986 on the then-current reference base of January 1974 involves a sequential calculation spanning thirteen consecutive years.

LINKING OF PRICE INDICES

The RPI expresses the level of prices at any given date as a percentage of the corresponding level at a previous date, called the "reference base". For example the "all items" index of 119.5 tor January 1990 (January 1987 = 100) means that prices in general increased by 19½ per cent in the three years to January 1990.

The reference base is left unchanged for long periods, recently for about a dozen years at a time, so that direct comparisons can be made between widely-separated dates. However it is sometimes necessary to compare dates which are not covered by the same index series, and this can be done in either of two ways, as follows:

a) Re-scaling to a common reference base

When the reference base is changed there is always an "overlap month" for which there is an index figure on both the old series and the new (the latter being 100). Using this link either index series can be converted to give it the same reference base as the other. In particular, dividing each figure in the old series by the last figure in that series (i.e. the figure for the link month) and multiplying by 100 will convert it to the same reference base as the new series.

For example, calculating the "all items" percentage increase in prices over the ten years to January 1990 involves two index series:

	Old series (Jan 1974 = 100)	New series (Jan 1987 = 100)
January 1980	245.3	A
January 1987	394.5	100.0
January 1990	..	119.5

The missing figure A can be calculated as:

$$A = 245.3 / 394.5 \times 100 = 62.2$$

allowing the percentage change between January 1980 and January 1990 to be calculated directly as:

$$\% \text{ change} = \{ 119.5 / 62.2 \times 100 \} - 100 = 92.1$$

b) Calculating percentage changes without intermediate rounding

Though the above method may be adequate for most purposes it has the disadvantage that some precision is lost through the rounding of the re-scaled index (A in the above example). When the greatest possible degree of precision is required it is therefore more satisfactory to calculate the percentage without intermediate rounding, from the formula:

$$\% \text{ change} = \frac{\text{New series index for later date} \times \text{Old series index for link month}}{\text{Old series index for earlier date}} - 100$$

which, with the figures from the above example, gives:

$$\% \text{ change} = \{ 119.5 \times 394.5 / 245.3 \} - 100 = 92.2$$

This is slightly different from, and more accurate than, the result of method (a).

Printed in the United Kingdom for HMSO.
Dd.292674, 3/91, C9, 3390/3, 5673, 142952.

CENTRAL STATISTICAL OFFICE PUBLICATIONS

ANNUAL

Annual Abstract of Statistics — has some 350 tables generally giving data for the last eleven years covering just about every aspect of economic, social and industrial life.

Social Trends — provides a valuable insight into the changing patterns of life in Britain. The chapters provide analyses and breakdowns of statistical information on population, households and families, education and employment, income and wealth, resources and expenditure, health and social services, and many other aspects of British life and work.

Regional Trends — with over 130 tables and 50 maps and charts, brings together a wide range of government statistics on the various countries and regions of the United Kingdom.

United Kingdom National Accounts — The CSO Blue Book is the essential data source for everyone concerned with macro-economic policies and studies and shows how the nation makes and spends its money. It is issued in early September and covers all aspects of the United Kingdom economy giving data for the last eleven years or longer.

United Kingdom Balance of Payments — The CSO Pink Book is the basic reference book for balance of payments statistics, presenting all the statistical information, for the last eleven years or more, needed by analysts who seek to assess UK transactions with the rest of the world.

Key Data — A "student" version of *Social Trends* with over 130 tables, maps and coloured charts covering a very wide range of social and economic data.

MONTHLY

Economic Trends — a compilation of all the main economic indicators liberally illustrated with charts and diagrams. The largest section gives time series and graphs over the last five years or so. It is the primary publication for quarterly articles on national accounts and the balance of payments as well as others commenting on and analysing economic statistics. The *Economic Trends Annual Supplement* contains long runs of annual and quarterly figures for the key series of economic indicators.

Financial Statistics — gives data on the key financial and monetary statistics of the United Kingdom. Tables usually contain at least 18 monthly and 12 quarterly or 5 annual figures. The biennial *Financial Statistics Explanatory Handbook* contains comprehensive notes and definitions for the tables.

Monthly Digest of Statistics — provides basic information on 20 subjects. Tables contain mostly runs of monthly and quarterly estimates for at least two years and annual figures for several more. The annual *Monthly Digest of Statistics Supplement of Definitions and Explanatory Notes* gives definitions for items and units in the *Digest.* It also applies to corresponding items in the *Annual Abstract* and *Regional Trends.*

OTHERS

United Kingdom National Accounts: Sources and Methods (third edition) — an essential reference book for everyone who makes use of national accounts data. It contains details of the concepts, definitions, statistical sources, methods of compilation and reliability of the various statistical sources which comprise the national accounts.

Statistical News — a quarterly journal providing a comprehensive account of current developments in British official statistics.

Standard Industrial Classification Revised 1980 — is a system of classification of establishments according to industry covering all economic activity.

Indexes to the Standard Industrial Classification Revised 1980 — contains lists of characteristic activities for each heading of the classification as well as an alphabetical index of activities. The publication is also indexed to the previous 1968 classification and to the European standard industrial classification (NACE).

CSO publications are published by HMSO and available from the addresses given on the back cover.